Schools Council
Research Studies

Evaluation in Curriculum Development: Twelve Case Studies

Schools Council
Research Studies

Evaluation in Curriculum Development: Twelve Case Studies

Papers from the Schools Council's project
evaluators on aspects of their work

Distributed by
APS PUBLICATIONS, INC.
150 Fifth Ave., New York, 10011

© Schools Council Publications 1973

First published 1973

SBN 333 14859 2

Published by
MACMILLAN EDUCATION LTD
Basingstoke and London

Companies and representatives
throughout the world

Printed in Great Britain by
Hazell Watson & Viney Ltd
Aylesbury, Bucks

Contents

Tables and figures

Tables

Figures

1 The role of the evaluator

F. H. Sparrow

He that judges without informing himself to the utmost that he is capable, cannot acquit himself of judging amiss.

—Locke, *Essay on Human Understanding*

In the early 1960s the men and women of imagination and insight who were responsible for curriculum development were determined to introduce new materials, new subject content and new methods of teaching into the schools. The first disciplines selected for change were science and mathematics; latterly the movement has spread to the humanities. The developers were certain that much irrelevant and out-of-date material was being taught in the schools, and that they could replace this outmoded curriculum with something much better—more relevant to the times and more interesting. The ideas for new content came from both outside the classroom and within it, from the universities and colleges, and from teachers who were called upon to help introduce the new materials. Indeed, the Nuffield projects were run by teachers for teachers.

The first concern of the developers was the production of teaching materials, and the urgency of the task left little opportunity for them to make a cool and careful evaluation of their product, or to formulate precise hypotheses to be tested by patient educational research of the traditional kind. It can be argued that much of the strength of the curriculum development movement stemmed from the stress that was placed on immediate needs in an essentially practical situation.

In such a situation the role of evaluation was limited. The developers were confident about the intrinsic worth of the new content, and fairly sure that the right way to expound the fundamentals of any subject was by using the inquiry method. This was particularly valuable in the sciences. The best of the curriculum developers were, however, characterized by their insistence on a process of materials refinement. Extensive try-outs of their materials (books, kits, teachers' guides, etc.) were organized in the ordinary schools of the country, and the resulting feedback of information, properly organized and taken account of, ensured that the final materials were very much improved and would actually work in the classroom situation. Thus a kind of evaluation began to take place, derived not from the use of a particular curriculum model (see p. 4) but from the immediate needs of a practical situation. The approach to evaluation in Britain has thus been essentially pragmatic. In a largely non-doctrinaire atmosphere, the very word 'evaluation' has come to be used with different but overlapping meanings. While this might well cause dismay for any who would prefer a single definition, universally recognized, it has helped the Schools Council project evaluators to appreciate the diversity of roles they can be asked to play. Of these roles, the most common is that mentioned above, in which the evaluator can be responsible for gathering and organizing the reactions of teachers and pupils to the project material. The methods adopted vary according to the nature of the project, and the case studies in Chapters 3–14 have been selected to cover as wide a range as possible.

The evaluator can also be expected to act as a critical friend to the project. Through his work, in addition to making a constructive assessment of new materials as they are being produced, he can also question the basic philosophy of the project and the appropriateness of those materials to its purpose. He may thus sharpen the definition of the project objectives.

The evaluator may also be responsible for tests and other instruments to measure the success of the undertaking—how far the project has achieved its intentions. In some cases this involves the use of existing test material; in other cases, evaluators have constructed their own test material to meet the needs of particular projects. Whatever the source of the tests, it is interesting to note that they are sometimes used not only to estimate the success of a project but also to help evaluate materials.

Even when the evaluator has performed all these tasks, still more can be asked of him. Headteachers, heads of departments and classroom teachers, when considering a new teaching method or course, rightly tend to ask exactly what it will mean for them. The fact that the success of a project can be demonstrated in some schools is no guarantee of universal success. Teachers want to know as much as possible of all the factors involved. The evaluator here has a descriptive role. He can show children's work from a variety of schools. His reports can include information on the neighbourhood of the project schools, their staffing, buildings, facilities and the like. He can use tape recordings and videotape to give teachers as much as possible of the 'feel' of the project. He can, of course, play a prominent role in dissemination and in conferences and in-service courses. His role is not that of a salesman but of an honest broker.

The work of the evaluator is thus essentially flexible, whether he functions as an expert on the organization and interpretation of feedback, as a critical friend, as a psychometrician, or as a purveyor of accurate information to teachers. Occasionally mention is made of other possible functions which lie largely in the future. It might be argued that the most vital question to be answered is not whether a project attains its immediate objectives—as demonstrated, for example, in the achievement of children at the end of a course—but how far it has been concerned with more long-term aims, such as the children becoming better scientists, better mathematicians or better citizens than those working on more traditional lines. Much of the most important evidence for this kind of judgement may only be available after many years, and usually after the pupils concerned have left school. Similarly, there are people awaiting some evaluation not just of individual projects in prescribed and limited areas but of the curriculum as a whole. This is a difficult field, but the setting up of the Schools Council Middle Years of Schooling Project at Lancaster University, covering the whole curriculum, and of the Council's Working Party on the Whole Curriculum for Thirteen to Sixteen-Year-Old Pupils could lead to evaluation exercises of great importance in the future.

Considerable interest has been expressed in the current position of evaluation in Schools Council projects. This book is intended to clarify that position.* It will provide information of interest and value to curriculum experts, to research workers, to university and college of education lecturers, to future project evaluators and to the growing number of classroom teachers who not only implement curriculum change by participating in projects but who, through their work in teachers' centres and in-service training courses, are also playing an increasingly important part in curriculum development.

* These case studies were compiled in 1971, at a time when the work described was still proceeding. Since then, in some cases, lines differing from those described have been followed.

2 Evaluation and curriculum development

David Tawney

The later chapters of this book report the thinking aloud of twelve evaluators evolving their roles and raising more questions than answers. As pioneers in a new sector of education, they were greeted with few certainties, so it is not surprising that they have approached their work in various ways. In their respective contributions, most have felt obliged to define their tasks, and their definitions vary widely. All would agree with Barry MacDonald when he says 'All evaluation is concerned with providing information for decision-makers', but there is a considerable range of opinion as to which decisions are relevant and what level of information is appropriate, even when evaluation is limited, as it is in most of the projects discussed here, to formative evaluation.

This chapter attempts to provide a framework in which the different accounts can be related to one another, by emphasizing three aspects of evaluation and its position in curriculum development. The first aspect involves the *level of thought* guiding the curriculum development, and hence the level at which evaluation is related to the project; the second is concerned with the area or *range* over which evaluation operates; the third is the *degree of rigour* employed in collecting information.

As pointed out in Chapter 1, the ideas guiding the first generation of curriculum projects in Britain were handled intuitively. The processes through which project teams embodied their ideas in learning experiences and teaching materials were largely pragmatic; it is not surprising, and probably entirely appropriate, that this should have been the case. Later projects have been influenced by the development, first in the USA and subsequently in Britain, of more theoretical approaches. The result has been that, although the curriculum developer is influenced by much the same aims and is working in much the same school situation as before, he is prepared to develop his ideas more carefully and more openly, so that the actions of the project can be seen to relate logically to its aims and the situation in which it operates. This structure of ideas, called a curriculum model, is refined to the extent that it will stand up to critical scrutiny from outside—a scrutiny which is increasingly invited by publication of the model in the project literature. Thus there has been a shift from the intuitive to the formally structured, from the implicit to the explicit; the potential customer is invited to inspect the design process instead of merely the end-product, and even to contribute to this process. The projects described in this book vary in the importance they appear to give to a theoretical basis for action; hence they vary in scope given to the evaluator.

Comparison of the evaluations described here can be achieved by considering the scope of each evaluation, the extent of what is being questioned. Some projects deliberately limit the area being explored. Wynne Harlen describes how the use of trial schools inherited from an earlier project allowed the evaluation to concentrate on the development of materials:

These were the kind of classes wanted for the trials, so that the value and effect of the materials could be evaluated without the interfering consequences of introducing a new way of working. Obviously it is necessary to reduce the number of uncontrolled variables in the trial situation, so the introduction of the material should be accompanied by as few other changes as possible.

The reader should note that although this was not an extensive study, it was a sophisticated and intensive one. Its narrowness can be contrasted with the broad scope of Peter Kaner's approach; he divided his evaluation into four main activities, ranging between a survey of the different aspects of the curriculum problem that the project team proposed to tackle and an attempt to measure the project's impact on the whole education system. Peter Kelly too takes a wider view, seeing evaluation as a necessity to ensure maximum objectivity at every stage of his project.

If we consider the degree of experimental rigour to which the evaluator works, here again we find a wide variation: few use statistical techniques and some do not use quantitative data at all. Anyone expecting the traditional standards of data collection which exist in most educational research would be well advised, before expressing his doubts, to compare the present efforts at evaluation with what J. F. Kerr deplores as 'the personal impressions or, at best, consensus of opinion' which guided some early projects.[1]

The data assembled by the evaluator should be judged by their appropriateness. Information must arrive in time for the material to be rewritten or it is useless; an evaluator is thus constrained by the programme of his project. J. S. Bruner describes formative evaluation as 'a form of educational intelligence for the guidance of curriculum construction'[2] and, continuing his analogy, if a military commander demanded the precision of a social survey from his intelligence service, the battle would be lost while the data were still being fed through the computer. Kaner comments on how little time the usual three-year project cycle leaves for classroom trials, and several evaluators point out that shortness of time has limited the scope of their investigations.

The criterion of appropriateness forces our attention to C. P. Ormell's comment that: 'Evaluation data as such do not generally *solve* any problems.

They may tell us when the material is not fully satisfactory, but they provide no substitute for the creative imagination needed to put that material right.' Increasing the precision at one stage in the process may be a waste of resources in view of this uncertain later stage.

The three aspects of evaluation described in the previous paragraphs help us see *where* a particular evaluation stands in relation to others. As to *why* the evaluation occupies that position, clearly the nature of the curriculum development, its aims and the situation in which it is working are important determinants: what is appropriate for the Science 5–13 Project is hardly likely to be appropriate for the English for Immigrant Children Project. Also of great significance are the personalities and experiences of the team members. These factors affect the role of the evaluator, who by his personality and experience adds yet other variables.

One measure of this variation in the role of the evaluator is his independence. Harlen sees independence as important: the evaluator should not be emotionally and intellectually committed to the material: 'Such commitment is bound to follow in anyone who has wrestled with the problems of developing and writing material, and clearly the person thus committed cannot stand back from the material, look at it objectively and gather evidence about it impartially.' She continues by describing the misunderstandings likely to arise if the evaluator is too independent to be a full member of the project team. In any event, the evaluator has a difficult role: there are few people who do not resent the attack on their professional competence implied by the criticism their material receives when put on trial—least of all the enthusiastic assertive person who may well be the best curricular apostle. Nevertheless, it is important that the evaluator should be able to make such criticisms, inhibited neither by his own involvement in the writing process nor by his relationship with other team members.

Kaner sees his task as including 'setting up a counter-image to that set up by the project', which must demand considerable independence. The present writer discusses an evaluation carried out by a separately funded, independent unit which reported directly to the Schools Council as well as to the project team—producing a situation which some may regard as potentially unsatisfactory. Kelly describes 'a policy of limiting the influence of individual personal commitment . . . by changing and redeploying personnel' as a way of avoiding the possible antagonisms which the critical approach of his project team to all their decisions could have engendered. Although certain team members had a special responsibility for evaluation, they were involved in the writing of some material, and the writers in their turn helped with evaluation; this enabled criticisms to be made without the team 'polarizing into a position of antagonism'.

These and other accounts refer to the position of the evaluator, his independence and the tensions he is likely to produce. It must be stressed that in certain projects these tensions have been strong enough to cause failures in the evaluation. An important factor appears to be the timing of the evaluator's appointment; the earlier in the life of the project he is appointed, the more acceptable his position seems to be. Whenever he is appointed, however, he is likely to produce some tension; he has a special responsibility to see that this tension is fruitful.

The first evaluations to be discussed in this book concern projects guided by well-defined curriculum models. The Science 5–13 Project used a model which is sometimes called classical. The evaluator helped other team members to clarify a list of behavioural objectives, i.e. the intended changes in pupil behaviour. This comprehensive list was prepared at the start of the project and, although originally intended as an internal working paper, was published in response to a demand from teachers in pre-trial schools. The purpose of the project was to develop teachers' guides to aid those teachers using 'active methods of learning'. As was pointed out above, the nature of the learning experience was not questioned; hence evaluation was restricted to the comparatively narrow task of determining how far the guides enabled the teacher to achieve his objectives, and of suggesting ways in which the guides could be modified to raise the level of that achievement. Statistical techniques were used to analyse the results of tests before and after trials, showing a significant gain in the scores of the experimental schools compared to the control schools, and a computer was used to group the questionnaire data; this evaluation was undoubtedly the most rigorous in quantitative terms. The information obtained had obvious and great value for the rewriting of the material: nevertheless, it did not answer every question, and the account is interesting also for its honest assessment of what the evaluation achieved.

Although less ambitious in the statistical techniques employed, the evaluation of the Cambridge School Classics Project was similar, both in the clarity of its aims and in the comparatively narrow area evaluated. The evaluator was appointed after the project had begun but found that clear aims had been formulated and trial schools carefully selected. Of the project's two main objectives, one was the attainment of translation skills; achievement in this area was measured by administering attainment tests at intervals to a large sample of trial pupils. Marking the tests was extremely time-consuming. When the evaluator subsequently asked herself the all-important question 'Could this information have been gained more cheaply?' she had to answer 'Yes':

In retrospect, it was not so much the test instrument that was at fault as the fact that it continued to be used when the primary aim of the tests [to discover if children were coping with the linguistic gradient of the course] could have been achieved by simpler and more economic means, and after it was demonstrated that the results relevant to writing the later stages were minor and not worth the time expended on them.

As to the project's second major objective, 'developing in the pupil an understanding of the content, style and values of classical civilization', the evaluator felt that here no measure of achievement could be devised without further definition of the cognitive skills and content matter involved. Teachers were asked to list in their reports, under a simple classification, any points raised in class discussion based on the material; this proved successful and led to an expanded classification being included in the *Teacher's Handbooks*, another instance of the evaluator helping to refine project objectives. Like Science 5–13, this project team seem to have had few doubts about the teachers' ability to interpret their intentions. There is an interesting summative element in the evaluation, the attainment of pupils following this course being compared with that of pupils following traditional courses.

The account of the Sixth Form Mathematics Curriculum Project includes a full discussion of the project's underlying philosophy; this is expressed in the form of a curriculum hypothesis that 'the use of relevance-enriched material will result in improved motivation, and will lead to better consolidation of concepts in the sixth former's mind'. Evaluation of this material is seen as an integral part of the project and is concerned with 'looking to see if [the material] behaves as well under classroom conditions as it was expected to behave'. The evaluation is thus seen as a continuing process, contributing as much to the quality of the next generation of material as to that of material currently on trial. The work on improving the material is intended not only to obtain data from the trials, but also to provide information leading to the establishment of filters through which these data are processed; this enables the decision-maker to discount the results of tests applied to classes where the conditions of trial did not satisfy certain criteria. Although the project calls for no radical changes in teaching method, and in fact does not specify how its material should be used, the evaluator believes that classroom results are likely to depend largely on how teachers interpret the project philosophy. Interpretation is highly variable: a teacher's understanding of mathematics, his attitude to teaching, to his class and to the project are just a few of the factors which would make open acceptance of feedback data of questionable value. The evaluation can be contrasted with that of the Science 5–13 Project, in which information about the trial schools was collected and collated systematically but was regarded as providing only a base line rather than a set of filters. The Sixth Form Mathematics Curriculum Project also differs from Science 5–13 in using statistical techniques infrequently; the trial situation makes it impossible to obtain statistically significant results, and the evaluator doubts whether statistical analysis would contribute to improving the quality of the material.

The Integrated Studies Project appears to have depended heavily on a carefully developed curriculum model, but one substantially different from those of the projects mentioned above. Committed to exploring 'the problems and possibilities of an integrated approach to humanities teaching in secondary schools', the project focused on a way of organizing the curriculum rather than on specific benefits that it was hoped the pupils would derive from using project material. Accordingly, the purpose of the trials was to generate, develop and clarify aims rather than to test material; integrating themes were studied in the trial schools, supported by packs of material produced by the project team. In this project it would have been inappropriate to use a 'vertical' curriculum model, in which aims were defined near the start of the project and attention thereafter devoted to refining the material so that these aims could be realized; instead, the project team adopted a 'horizontal' model in which aims, learning experiences and material were developed concurrently. Evaluation was seen here as less concerned with measuring and recording the results of an experiment and more with analysing and judging a complex and growing organism against a gradually developing consensus of opinion. The area evaluated was wide, ranging from the packs of material to the problems in human relations which arise when an innovation demanding collaborative planning and teaching is introduced to a school. The evaluator used no quantitative data but relied heavily on participant observation; such judgements, necessarily subjective, were sharpened by the theoretical approach of the project and validated to quite a high degree by discussion between all those involved.

The Humanities Curriculum Project team adopted a similar approach, discarding the vertical model with its pre-defined objectives as being inflexible and as begging the very questions they wanted to raise; they felt that trials should not merely test hypotheses but also originate them. The project's brief was 'to provide stimulus, support and material for schools teaching the humanities to pupils aged 14–16 of average and below average ability'. The project team responded by providing 'collections of original source material' which were 'gathered around inquiry areas and used as evidence for discussion. Teachers, in the role of discussion group chairmen, took responsibility for feeding in evidence that the pupils could study and interpret.' Within this broad context, a range of hypotheses was explored. The account shows that the team gave considerable thought to development of the project philosophy —a philosophy so novel as to place the role of the evaluator in some doubt: 'In an approach which is not based on objectives, there is no ready-made niche for the evaluator.' During the first year the evaluators carried out a wide and all-embracing but entirely qualitative investigation of what was happening in the trial schools, and of the many factors within and outside the schools which were affecting the results; checklists, questionnaires, tape and videotape recordings were all used to provide as complete a picture as possible. Towards the end of the first year and throughout the second, the evaluators narrowed their attention to some half-dozen carefully selected schools. Of great interest in this account are the comments on trial schools and on the summative evaluation planned for 1970-2. This evaluation falls in the category of supplying information about the project and is described as evaluation for 'consumers', or 'decision-makers'—'sponsors, local education authorities, schools and examination boards'. This work has been carried out by an expanded team and is designed to make considerable use of statistical techniques.

The chapter on the evaluation of the Nuffield A Level Biological Science Project gives prominence to the curriculum model which guided the project and includes a diagrammatic representation, which illustrates the vertical features of the model. Aims were stated at the beginning of the project and then refined into objectives of different kinds; teaching strategies were developed in order to fulfil these aims and material produced to support them; the strategies and material underwent trials and as a result were refined; the final products were disseminated to teachers. Nevertheless, although objectives were defined at the beginning of the project, 'it was . . . a deliberate policy to emphasize that the objectives were mutable, so as not to restrict the exploratory and creative aspects of development, in which new ideas and new approaches are sought continually'. The evaluator demonstrates how this horizontal aspect of the project team's policy, resulting in the modification and discarding of some objectives during the course of the work, was fully justified. The team used a range of techniques to collect and handle data. Of particular interest is the section which discusses how far students were successful in handling quantitative information. At first achievement of this objective was low; teachers said this was due to the poor standard of the pupils' mathematics. A simple statistical analysis of the O level mathematics results showed that, on the contrary, the great majority of pupils had reached a reasonable standard; furthermore, the analysis was able to show why teachers had thought otherwise. Having removed this misconception, the project team narrowed their search and finally attributed the low standard of achievement to inadequate course material. The material was modified; as a result, teachers were able to report a considerably higher achievement. Few accounts illustrate such a direct use of formative evaluation.

The scope of the evaluation in this project was very wide, ranging from the formulation of objectives to follow-up studies of pupils in higher education. 'Evaluation was geared to decision-making throughout this work, being concerned in the broadest sense with the collection of data on which reliable judgements could be based.' It was equally wide-ranging in its appearance at every stage of the project, and in the number of people involved: 'it was considered important that, within the limits imposed by time and administration, a range of people concerned with the products of development should play a part in as many stages of the evaluation process as possible'. Although the evaluation was mainly formative, the evaluator sees the project as part of a continual process of curriculum development and so claims that there can be no sharp division between formative and summative evaluation. His account ends with a brief outline of investigations still proceeding after the project's development phase had ended.

The remaining projects appear to have paid less attention to theory. This is not to accuse the project teams of woolliness: some areas of the curriculum may not be as amenable to the use of curriculum models as others, and it might also be the case that a project had a well-developed philosophy which was not felt to be essential to the evaluation account included here. The chapter on Language in Use (part of the Programme in Linguistics and English Teaching) explains why the team was unable to develop a more precise curriculum model or carry out a more fundamental evaluation. For tactical and logistic reasons, trial teachers were given considerable freedom in the units of material they could choose to test, and further freedom within each unit, which comprised a planned sequence of suggestions about activities, based on a particular topic such as sports reporting. Thus not all 110 units were tried out, and there was a substantial variety in the work engendered by each unit. However, a more important factor was the difficulty of testing the project objectives, since this postulated an awareness of the nature and function of language and a competence in its use in a variety of situations.

It is precisely in the nature of awareness and competence that a sampling procedure cannot adequately test them. We can never know whether a person has the language for a situation until the situation occurs, and in language activity we have to define 'situation' realistically, which in turn excludes test situations. It follows that it is not practicable to *measure* a student's awareness of, or competence in, the diversity of situations which life presents and which make a specific linguistic demand on him.

In addition, the evaluator points out that little is known about the language development of secondary school children and that the assessment of language skills is extremely complex. For these reasons evaluation did not derive from a curriculum model, but took a more pragmatic approach, restricted to assessing the design of the material. The work was therefore largely qualitative: questionnaires, oral reports made during visits (coupled with observation of classes), extended written reports and continuing discussion were used, and the high level of agreement between the data obtained through these different channels encouraged confidence in the conclusions reached.

Sometimes the evaluator appears to work almost outside the project rather than being a full member of the project team, and it may be significant that reports from such evaluators are characterized by less discussion of the theoretical framework of the project. This apparent detachment may be attributable to the late appointment of the evaluator, the pragmatic approach of the project or the fact that evaluation was entrusted to a separate unit. The evaluator of the Mathematics for the Majority Project carried out a wide-ranging and thorough set of investigations using standardized tests and statistical techniques. One investigation was a careful survey of the different aspects of the curriculum problem with which the project was concerned; here he was able to provide a fairly precise description of the mathematical attainments and attitudes of early school leavers in the third and fourth years and of the members of staff teaching them mathematics. The evaluation also helped the project team to reach a common set of objectives, although little use seems to have been made of this. Questionnaires completed by trial teachers and reports of criticisms which the teachers raised at their meetings provided information for rewriting the material; the overall impact on the pupils was assessed with standardized tests. The evaluator comments shrewdly on the value of these tests, pointing out the difficulty of relating results to items of material; he concludes that case studies of particular schools have greater formative value. His account is interesting for its comments on the use of college of education staff and students as observers and for the great store he attaches to group meetings of trial teachers. The obvious independence of the evaluator is emphasized by the summative element he sees in his work, and by his obligation to act as an honest broker and 'provide a description which will inform a headteacher or an adviser of the sort of outcome he can expect if he encourages the adoption of project methods and material'. However, since this evaluation does not seem to have been an essential part of the project, the extent of its influence on the project's course is not clear.

The English for Immigrant Children Project appears to have placed little emphasis on a curriculum model, probably because there were severe external pressures, which undoubtedly prevented the evaluation from using tests and numerical measures. The projects discussed previously have been operating in well-defined areas of the school curriculum—areas in which teachers already had considerable skill and experience; such projects can be regarded as reforming rather than pioneering. English for Immigrant Children, however, was grappling with a new and very urgent problem, aiding teachers who were working in varied but generally unfavourable conditions and who were grateful for any help that they were given. Far from viewing the material with scepticism from a background of experience, the teachers clutched at it: 'To criticize the scheme or the materials would have been like cutting off the branch on which I was sitting,' said one. In view of the desperate need, the project team decided to involve as many teachers as possible in the trials, so that dissemination and support took precedence over objective evaluation. The evaluation, which involved questionnaires, area meetings and reports of visits, must be considered to be narrow and crude, but in the circumstances anything broader and more refined would have been irrelevant. This account is valuable not only as a record of what can be achieved under adverse circumstances but also for its discussion of evaluation problems in an area of the curriculum where teachers have little experience.

Project Technology was again working in a new curriculum area and also saw its role as the dissemination of ideas and the provision of support for teachers through regional groups and technology centres, rather than merely the production of teaching materials. The evaluation, carried out by an independent, separately funded unit reporting direct to the Schools Council as well as to the project team, seems to have operated on the periphery of the project and, although providing interesting information, to have lacked integration with it. Bruner says:

Evaluation can be of use only when there is a full company on board, a full curriculum building team consisting of the scholar, the curriculum maker, the teacher, the evaluator and the students. Its effectiveness is drastically reduced when it is used for the single purpose, say, of editing a chapter, making a film, devising a test.[3]

This evaluation has apparently been used for a number of such disparate single items; the account says nothing about any theoretical structure which the project may have developed to link these items together. Possibly the vastness of the project's brief may have made the development of an all-embracing philosophy daunting, if not impossible. Furthermore, during the first year of trials, the project was considerably understaffed and the evaluators found they they, like the evaluator of English for Immigrant Children, had to offer support to teachers rather than collect information from them. The regional group structure served one aim of the project well, namely the dissemination of ideas; it was, however, less successful for the refinement of teaching materials, since it proved a cumbersome system of communication and made the trial schools difficult to identify. It was because the channels of communication between the project and its associate schools were not working well that the evaluators' reports were particularly useful, but this also forced the evaluation to be simple. The report on the evaluation of *Photocell Applications* is valuable in showing how some measure of objectivity can be established in an unstructured trial situation. Nevertheless, the account must raise some important questions:

why was an independent evaluation unit established?
what are the advantages and disadvantages of separate evaluation units?
what is the place of evaluation in a project which appears to attach relatively little importance to teaching materials and trials?

The evaluator of the Nuffield Secondary Science Project was appointed too late in the life of the project to have had any part in formulating objectives, and hence too late for the evaluation to be truly integrated with the project or indeed to be truly formative; furthermore, she worked only part-time. She therefore decided to restrict the scope of the evaluation to two investigations: first, whether the pupils following the course over a year showed any change in attitude towards science, and second, what type of activity in the school laboratory was engendered by the materials. She decided on the first because the project team placed affective objectives high on their list, and on the second because 'the aspect of activity and element of investigation in the pupils' work, coupled with repetition and variety for consolidation' were points raised repeatedly in the written materials and in the advice given by the project to trial teachers. Pupil attitudes were measured by the pre-trial and post-trial application of a standardized test, but the second investigation, despite the use of an observation schedule, was more subjective. The account raises the important question of how the results of the evaluation will be used.

Although the evaluator of the Infant School part of the project on Bilingual Education in the Anglicized Areas of Wales had the advantage of being thoroughly familiar with the project's methodology, his evaluation does not truly seem to have been part of the project. It lasted only a short time and its purpose, 'to make a judgement of the progress made so far and to assess whether the scheme was worthy of continuation and expansion at a later date', was as much summative as formative. With such a brief, it was clearly important that the evaluator should be independent. The lateness of his appointment and the shortage of time prevented him from using tests although these were available; instead, he visited classrooms and made careful observations. Although it is not clear what steps he took to make these as objective as possible, the account is interesting for its comments on the tactics of the observer in the classroom, and for the conclusions reached. As with the Humanities Curriculum Project, the evaluator sees the necessity of writing his report for the decision-maker: 'Whilst the evaluator might have spent months or years in making his judgements, policy decisions are often made in a single meeting and a long report, no matter how interesting, may in the final analysis fail to persuade the decision-maker to take action.'

These twelve accounts of evaluations must raise a number of questions.

(a)   What is the place of the curriculum model, the formally argued plan of action? Does it seem out of place in education, where activities so frequently appear pragmatic?

(b)   What should be the scope of evaluation in a project? How long should it last and how many people should be involved? How independent should the evaluator be?

(c)   What techniques should the evaluator use? Here the full range is described, from the use of tests, with a computer to collate the data obtained, to subjective judgements based on observation.

(d)   Finally, the reader may be tempted to ask himself whether, even allowing for the wide range of circumstances, it is right that all these evaluations should be so different. Or does this diversity suggest a lack of experience? And he will surely ask: 'Is evaluation worth while, worth the money spent on it?'

This chapter has sought to review the accounts and to relate them, by the degree to which each project and its evaluation possess a formally developed basis, the scope of the evaluation within the project, and the rigour with which data have been collected and analysed. In the effort to simplify and clarify, distortion has inevitably occurred. It is important, therefore, to regard this chapter as an introduction only, and to consider the questions above in the light of the detailed accounts which follow.

References

1   J. F. Kerr (ed.). *Changing the Curriculum* University of London Press, 1968, p. 21.
2   J. S. Bruner *Towards a Theory of Instruction* New York: Norton, 1968, p. 163.
3   Bruner, op. cit., p. 164.

3 Science 5–13 project

Wynne Harlen

This project, sponsored jointly by the Schools Council, the Nuffield Foundation and the Scottish Education Department, was set up in 1967 at the University of Bristol School of Education to consolidate and extend the work of its predecessor, the Nuffield Junior Science Project. Initially intended to run for three years and later extended for a further two, it concerns children throughout the age range 5–13.

The terms of reference for the project included 'the identification and development, at appropriate levels, of topics or areas of science related to a framework of concepts appropriate to the ages of the pupils. The aim of the development [was] to assist teachers to help children, through discovery methods, to gain experience and understanding of the environment and to develop their powers of thinking effectively about it' (Table 3.1). The project was also to take account of the needs of children with varied knowledge of science, to advise colleges of education on the science content of curriculum courses and to maintain close liaison with other related projects.

A search through the literature for 'a framework of concepts appropriate to the ages of the pupils' revealed that it did not exist. The attempt to create such a framework, although an unreliable guide in itself, proved a useful starting point from which to consider the project objectives. It was relatively easy to state the broad aims in general terms, but breaking these down into more specific statements expressed in behavioural terms occupied a large part of the team's time, and particularly that of the evaluator, during the first year of the project and at intervals throughout its life. That the statement of objectives eventually took the form it did and was included in the project's material for teachers (see, for instance, *With Objectives in Mind*, Macdonald Educational, 1972, pp. 59–65) was due to two circumstances in particular. One was the presence of an evaluator as a team member; the other was the reaction of various groups of teachers who were consulted about the objectives whilst these were being drafted. The teachers' immediate response was to request a copy of the objectives and start using it as guide for their work in the classroom; it was realized that part of the help the project could give was in supplying teachers with clear objectives for their children. So the statement of objectives, initially drawn up as a necessary step to clarify the minds and guide

Table 3.1 Organization of the Science 5–13 Project

	MAIN TEAM		EVALUATION		SCHOOLS INVOLVED		LEAs INVOLVED (England & Wales)	
	Staff	Budget*	Staff	Budget*	With trials	Associated informally	With trials	Indirectly
August 1967	3		½		—		—	
1968	4		½		—		—	
1969	5	£141 000 approx.	½	£20 000 approx.	130	111	12	141
1970	5½		1		90		19	
1971	1½		1		200		19	
1972 } extension	1		1		—		12	
1973					—		—	

*The division between main team and evaluation is only approximate, since evaluation was not costed separately. The total grant of £161 000 was provided by the Schools Council, the Nuffield Foundation, the Scottish Education Department and the Plastics Institute.

History

Set up a year after the Nuffield Junior Science Project ended, with the intention of building further on the ideas of that project and taking note of other work in primary science.

Aims

To help teachers in that part of their work concerned with educating children through science.

To advise colleges of education on the science content of curriculum courses; to study how to increase primary school teachers' knowledge of science.

Scope

For teachers in any primary school and any kind of secondary or middle school in which children up to the age of 13 are educated.

For teachers of children with a wide variety of ability and environment.

Activities

The development of materials to guide teachers in the provision of suitable science activities for their children and the supply of background information for the teachers.

Helping with courses for teachers in local centres and running large national courses about twice a year.

Disseminating the project's ideas to schools and colleges through lectures, visits, newsletters.

Materials

Units for teachers on various topics, e.g. time, metals, trees, coloured things. Some consist of a book of classroom activities and a separate book of background information. Others consist of one book which includes background information.

A book introducing the project's ideas, giving its objectives in detail and generally supporting the units.

Material suitable for teachers to use with children reaching the stage of formal thinking, in upper junior and lower secondary classes.

the writing of team members, became an important part of the project material.

The objectives, 150 or so statements, were grouped according to stages of children's intellectual development; the concept of stages was for convenience in accommodating the changes in modes of thought of children in the age range 5–13. Three stages were chosen; they had the same properties as those of Piaget, whose ideas and findings were widely used, but the boundaries and definitions of these stages were such as to be more useful in the context of school organization:

stage 1: the transition from intuitive to concrete operational thinking and the early phases of concrete operational thinking;
stage 2: the later phases of concrete operational thinking;
stage 3: the transition from concrete operational to formal operational thinking.

Project material

Material has been written for teachers in the form of units, each concerning one topic area for science activities. A unit is intended to guide the teacher on activities suitable for children at one or another stage of development, to suggest objectives he might keep in mind for the children during the activities, and to provide suitable background information which the teacher himself may lack and not be able to find easily in a suitable form. The introductory book, *With Objectives in Mind*, gives a general explanation of the project's philosophy and includes the list of objectives.

The units each take a selection of objectives from this list[1] and show how these objectives could be achieved by children if they are working in a particular subject area or with particular material. They suggest activities relating to a study of the unit's content area, through which it is possible for children to achieve specified objectives. They do not provide a course, but are rather seen as illustrations which will help teachers to provide children with experiences to suit their individual requirements and preferences.

The four units which were the subject of the evaluation plan described here are:

Working with Wood, stages 1 and 2
Metals, stages 1 and 2
Time, stages 1 and 2
Trees, stages 1 and 2

All except *Trees* comprised two books—one relating to classroom activities and one of background information for the teachers. They were to be given trials in junior schools or junior departments of primary schools with children aged seven to eleven. Before describing these trials, it seems important to clarify the role of the evaluator in the project and describe her activities during development of the unit material.

The evaluator's role

The purpose of the evaluator's work on the Science 5–13 Project was to assist in the development of the project's ideas and material. The form of assistance was different from that given by the other members of the team, since the evaluator was not directly involved with researching and writing the units, but rather with clarifying the objectives of the project's material and providing information as to how well it was achieving its intended purposes. The roles of the writers and the evaluator were therefore distinct and yet intimately interconnected. Evaluation was an integral part of the project's development from the start, but was separated from other functions of the project by being the sole responsibility of one person.

There are advantages and disadvantages to this close relationship between evaluator and other team members but on the whole the advantages, which centre round ease of communication, outweigh the disadvantages, which arise from loss of objectivity on the part of the evaluator. It is no doubt important for the evaluation of material to be in the hands of someone who is not emotionally or intellectually committed to it. Such commitment is bound to follow in anyone who has wrestled with the problems of developing and writing material, and clearly the person thus committed cannot stand back from the material, look at it objectively and gather evidence about it impartially. It is not a fault in the writer, but a result of his necessary involvement in his work, that what he produces is more likely to be improved if it is evaluated by another person. But this is only so if the other person is sufficiently well informed about the purpose, content and context of the work to enable him to gather useful evidence. The uncommitted evaluator is faced with the problem of communication: if he tries to remain impartial and objective, he may end up also ignorant of many things which he should understand to do his job properly. It is no easy matter for an evaluator who is not close to the project team to understand the aims of their work sufficiently to plan a valid and useful evaluation. This is particularly so in the case of on-going or formative evaluation, but also true to some extent in the case of final or summative evaluation. When the evaluator is a team member, the communication problem is reduced but at the risk of too much involvement in the development of material. So there are drawbacks to both situations, which cannot be avoided but only minimized by being fully aware of them and consciously taking appropriate steps.

In this project the evaluator took no part in writing the units but kept in close contact with the material at all stages of its production. Fig. 1 shows the parallel development of unit material and evaluation material. The unit,

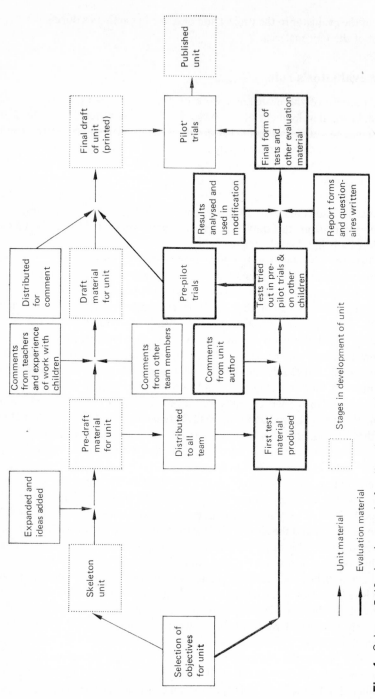

Fig. 1 Science 5–13: development of unit material and evaluation material

beginning as a skeleton, was first read by the evaluator in its pre-draft form, at which point it was possible to develop the first ideas about suitable evaluation material. After small-scale informal classroom trials and discussion amongst the writing members of the team, the pre-draft material was revised. The ensuing draft form had a wider circulation to people whose comments were invited, and was tried out by more teachers. These later classroom trials, called pre-pilot trials, were used to provide examples of children's work and give further immediate feedback for revision. They were also used by the evaluator as pilot trials for test material.

Of the instruments which might be used in the evaluation, the tests for children were the most elaborate and took the greatest time to produce, so these were the first to be given attention. The first draft of some possible test items was discussed with the unit's author before any test production was begun. These discussions were of considerable benefit to both participants, being part of the close communication which was established in this project. Each found value in seeing how the other had interpreted the unit's objectives and, without necessarily changing any ideas or opinions, appreciated another point of view. The chief reason for discussing the test items at this early stage was to ensure as far as possible that the items would detect the kind of behavioural change which the unit's author intended to promote, that they were acceptable in terms of their content, and that they covered adequately any aspects of the unit which the author particularly wished to be explored. To do this involved digging deeply into the meaning of the objectives, analysing situations in which achievement could be promoted or could show itself, considering the expected degree of achievement, and so on. Such exchanges, early on, before ideas had become too firmly rooted, caused both writer and evaluator to think more carefully about the purpose and effectiveness of what they were producing.

Arrangements for trials

The project inherited the arrangements for trials set up by its predecessor, the Nuffield Junior Science Project; this limitation must be remembered in considering the descriptions which follow. The trials were to be conducted in schools in 12 LEAs in England and Wales and in 4 counties of Scotland. Although there were disadvantages to having the pilot areas pre-selected, the advantage was that within these areas it would be easy to find classes which already had experience of active methods of learning—derived in part from the previous project—and in which it might be hoped that learning through discovery was already going on. These were the kind of classes wanted for the trials, so that the value and effect of the materials could be evaluated without the interfering consequences of introducing a new way of working. Obviously it is necessary to reduce the number of uncontrolled variables in the trial situation, so the introduction of the material should be accompanied by as few other changes as possible.

The project laid considerable emphasis on thorough preparation of teachers for taking part in the trials. This was necessary to overcome the anxiety and suspicion which the word 'evaluation' evokes in many teachers. To most the word is taken to be synonymous with 'testing' and in primary schools generally, particularly the more progressive ones, there is an understandable dislike of testing. The project evaluator consciously tried to improve the attitude towards evaluation held by teachers taking part in the trials, and felt that the efforts in this direction met with considerable success. Through lectures, courses and discussions it was possible to explain the reason for the evaluation and the plan devised for it. Experience showed that when teachers realized that the evaluation was essential to the development of the material, that it was concerned with this material and not with assessing their children or themselves, and that they had a valuable part to play in it, then they were prepared to co-operate and not prejudge the work. The teachers became genuine partners in the project's attempt to help them.

Guidelines for the evaluation

Five guiding principles were drawn out of experience and deliberation during the first year and a half of the project.

(a) An evaluator must be prepared to spend a great deal of time and effort to find out exactly what it is that the project aims to do through the material it is producing. This means breaking down such statements of aim as 'helping teachers to help children learn science' until these can be expressed as identifiable behaviours; only then can the achievement of the aim be evaluated. Such analysis is essential, exhausting and apparently unproductive but unless it is done thoroughly everything which follows is insecurely based.

(b) Evaluation must be concerned with children's behaviours; the material being evaluated is an agent of change in this behaviour. Since behaviour is very complex, the problem must be looked at from all angles, different kinds of instruments used, both subjective assessments and objective methods of testing employed if appropriate, and evidence gathered about changes in attitudes as well as in cognitive abilities.

(c) It is most important to find or develop techniques of evaluation which are appropriate to the behaviours being investigated but which interfere as little as possible with these behaviours and the activities in which they are made evident. The evaluation techniques should be enjoyable, if possible, but in any case as easy and straightforward to use as can be. A project's material is invariably intended to be stimulating and interesting for both teachers and pupils, and if this positive, enthusiastic response is found, the evaluation must do nothing to diminish it.

(d)   There is an obligation to think ahead very carefully about the probable results of using any evaluation instrument, to consider how usable the collection of certain information may be and whether the amount of data it would yield could be handled in the time available: this may save wasted effort on the part of the evaluator and all those who provide the information. It is as important not to over-collect as not to under-collect information. Assembling data about behaviour always involves other people, whose time and efforts must be respected. It falls to the evaluator to consider carefully what questions need to be asked, to ask only 'real' questions—those whose answers are honestly needed and can be used.

(e)   Finally, the project will benefit greatly if teachers are really involved in evaluating the material. It helps both the evaluation and the teachers if they are not merely required to fill in forms, send them back, and hear no more until the next set of questions arrives. Meetings arranged to discuss questions on the forms can encourage better observation and reporting on the part of the teachers when they appreciate the purpose of the questions, and better questioning on the part of the evaluator, who realizes how teachers have struggled with inadequate questionnaires. Where possible, the teachers should carry out the direct testing of children, since this reduces the interference with normal work caused by the arrival of an outside administrator.

Formation of the evaluation plan—a four-sided attack

These guidelines were applied to the material being evaluated and the situation in which the trials would take place, in order to choose what kinds of information should be gathered. Any data would have to be readily gathered and rapidly interpreted, be the most relevant, interfere as little as possible with the progress of the trial work, and be such as could combine with other data to produce as complete a description of the trial work as possible. Of course there had to be a compromise, for it would have been an advantage to gather all possible relevant information, exploring many aspects of the learning situation, but this would undoubtedly have caused too much interference. So the compromise was that there should be an attempt to gather evidence about four main aspects. The choice of these four followed from the nature of the project.

The ultimate aim of the project's material was to change the children's behaviours, as expressed in the objectives. Therefore it was necessary to investigate whether or not any of the expected changes had taken place. Yet the material only affected the children indirectly, through the teachers for whom it was written. There were two important links in the chain from the project's material to the children: from the material and the teachers and from the teachers and children. If the material was not adequately communicated to the teachers, then no matter how successful the project's ideas might be in theory, they would fail to produce any results in practice. If the teachers understood the material but the material was not effective in helping children learn, then again there would be no practical results. To have any chance of estimating cause and effect relationships, both these links had to be investigated. Finally, the learning environment was thought to be very relevant to the effect of the material, and included the social as well as the physical environment, both within and outside the school.

These, then, were the four aspects to be investigated: changes in children's behaviours, teachers' reports and opinions of the material, the interaction of teachers, children and material, and the learning environment. The techniques chosen for each investigation are indicated in Fig. 2 and described below.

CHANGES IN CHILDREN'S BEHAVIOURS

Since interest was in the changes in behaviour and not in any particular level of attainment or in differences between individuals, a 'before' and 'after' pattern of testing was planned. Since the trial work might have no connexion with any changes observed in this way, a control group of children had to be tested in the same manner as the group undertaking the trial work. The control group made it possible to estimate what part of the trial group's behaviour changes was the result of experiences connected with the trial material, and what part was due to the combined effect of test sophistication, maturation and other experiences.

The control group would only serve this function adequately if it matched the trial group as fully as possible. Complete matching on a large scale is impossible, so in this case differences between classes in the two groups were randomized. The mechanism for this was as follows. Pairs of classes were suggested for participation in the trials, the classes in each pair being as similar as possible in respect of the children's age range, type and size of school, characteristics of the neighbourhood and teacher's experience. These classes were then assigned randomly to either the control or trial group, so that no systematic bias was introduced.

The form which the test items should take was decided in the light of previous work by the evaluator which had dealt with the problem of measuring young children's achievement in science. This work led to the development of a method in which the test items were introduced by a film sequence showing a demonstration, a situation or some objects, which posed the problem the children were to solve. The answers were recorded by the children in booklets by ticking one of the alternative responses given. This form of test was preferred to the conventional pencil and paper type because it drastically reduces the dependence on verbal ability and enables the presentation of the problems to be as real as possible. Since the objectives of science teaching are concerned with how a child will act or deal with practical problems, the most obvious way

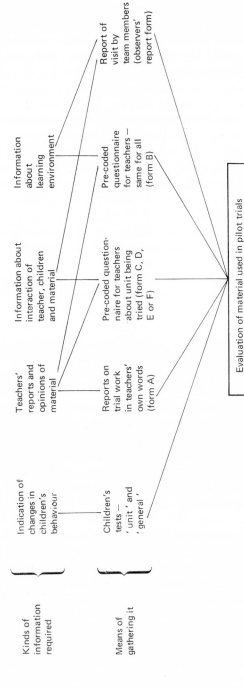

Fig. 2 Science 5–13: evaluation plan

to find out whether he has or has not developed a concept or idea is to present him with a real situation, so chosen that he cannnot deal with it successfully unless he has developed the concept or grasped the idea. However, since this would require individual administration, it was completely impracticable in the present case. The most attractive alternative, which would avoid the disadvantages of the pencil and paper form of test, was to use moving film. Although film is a two-dimensional medium, the movement of objects and apparatus provide the necessary cues for their real nature and form to be appreciated. The most practical kind of projector was chosen—one suitable for use in daylight, and with an integral rear projection screen, for convenience. This projector has the added advantage of resemblance to a television set, so children are already familiar with it as a source of information.

The test items were so written as to detect the various kinds of behaviour described in the project's objectives. Only a fraction of these objectives relate to 'knowledge'; by far the majority deal with the many other kinds of behaviour involved in learning. The old idea that only knowledge can be tested has been largely dispelled, but it still remains true that knowledge is the easiest to test by conventional means. Fortunately, the film medium is a good one for presenting items which are not testing merely for knowledge. The film can, for instance, present a problem where solution calls for ability to identify and manipulate variables, in a way which is much clearer than a verbal description would be. It can also introduce problems which test understanding of such things as sorting, grouping and classification. It can provide data in an easily grasped form and be used for items in which all information is provided and the question demands reasoning or explanations. The use of film is not, of course, restricted to cognitive abilities—in fact it may well have greater relative value for testing behaviours in the affective domain.

The test items contained situations or problems so designed that the children's responses would show whether they had achieved a particular objective. Where possible, care was taken to avoid using problems described or suggested in the units, because the criterion of success in this part of the evaluation was the achievement of objectives, not how thoroughly the problems in the units had been studied. To have based the items directly on problems selected from unit activities would not only have implied that those activities were more worthy of attention than others, but would have indicated that the teachers were expected to follow the unit in a way which the project never intended. As has already been said, the units are not a course, therefore a test based on a course could have no relevance.

A separate test was thus required for each unit; four 'unit' tests were produced, each consisting of thirty-four items. But in addition there were objectives common to all units—objectives chosen to guide the approach to active learning in science which pervaded all the project's material. A 'general' test was devised to assess the achievement of these general objectives. The items in it tested application and transfer to other problems to an even greater degree than the unit test items. For example, in one item the film shows two equal-sized pieces of paper, one plain writing paper and the other news-paper. They are picked up and a strip is cut from each; the strip of newspaper is wider than the plain paper but they are the same length. These strips are then attached to separate bulldog clips hanging from a frame. Similar clips are put on the bottom of the strips and weights hung from them as the first part of the sequence ends. At this point the commentator administering the test asks the children to record in their booklets whether or not they think this is a fair test of which kind of paper is the stronger. The film sequence then continues: two more strips of paper are seen hung side by side on the frame. This time they are of equal width as well as equal length, and again weights are being hung from them as the sequence ends. The children are then asked to record in their booklet their judgement of this test of the paper, by ticking 'Fair' or 'Not fair' in the second part of the question. The objective under test here is 'awareness that more than one variable may be involved in a particular change' (stage I).

The general test was in two parts: the first dealt with the general cognitive objectives, and the second with the objectives of the affective domain. In the latter an attempt was made to measure children's liking for certain activities, both in science and in other areas of work. The children were asked to state their liking for the various activities in terms of a three-point scale presented visually to them. In the introduction to this part of the test, the film sequence showed two children eating ice cream. The children taking the test were asked to imagine themselves doing this and say how much they liked doing it. It was imagined that almost all would like this 'very much', so a personal standard for liking something 'very much' was established. The second sequence showed children polishing shoes, which provided a standard for liking some-thing 'not very much'. After this the sequences showed other activities; in each case the children were invited to imagine themselves doing the same things and to note how much they liked it—'very much', 'a little' or 'not very much'. The point of filming these activities rather than simply giving the children a list was that titles such as 'looking after animals' or 'gardening' could be interpreted in many different ways by different children, whereas the film shows a definite activity. All the children can thus respond to the same situation, not to their own idea of what the activities involve.

The general test and one of the unit tests were given to each child in both the trial group and the control group at the beginning and end of the trial period. The same test was used on both occasions; the limited advantages of using two parallel forms of the test were not considered to justify the extra expense and time involved in producing them. The tests were administered in most cases by the class teacher, who was supplied with a suggested film comment-ary as well as the film loops and children's booklets. The teacher also marked the tests, using the mark scheme and score sheets provided. As the marking was objective throughout, re-marking by the project was not thought necessary.

A disproportionate amount of attention has been given here to the children's tests because they were of a novel kind. However, it must be stressed that the tests were but one of four types of evidence which contributed to the evaluation, and were not considered to be any more important than the others. There is plenty of experience to show that evidence of behaviour changes by itself is of little consequence for evaluation of curricular change. It is only of value if the conditions under which such changes did or did not take place are also known.

TEACHERS' REPORTS AND OPINIONS

These were collected formally by questionnaire and informally at meetings and during visits of team members and others to the classrooms. Three forms, to be completed by all the trial class teachers, were distributed at the start of the trials:

form A   mainly blank paper on which teachers were invited to write an account of the relevant activities of the children during the trial period;

form B   a questionnaire, mostly pre-coded, asking for information about the class, school, relevant biographical data about the teacher, details of the test administrations, and opinions about the project's introductory book, *With Objectives in Mind;*

form C   (one of these according to which unit was being tried by the
D, E, or   teacher): another pre-coded questionnaire asking for infor-
F   mation, observations and opinions about the unit.

In planning these forms, an attempt was made to arrange the questions in the order in which things might be encountered. This was to encourage teachers to record their impressions at frequent intervals rather than leaving all the recording to the end of the trial period, when they might have forgotten certain points which occurred to them weeks before.

INTERACTION OF TEACHERS, CHILDREN AND MATERIAL

Because of the difficulty of arranging the prolonged observations and records in the classroom which are needed if interaction is to be analysed on a formal basis, this work was done only by informal observation. A team member visited each trial class whilst work was in progress. After the visit the team member filled in a form, recording what had been observed about such things as the class organization, the use being made of the material, the attitude of the teacher to the project's ideas, the teacher-pupil relationship, etc. There were also some questions on the teachers' report forms designed to indicate how the material was used and how the children reacted.

THE LEARNING ENVIRONMENT

Information about this was gathered from the teachers and from the visiting team members. Questions which required factual answers and did not depend on making a decision or a value judgement were included in the teachers' report form B. The other questions were included in the observers' report form. This was not because teachers were thought to be incapable of making judgements of the kind required, but because they were not in a position to do so. For example, a teacher might consider the children's working space was 'adequate' if she had always been used to teaching in very poor and cramped conditions, but for the purposes of the evaluation the judgement needed to be made on standards which are more widely applicable. The team member, visiting many schools in many parts of the country, was able to make a more useful judgement of such things as the adequacy of space within and outside the classroom, and its adequacy not only in quantity but also in quality, and of the use which was being made of it.

Organization of the trials

NUMBERS TAKING PART

There were four units ready for trials starting in September 1969 (see p. 18); these were allocated to the twelve pilot areas so that each area tried only one unit. Thus three areas were concerned with the evaluation of each unit except in the case of *Time*, which was also given trials in Scotland. In each English

Table 3.2 Basis of sample for evaluation of one unit (provided jointly by three pilot areas)

Age range	Type of school	No. of classes	
		Experimental	Control
Younger (7–9)	Rural	3	3
Older (9–11)	Rural	3	3
Younger (7–9)	Urban, prosperous catchment area	3	3
Older (9–11)	Urban, prosperous catchment area	3	3
Younger (7–9)	Urban, disadvantaged catchment area	3	3
Older (9–11)	Urban depressed catchment area	3	3

or Welsh area six classes helped evaluate the unit and six control classes were involved in the testing. Scotland had eight trial and eight control classes. Thus the number of classes trying out a unit was eighteen for *Metals, Working with Wood* and *Trees*, and twenty-six for *Time* (a total of eighty).

DURATION OF TRIALS

The pre-trial testing took place in the first half of the autumn term 1969; trial work was begun in any trial class as soon as the tests had been completed in that class. By the end of the spring term 1970, the trial work and post-trial testing was completed for *Metals, Working with Wood* and *Time*. The working time of the trials was one full term, spread over two terms. To give *Trees* a proper trial, the work was spread over a full year so that all the seasonal changes could be included in the trial period.

Table 3.3   Programme for trials

	Sep–Oct 1969	Nov–Dec 1969, Jan–Feb 1970	Mar–Apr 1970
Trial classes	All take both unit and general tests	Children's activities guided by teacher using trial unit	All take both unit and general tests
Control classes	All take both unit and general tests	Children's activities continued as previously	All take both unit and general tests

Report on the trials

The trials were completed as planned with a loss by the end of only three experimental classes out of the eighty constituting the original sample. This very low rate of drop-out probably resulted from careful selection and preparation of classes in the first place, and from the fact that teachers were supplied with necessary materials or means to purchase them, and visits were paid to the classes during the trials. Much of the credit for this must go to the local organizers; these were local inspectors, advisers or teachers who undertook the distribution of materials and were responsible for liaison with the project team. Team members also played an important part in the trials by visiting the classes and attending local meetings of trial teachers. The observers' report forms completed by the team members after their visits were found to be of great value, and without the information they contained it would not have been possible to interpret the teachers' questionnaire responses as usefully as was in fact done.

Administering the tests to the children took longer in many cases than was anticipated. The reasons for this were chiefly lack of experience with the use of film loops on the part of many teachers, the failure of some loops to run, due to being inefficiently put into the cassettes, and the malfunctioning of many of the projectors. These technical problems tried the patience of many teachers, and of the evaluator (who tried to put things right as quickly as they went wrong) almost to the limit. Teachers were asked to report on the testing and a few expressed their feelings clearly:

Whilst the method of testing might appear very attractive in theory, in practice I found it to be unreliable, time-consuming and a great tax on one's patience. The children seemed to enjoy the films and generally found the method of answering easy to understand. Nevertheless ... they found the constant interruptions very tiresome.

However, the problems were overcome and it was encouraging to find that, despite the trouble, teachers saw the point of the work:

I cannot see how this administration could be made easier, but a section in the unit on *Time* explaining how twenty-four hours in a day could be extended to about thirty hours would have been useful! To be serious, it meant extra work but we felt it worth while!

Analysis of results

Class mean scores, rather than scores of individuals, were the basis for statistical analysis of the children's test results; the sample size was thus quite small, being the number of classes and not the number of children involved. The mean scores were derived from the scores of children who completed both tests on both occasions. In the case of three unit tests, the difference between post-test scores for trial and control was statistically significant (at the 0·05 level). For each of these three units an analysis of variance showed that variance attributable to difference between trial and control classes was negligible for the pre-trial test scores but highly significant (beyond the 0·001 level) for the post-trial test scores. The results for the fourth unit were complicated by considerable initial difference between the trial and control scores, but they showed the same trend—a greater rate of increase in the trial group as compared with the control.

Satisfying though these overall test results were, they had little consequence for rewriting. To give some indication of which parts of the unit were most effective in terms of the children's performance, the scores for different groups of items in the tests were calculated separately. Change in score on the groups of items relating to each of the objectives represented in the tests were compared, trial with control. This gave some guidance as to the relative effectiveness of the parts of the units relating to these objectives. Such a procedure could only suggest hypotheses, and other information was examined for evidence to support or reject them.

Alongside this analysis of children's test results, data from the various questionnaires and report forms was used in two main ways: information, suggestions and comments of teachers which could not be coded were extracted and collated; the rest was coded and transferred to IBM cards along with other information about the classes. The coded information—about 300 items for each class—was analysed by computer, using a program for classifying qualitative data by cluster analysis. This greatly helped the treatment of questionnaire responses, which would otherwise have been very clumsy, since on almost every question there is a range of opinion and mere totals of replies in one category or another convey little more than that some like one thing and some like another. It is much more helpful to know whether a certain reply to one question tends to occur with a certain reply to another, whether there are patterns in the responses and, if so, what conditions are associated with particular patterns. The cluster analysis program sets the computer to search through the lists of code numbers to find those numbers which occur together in the lists more frequently than would be expected to happen by chance. It collects together a group of numbers which each have a value of observed coincidence greater than the expected coincidence with other numbers in the list. Several groups of numbers are found in this way, many of which overlap to a large extent. With the help of a further part of the computer program it is possible to identify the two most useful groups—those where the coincidence between the numbers is greatest in opposite directions. These two groups form the opposite ends of a dimension, and when the numbers in them are decoded, it is quite easy to see which, in the terms of the project, is the 'positive' end and which is the 'negative' end.

This program was used separately on five different sets of information, one for each unit and one for all classes combined. The latter included all the information which was not specific to any unit, i.e. from teachers' form B, from the observers' report form and from the children's test results. Here are some of the items in the positive group found in the analysis of combined class results:

(a)   The children's test score on attitude to science activities increased during the trial.

(b)   The class had previously been working through active discovery methods.

(c)   The desks or tables in the classroom were arranged in irregular groups.

(d)   The class timetable was fully integrated.

(e)   At most times of the day the children worked individually or in groups at their own tasks.

(f)   The children regularly worked outside the classroom.

(g)   The children formed their own groups for working.

(h)   Science activities were carried on by different groups at different times, as chosen by the children.

(*i*)   The children could work on their own ploys.

(*j*)   The teacher had warmly approved the ideas project's on first being introduced to them.

(*k*)   The teacher appreciated very well the meaning of objectives.

(*l*)   The teacher used a discovery approach in most areas of the curriculum.

(*m*)   The teacher had made some use of the project's statement of objectives apart from using it in connexion with the trial work.

And in the negative group:

(*a*)   The class had previously been used to working through formal methods.

(*b*)   The children's activities were very largely directed by the teacher.

(*c*)   The desks or tables in the classroom were arranged in regular groups or rows.

(*d*)   The children worked as a whole class at most times of the day.

(*e*)   Science activities were organized so that all groups always worked at the same time.

(*f*)   Science activities were organized so that all the children worked on much the same problem.

(*g*)   The teacher allocated the children to groups for science activities.

(*h*)   Science activities had not been included in the children's work before the trials.

(*i*)   The teacher had a poor appreciation of what objectives are.

(*j*)   The teacher used a discovery approach hardly at all.

(*k*)   The teacher thought that evaluation of whether or not objectives had been achieved was unnecessary.

Interpretation and use in rewriting

An internal report for each unit gave the results of the cluster analysis and an interpretation of the statistical analysis of the children's test results. In addition to the data constituting the positive and negative groups, the weightings of other responses or items of information were used to indicate the degree to which each was associated with the positive or negative group. A bonus from this process was the light it shed on the value of collecting different kinds of information and on the usefulness of various questionnaire items; had this been done at the pre-pilot stage, more efficient questionnaires could have been written for use in the trials.

In general it was found that the items of information in or closely associated with the positive groups expressed success and satisfaction with the material, whilst the reverse was true for the negative groups. By treating the negative group responses as reasons for dissatisfaction, points requiring attention in rewriting were identified. For instance, nearly all the negative groups con-

E.C.D.—2*

tained the item 'teacher wanted help with class management and group work organization, which was not supplied by the unit'. This was evidently a cause of dissatisfaction which could be met during the revision by writing in suggestions to provide the help needed. Usually it was possible to find ways of correcting the cause of dissatisfaction without upsetting those who were satisfied with it; in this case, it was unlikely that including help with class organization would upset those who had been able to use the units successfully without it.

A good example of how the results of evaluation were used is provided by the unit *Working with Wood*. The material in this unit was completely reorganized in response to the discovery that teachers felt the topic was too narrow to suit the wide-ranging exploration which is appropriate in the junior years. The suggested investigations concerning wood were consequently rewritten to fit into a wider context, and more trouble was taken to explain how they could lead to and support other classroom activities. In doing this, much more practical help with classroom management was brought in.

The cluster analysis results also cast more light on teachers' written comments and suggestions. By looking to see which of teachers' questionnaire responses were in the positive and negative groups it was possible to estimate to what extent a teacher making any particular comment was one who was satisfied and able to make use of the unit or one who was dissatisfied and not helped much by the unit. The comments had much greater value when examined in this way than if they were treated as all coming from the same background of opinion.

Whilst the computer sorted out the information, it did not, of course, make judgements. Criteria for rewriting still had to be decided by discussion amongst the team. For whom were the units being written? For teachers at one end of the dimension or the other, or those in between? Was it possible to cater for people at all points along the dimension? These were the questions which still had to be answered after the computer had done its work.

Unanswered questions

The evaluation results did not provide answers to several questions which seemed very important at the time of rewriting but which had not existed at the time of the trials. The interval of time between the beginning of the trials and the revision of the units was eighteen months—at least six months longer than necessary, on account of delays caused by constant failure of the computer to complete the five long analyses. During this time the writers in the team had produced two further sets of units, and in doing so had made use of their subjective impressions of the way the trials described here were progressing. Changes were thus made in the writing style and form of guidance given in the new units because the team had absorbed some of the evaluation results before they were fully analysed, but also, and probably more so, because ideas had developed in the intervening time. So when the first set of units came to be revised, questions to which the writers most wanted answers were:

Are the new ways of writing preferable to the old?
Which is the more acceptable form of guidance?
Shall we rewrite the first units in the style of the latest ones?
Should an index to objectives be included?

The evaluation could not supply answers—the index of objectives, for instance, was brought up several months after the trials of the first units had ended! In these trials teachers each tried only one unit and could not compare one with another even on the same set, let alone make comparisons with units still unwritten at the time of the trials. Many liked what they tried, but might have been less easily satisfied had alternatives been known. The plans for later trials were drawn up so as to enable comparative judgements to be made—another example of the way the results proved formative in refining evaluation items rather than the material.

It would seem that one of the main problems confronting anyone attempting formative evaluation is to define the areas to be investigated, i.e. formulate the objectives of the evaluation. But the main obstacle to achieving what the evaluator sets out to do is that these objectives will be constantly changing with the inevitable development of the project team's ideas. Formative evaluation could only be completely 'successful' if the writers' ideas stood still—hardly a characteristic of a lively and creative team. Maybe the measure of a good team of writers is the failure of its formative evaluation!

Publisher for the project: Macdonald Educational.

Note

I   The first units to be produced were written according to this pattern. The evaluation showed that this pattern had serious disadvantages; in revising the first units and writing later ones, the activities were directed towards a wider range of objectives.

4 Cambridge School Classics Project

Patricia Story

The Cambridge School Classics Project, financed jointly by the Nuffield Foundation and the Schools Council, was set up in January 1966 with a two-fold brief: first, to investigate methods of teaching Latin in the early stages and to produce an O level language course; second, to provide materials for a classical studies foundation course which would be suitable for pupils aged 11–12 and of a wide range of ability. The project has since produced draft material for both courses which has been used in a large number of trial schools and is now being revised for publication. The first unit of the Latin language course was published in 1970 and the classical studies foundation material followed suit early in 1972.

What follows is concerned with the evaluation of the experimental O level Latin course. The pupils' material is divided into five units, all comprising a number of stages. Each stage takes the form of a pamphlet containing stories in Latin, linguistic information and exercises, and further discussion in English of the theme of that particular pamphlet. Unit I, for example, describes life in Pompeii in AD 79, the year of the eruption, and ends with the destruction of the city. The twelve pamphlets that make up the unit each describe a different aspect of life in the city, usually seen through the eyes of the family and friends of Lucius Caecilius Iucundus, a Pompeian *entrepreneur*. Caecilius himself appears in a variety of situations—buying a slave for his household, falling victim to a confidence trickster in the forum, taking part in the social life that centred on the public baths in the city. In another stage the family cook, a slave named Grumio, pretends that he has the right to vote (and to accept bribes) in the local elections and comes to grief. In yet another stage a serious riot breaks out at a gladiatorial show in the amphitheatre, and in another the excitement aroused by the arrival of a troupe of actors is described.

The pamphlets of unit I are accompanied by a set of sixty slides of Pompeii, a tape recording of some of the Latin text, and a *Teacher's Handbook* which contains a detailed analysis of the unit's linguistic scheme, suggestions about teaching methods and further information about the content of the material.

The evaluator's task

An evaluator was appointed in September 1967 to assess the O level Latin language course. Her work was seen as essentially formative: she was to assess the progress of the course in the schools which, from that month, had started to use the experimental material; and she was to help to revise the material for publication in the light of suggestions and criticisms made by the schools. It was also hoped that the information gained from the schools would be useful to the writers who were at that time working on the later stages of the draft material.

The timing of the appointment is worth discussing in connexion with the role of an evaluator. When she arrived in Cambridge the aims of the course had already been formulated, the early material written and the group of trial schools selected. The general aims of the course were to enable pupils to read a selected group of Latin authors and to understand the content, style and values of classical civilization. These general aims were further defined and discussed in the *Teacher's Handbooks* to the course. In this instance, the evaluator was fortunate in having colleagues who had been impressed with the importance of having clear aims, particularly about the linguistic aspects of the course, and of relating their aims to classroom practice. The group of trial schools had also been selected with great care, and was as representative as possible in a situation where local authorities, headmasters and teachers were free to decide whether they wished and could afford to embark on a new course. However, one can envisage a situation where the presence of an evaluator might have been helpful in clarifying aims and organizing a test programme.

There was also the fact that no 'testing of tests' could be carried out before the main assessment programme began in September 1967; this precluded the use of multiple-choice tests where a bank of pre-tested items is essential. It was not possible to postpone the start of the main assessment programme to provide this: the evaluator's appointment was in the first instance for two years only, and if the information from schools was to be helpful in the writing of the later stages of the course, it was obvious that it would have to be collected and analysed as quickly as possible.

Certain advantages would have resulted from postponing the main assessment to the second year of the trial programme, or at least the provision of sufficient evaluation resources to take into consideration both the first and the second year's work. Certainly, in the second year the 'Hawthorne effect'[1] would be much less apparent and teachers would be more at home with the course, which involved the adoption of new or unfamiliar teaching methods and subject matter.

In the preceding paragraphs it has been assumed that an evaluator's role is a complex one. He is to help with the clarification of the aims of the course, if not with their actual formulation; he has a knowledge of sampling techniques and can organize test programmes; and presumably he must be familiar with the content and teaching methods of the course he is testing, and preferably have some teaching experience. Even if the evaluator is not expected to possess or exercise all these skills, the fact remains that he needs to be a person of protean ability or at least to have very good advisers. In the case of the Cambridge School Classics Project, the evaluator had considerable teaching experience, some knowledge of experimental examining and an almost total ignorance of statistical techniques. She was therefore very grateful for the help given her by the project's evaluation committee, the members of which were an HM Inspector, a practising teacher of classics, an educational psychologist, a mathematician and the project director. With the help of this committee, an extensive assessment programme was arranged, involving the use of verbal reasoning (VR) and attainment tests, teachers' report forms, pupil questionnaires and school visits.

Outline of assessment for unit I

VERBAL REASONING SCORES

These were obtained for nearly all pupils, either from their eleven-plus examinations or from the standardized test supplied by the project for the purpose of the trial. Both from the administrative and from the statistical point of view, it would have been simpler to give the same standardized test to all children in the trials; in fact, only pupils who took the project's test (about two-thirds of the total sample) were included in the selected sample whose attainment tests were to be analysed. As the VR scores were to be used not to make fine discriminations between pupils, but to assign them to three broad bands of ability, the one group test was considered adequate.

ATTAINMENT TESTS

The attainment tests were designed to check the effectiveness of the project's material. This had been constructed in the hope that it would be understood by the great majority of pupils taking the course, the less able as well as the able. The tests, which were constructed on the same principles as the material, sought to demonstrate this fact. They were therefore not intended to discriminate sharply between able and less able pupils and produce a good scatter of marks, which would have meant devising a new set of tests. In addition, it was hoped that the tests might supply useful information to those who were then writing the material for unit III.

The tests were worked by all pupils after every fourth stage of the material (i.e. after stages 4, 8, 12). Each test took the form of two Latin stories (only one in the first test) for translation. The first story in the pair contained themes and characters familiar to the pupil from unit I; the second story, apart from its classical setting, had no close connexion with the material in the unit.

Linguistically, the stories were pitched at the level found at the beginning of every fourth stage. New sentence patterns and morphology were lightly represented in easy contexts, as the pupil was not necessarily expected to have mastered new features by the end of the stage in which they were introduced. In all tests except one, the teachers were asked to supply any vocabulary requested by the pupils. There were two reasons for this:

(a)   it was not intended that the pupils' grasp of sentence patterns and morphology should be obscured by ignorance of vocabulary;

(b)   as the project had suggested that vocabulary should be learnt gradually in context through frequent exposure rather than by rote in lists of isolated words, and as the range of vocabulary was very wide, it was felt that the pupils should be given time to acquire knowledge of common words.

However, it was hoped that by the end of unit I the pupils would have begun to acquire a basic vocabulary, and in the first part of the stage 12 test the pupils were given no help with vocabulary except for a few words provided in the test paper.

The teachers were asked to devote one lesson period to each of the tests; the test length was kept short in the hope that all pupils would finish in 35–45 minutes. No strict time limit was applied, as this was felt to be unimportant. The teachers were asked to treat the tests as far as possible as part of the regular work of the class; the scripts were to be marked by the teacher and returned to the class for correction in the usual way before being sent to the project office.

It was found that in general pupils encountered little difficulty with the sentence patterns and morphology incorporated in the tests. Lexical difficulties were fully demonstrated only in the stage 12 test, which showed that unless pupils recognize a certain proportion of the words in a passage, they tend to distort the morphology and sentence patterns in an attempt to arrive at some meaning. Although basic vocabulary occurs frequently in the material and although the project suggests that it should not be taught by rote, the unit I *Teacher's Handbook* had not sufficiently stressed that vocabulary does need constant consolidation.

Assessment of English expression caused little difficulty in the early tests, as the stories consisted of easy narrative or dialogue and few demands were made on the pupil's command of his native language. In the later tests, however, it became clear that the grading system adopted tended to emphasize the technical aspects of language and did not give much scope for an adequate assessment of the pupil's work as a coherent idiomatic piece of English. In later tests the balance was redressed by giving two grades, one for the pupil's grasp of the linguistic structure of the Latin, the other for his understanding of the passage as a whole and for the quality of his translation into English.

TEACHERS' REPORT FORMS

No particular difficulties were experienced in collecting the teachers' observations on the course. They filled up a standard report form at the end of each stage in the material and sent these for analysis to the project office. Because nearly all the teachers had volunteered to teach the course and had previously undertaken to do any paperwork required by the project, the percentage of report forms returned was extremely high. The information on the forms that could be codified was recorded on two series of grid sheets; one formed a record of the individual schools' reactions to stages 1–12; the second summarized the attitudes of all the schools in one age group to a single stage. To give an example, it was possible to discover at a glance how many schools with beginners aged eleven thought the amount of new vocabulary given in any one stage excessive.

Information that could not be conveniently codified was entered directly on the revision copies of the material. Fortunately for the evaluator, the teachers showed a remarkable degree of agreement about the successes and weaknesses of the material. Apart from a plethora of minor blemishes, the only defects of any seriousness appeared to be the presentation of the imperfect and perfect tenses in stage 6, the static nature of the stories in stage 10 (which did not appeal to pupils in this age group), and the guided compositions in Latin. These were intended as creative exercises but generally left pupils feeling frustrated because of their difficulty.

Initially, there was also a supplementary data sheet, which was an attempt to obtain a synoptic view of the difficulties presented by every group of four stages. This data sheet, however, did not commend itself to the teachers, who preferred to write about continuing problems on the standard report forms, and the questions on the data sheet were incorporated in the revised report form which came into use for the end of unit II and subsequent units.

THE PUPIL QUESTIONNAIRE

At the end of stage 12 each pupil was asked to answer a questionnaire about his attitude to the material and his reactions to various classroom activities. A few examples serve to illustrate the kind of question asked and responses obtained.

One question listed the main characters appearing in stage 1–12 and asked pupils to pick out the ones they liked best and least. Grumio the cook emerged as the clear favourite: he was variously described as funny, jolly, good at his job, daring, always in trouble, always after the girls (a characteristic that met with the approval of both girls and boys). He was also popular 'because we hear a lot about him'. It is clear from the comments made about other characters that their popularity often depends on their number of appearances in the project material.

Caecilius and his faithful slave Clemens were also popular with all ages and both sexes, but particularly with the boys. In their attitudes to several characters there was a tendency for pupils to show more sympathy with members of their own sex. Even the most unpopular character of all, the mother Metella, was less unpopular with the girls than with the boys. Both sexes, however, could not forgive Metella for her jealousy of the pretty slave girl Melissa, although this is mentioned in only one story; elsewhere Metella and Melissa appear to co-exist quite amicably. The fact that the pictures of Metella suggested to the pupils that she is vain and snobbish and 'does nothing but sit around in the atrium all day' only served to strengthen the pupils' dislike of her. This strong negative reaction was entirely unexpected by the project writers—a fact which may provide justification, if justification is needed, for this particular piece of consumer research.

Another question which inquired about the kind of reading material preferred showed that all groups of pupils were strongly in favour of mystery and adventure stories. Plays were extremely popular with the boys aged eleven but their appeal seemed to diminish with advancing age and growing self-consciousness, although over half the thirteen-year-old girl beginners and a third of the thirteen-year-old boys still enjoyed them.

The pupils were also asked about their preferences for activities associated with translation. Translation in pairs and groups proved to be the most popular activity, the eleven-plus boys and girls preferring to work in pairs and the twelve-plus pupils and thirteen-plus girls in groups. There was some support for translating silently on one's own, and three groups were moderately pleased to hear the teacher reading aloud to them. Listening to the tape was the least popular activity, which was hardly surprising in view of the poor technical quality of the experimental version. Girls of eleven- and twelve-plus and boys of thirteen-plus disliked translating aloud by themselves to the teacher and class, although the eleven-plus boys placed this activity third in their order of preference. This may perhaps be a reflection of the fact that a large proportion of the boys in this part of the sample had high VR scores and were highly successful at oral translation. It was a little disappointing that 18 per cent of the eleven-plus boys and 14 per cent of the twelve-plus girls had apparently not experienced working in either groups or pairs.

A further question concerning a broader range of activities revealed that looking at slides was the most popular activity of both sexes and all age groups. This may be regarded as a compliment to the good quality of the project slides, but it may also reflect the fact that this activity does not count as work in the pupils' eyes and is still a special treat once or twice a term, when the classicist can arrange to take over the geography room for the odd lesson. Visits to schools and teachers' reports show that the project's suggestion of showing four or five slides in any lesson where they seem relevant is quite impracticable in many schools.

Some problems of general interest

Of the many issues arising in this evaluation, three only are chosen for discussion as being of general interest.

The first relates to the size and nature of the sample and the difficulties of dealing with a large amount of test material. The project course was initially tried out in a representative group of 74 schools; 3581 pupils and 121 teachers were involved. The wisdom of drawing up such a large sample in the first place may be questioned, but there were good and obvious reasons why this was done. It provided for comments from a large number of teachers; it made possible an adequate sampling of the widely varied patterns of school, course and timetable organization in which Latin may be taught; it permitted the inclusion of enough less able children in the sample, which was felt to be very important since the project's course was designed for classes with a wider spread of ability than in the traditional grammar school; and finally, it provided the capacity to tolerate the inevitable loss of trial classes, for one reason or another, without unbalancing the sample.

The marking of attainment tests, however, presented difficulties which have not been successfully resolved. One concerned the numbers involved and was associated with the methods of marking adopted. With 3581 tests flooding into the project office every six weeks or so, it was obvious to the evaluator that if she were not to be completely overwhelmed, she must select an inner sample of papers to mark. Eventually, a representative sample of 426 pupils was selected. This seemed manageable from the marking point of view and also appeared to yield adequate sub-groups in most areas, although the number of less able children was too small to produce significant results. This deficiency was remedied by reference to the performance of all the less able children in the original group of 3581—again an argument for a large initial group of schools.

Even with this relatively small number of pupils, the marking of attainment tests in considerable detail occupied the evaluator for too much of her time, and some of the results obtained were not worth the effort expended on them; e.g. the analysis of pupils' mistakes did not affect the writing of the later stages or the revision of the material. There were two reasons for this: first, information about the early stages of the course bore little relation to the sophisticated linguistic structures which were then being incorporated in the later stages; secondly, many of the pupils' mistakes seemed to be specific to the test pieces themselves, and although they were very useful in revising the tests for further use by teachers, they were largely irrelevant to the revision of the course material.

Certainly, the tests did fulfil their primary function of showing whether or not the pupils could cope with the linguistic complexities of the various stages of the course. However, this could have been established by adopting the quite simple procedure of dividing the pupils into three groups according to whether they performed well, badly, or indifferently on the tests. Their performance could have then been easily correlated with the variables of VR scores, age and sex, and this was in fact eventually done. Had the tests showed up serious deficiencies in the course material, no doubt the detailed marking would have benefited the revised version of the material and could have led to some re-planning of the later stages of the course. It is a measure of the material's success that the tests revealed quite clearly that most children could cope with the linguistic gradient of much of the course and that the mistakes that the majority made were few and not very serious. In retrospect, it was not so much the test instrument that was at fault as the fact that it continued to be used when the primary aim of the tests could have been achieved by simpler and more economic means, and after it was demonstrated that the results relevant to writing the later stages were minor and not worth the time expended on them.

Another problem of general interest was presented by the second of the two major aims of the course, that of developing in the pupil an understanding of the content, style and values of classical civilization. This aim was regarded as extremely important by the project team; this is shown by the fact that all the reading matter in the course is set in an ancient context and its content explained and amplified at the end of each stage. The *Teacher's Handbooks* contain further information and a bibliography, and sets of slides are produced to illustrate the material in the pupils' texts. It seemed to the evaluator, however, that no coherent evaluation of the achievement of this aim could be attempted until it had been clearly defined what cognitive skills and content matter were involved.

On the report form for unit I, teachers were asked to list the questions discussed in class which went beyond linguistic problems. In this way it was hoped to discover the range and depth of interest shown by pupils in the subject matter of the course. This proved useful for the revision of the material for publication; it revealed, for instance, that the historical introduction about Pompeii in stage 3 does not mean very much to pupils of this age group who have no historical framework to which they can relate it.

At the same time the questions that were discussed in class might be shown to differ not only in their subject matter but also in the kind of cognitive skill they presupposed. As a result, it might be possible to persuade teachers that such skills could be identified and classified, and that their teaching should be consciously directed to produce them. An early attempt to impose on a group of local teachers B. S. Bloom's analysis of cognitive objectives,[2] and to ask them to analyse *en passant* a class discussion in Bloom's terms, met with a deserved lack of success. It was quite apparent from this experiment that any classification of cognitive skills would have to be straightforward and involve as little technical jargon as possible.

It occurred to the evaluator that it would be possible on a revised report form to ask teachers to continue to record pupils' questions and comments but to classify them under three headings: information, analysis and evaluation. This was done for unit II and the following notes added to explain the meaning of the headings.

'These headings are arranged in ascending order of complexity. Thus analysis presupposes a knowledge of the relevant information and evaluation presupposes analysis of a problem. Some examples may be helpful.

'(a) *Information:* Under this heading should be recorded information volunteered by pupils and requests for further information, e.g.
How was the Fishbourne villa discovered?
Did Cogidubnus pay tribute to Rome?

'(b) *Analysis:* Attempts by the pupil, prompted or unprompted by the teacher, to explain the information, e.g.
The reasons why Cogidubnus' father supported the Romans.
The evidence for associating the villa at Fishbourne with Cogidubnus.

'(c) *Evaluation:* This may be of various kinds.
Historical, e.g. an assessment of the evidence associating the villa at Fishbourne with Cogidubnus: is it convincing?
Aesthetic, e.g. a discussion of Romano-British taste.
Ethical, e.g. a discussion of the character and behaviour of Cogidubnus.'

The response of teachers has been encouraging and as a result the following expanded classification has been included in the revised teacher's handbook for unit I (see *The Cambridge Latin Course,* unit I, *Teacher's Handbook,* Cambridge University Press, 1971, p. 24):

We suggest that the following objectives, already being pursued in many schools, should be kept in mind. Pupils should be encouraged to:
(a)   make comparisons between the ancient and modern worlds,
(b)   ask for and suggest explanations of the facts presented in the pamphlets,
(c)   produce original work of their own; this may take the form of an imaginative essay or of drawing conclusions from the facts they have acquired,
(d)   realize what is involved in making valid judgements, whether they be historical, aesthetic or moral.

It is not suggested that children of eleven and twelve will be able to proceed very far with (d), but it is better to err on the side of over-ambition than to underestimate the capacity and interests of young adolescents.

It is thus hoped to familiarize teachers with the idea of a hierarchy of cognitive skills which their pupils should be trained to develop. Questions in the project's special O level examination have been framed with these skills in mind.

The third and final problem to be discussed is that of making valid comparisons between experimental and other courses. Since one of the main aims of the project course is to develop competence in reading Latin, and since so much time in the classroom is devoted to this end, it is proper to ask how the reading performance of project pupils compares with that of pupils taking traditional courses. Such a comparison was impossible in the early stages of the project course, since the experimental material is very different from traditional courses in its linguistic scheme, vocabulary and content, and no test could be devised that would be fair to both groups of pupils. However, at the O level stage, when all pupils would be reading Latin authors, albeit different ones, some comparison might be made. The situation was still far from being an ideal one experimentally, in that it was impossible to isolate reading skill as the one independent variable. For example, the project and traditional courses differed in ways other than their approach to reading. Pupils taking traditional courses would have spent a considerable amount of their time learning grammar formally and translating from English into Latin. Project pupils would have done neither, but would have concentrated instead on learning to read Latin and studying Roman civilization. There was also the difficulty of matching groups of pupils in terms of VR ability, length of course, number of lessons per week and the competence of their teachers. To mount a large experiment involving schools other than the project ones was out of the question, in view of the time and money available.

As an alternative, a longitudinal experiment within the existing group of project schools was devised. Pupils in a selected group of project schools, who were taking O level in the summer of 1969, were asked to translate a passage of Latin just before their examination. These papers were sent to the project to be marked. These pupils had of course been traditionally trained, as the project course had started in these schools only in September 1967. The experiment was repeated in the summer of 1970 with the next year's O level pupils, a group composed mainly of pupils who had been traditionally trained but with a few pupils who had completed the project course in three years. In 1971 and 1972 it was planned to repeat the same experiment until all the project pupils had taken the O level examination. Comparison between successive groups in the same school may be rather unreliable as they have not been formally matched in ability or necessarily taught by the same teacher. However, schools where the composition of successive classes has radically changed, perhaps because of secondary reorganization, have been excluded from this sample. Taking the sample as a whole, the evaluator hopes to establish whether there is any significant difference between pupils who have followed different courses within the same school.

Publisher for the project: Cambridge University Press.

Notes and references

1   The performance of people taking part in an experiment is often favourably affected by the fact that they are taking part in an experiment, regardless of the subject of the experiment itself. This effect was first noted during experiments on working conditions at the Hawthorne factory in the USA.

2   See Bloom, B. S. (ed.) *Taxonomy of Educational Objectives: the Classification of Educational Goals*, Handbook I, *Cognitive Domain* Longmans, 1956.

5 Sixth form mathematics curriculum project

C. P. Ormell

Introductory: the project's aims

This essay attempts to describe methods of evaluation and ways of thinking about evaluation which have emerged in one particular curriculum project. The Sixth Form Mathematics Curriculum Project was set up by the Schools Council in 1969. The following discussion relates to the pilot stage of the project (1969–70) in which the author combined the roles of project director and evaluator. The methods described here seem to be suited to this project, but projects differ a great deal, and it is not necessarily true that they would be equally suited to other projects. In order to see the situation in perspective, it is necessary to consider first what the project is trying to do, and the degree of rethinking which this embodies. As a preliminary to this, we should begin with a few words about the origin of the project.

The Project began in January 1969 as a study of the sixth form mathematics situation.[1] That such a study was necessary after ten years of radical change in the pre-sixth form curriculum was evident enough. A situation of some confusion had developed in sixth form mathematics and there was a clear need to make sense of this. The confusion arose from several unresolved issues: the wide gap which existed between 'new maths' syllabuses on the one hand and the current versions of the traditional syllabuses on the other; the wide diversity of content within new maths syllabuses;[2] the problem of providing a suitable kind of mathematics in the sixth form as ancillary to a range of subjects including physics, chemistry, biology, economics, geography and social studies; the problem of providing a suitable kind of mathematics in the sixth form which would have a general educational effect and which would enable mathematics to be studied usefully in the sixth form by a much wider range of students than before.

As a result of reflection and analysis, the author became convinced early in 1969 that these problems were interrelated, and that the single main cause of trouble in sixth form mathematics stemmed from the lack of clearly apparent *relevance* in much of the work done, both in new maths and traditional courses, and in specialist syllabuses in recommended ancillary syllabuses. It was also concluded that the motivational advantage which could be gained from adopting a conspicuously new maths style was to some extent a spent force at the sixth form level. Much of the steam of the new maths movement came from attempting a greater diversity of work; but at the sixth form level the object was rather to bring together strands of thought previously developed to form a coherent, integrated, consistent whole. It would be an understatement to say that this presented problems: some resolution of thinking was needed at the sixth form stage if the student was to maintain self-confidence and momentum.

In 1969 the project began to produce units of material of a new kind, based on the concept of 'hypothetical relevance', by which was meant the application of mathematical models to posited, proposed or projected *non-actual* situations. This concept arose from an analysis of how mathematics is useful, and how this usefulness can be brought out most strongly. It became clear that the whole of mathematics could be seen in this light, as a kind of symbolic apparatus from which models of non-actual situations could be built. The models were useful because manipulation of the model enabled one to foresee in a wide range of particulars what the consequences of these not yet actual situations would be. Mathematics could be regarded as a discipline which, on being built up, gradually produced the ability to explore the implications of *possibilities*; i.e. proposals, plans, theories, suggested innovations, contingencies, opportunities.[3] The conversion of this idea into teaching material resulted in what might be described as relevance-enriched material, compared with the relatively formal material of the past.

Thus the project began to produce a new kind of material at a level of difficulty suitable for sixth formers of average ability. It was felt that if a great quantity of such material were available for use in sixth form courses, a new kind of approach could be used in this level of mathematics teaching which would make the subject more accessible to a wider range of sixth formers than before, which would contain its own built-in motivation (through the imaginative interest of the situations), and which would therefore enable sixth formers to consolidate a wide range of simple techniques used in conjunction with one another. The project initiated trials of the material, regarded as curriculum experiments, in the autumn of 1969. What were the trials designed to do? What hypothesis might their results be said to confirm or disconfirm? (It is of the essence of the scientific method that one performs experiments to confirm or disconfirm hypotheses.) Reflection on these questions led to the formulation of a definite curriculum hypothesis—an attempt to sum up the aims of the material and its method of use. Although the terms of the hypothesis, stated below, are general, they are nevertheless the ones of most concern to the project. Some problems arising from the generality of the terms will be examined later on.

THE PROJECT'S CURRICULUM HYPOTHESIS

(*a*) The main problem at the sixth form stage in mathematics is one of establishing a coherent kind of mathematical thinking.

(*b*) The aim of the project is to enable the sixth former to think freely about a wide range of mathematical patterns: for example, to monitor a range of formulae and to select successfully from the range the one which is appropriate to a particular problem.

(*c*) Motivation is the key to developing this facility. Unless the sixth former is given a strong sense of purpose, preferably via a clear perception of how and why mathematics is useful, he is unlikely to develop the kind of inner 'freedom to think' which is being sought.

(*d*) Such a sense of purpose can be built up and sustained by using material in which the characteristic value of mathematics as an instrument for exploring possibilities is made fully explicit throughout.[4]

(*e*) The material should centre on the discussion of significant situations and involve the posing of significant questions in these situations. A range of questions should preferably be asked, so that each situation may be examined 'in the round' rather than merely in certain semi-formal aspects.

(*f*) Continued employment of this kind of material ought to develop the sixth former's imagination, strengthen his recognition of pattern in situations, raise and sustain interest, generate a sense of purpose, and lead to the development of a kind of clarity about the use of mathematical methods to solve real problems.

The main burden of this hypothesis is that the use of relevance-enriched material will result in improved motivation, and will lead to better consolidation of concepts in the sixth former's mind.[5] These are the effects that the material might be expected to produce if the thinking on which it is based is valid. But the case for using such material is not wholly concerned with the effects mentioned in (*f*) above, i.e. the immediate classroom response. It is also related to the changing role of the mathematically educated person in an increasingly computer-rich society. The mathematically educated person no longer needs the same kind of mental equipment as he did previously, because many of the manipulative tasks of mathematics (not only computation) can now be accomplished by computer program. It is probably a fallacy to argue that in consequence we should mainly teach concepts, for a diet composed wholly or mainly of concepts is not very palatable for the average sixth former. Work devoted wholly or mainly to concepts—i.e. pattern and structure recognition—is relatively unrewarding for all but a highly able minority. (This is connected with the fact that the main motivation for such work is the ability to do it successfully without undue effort!) More generally such work is not likely to be closely enough related to experience, for the average sixth former to build up a strong framework of mathematical ideas. In other words it is difficult to capture sufficient interest and involvement for long enough to achieve the high standards of manipulative and intellectual (i.e. logical) accuracy which are needed.[6]

What the non-specialist mathematician requires today is not so much the possession of a great variety of formal mathematical concepts, but the imagination to foresee useful mathematical investigations in real situations. He needs, first, a thorough familiarity with mathematics-to-situation and situation-to-mathematics translations, and second, sufficient imaginative energy to see what can be done in these situations. The change-over from the concept approach to the relevance approach corresponds to the change-over from a social situation where possession of knowledge as such conferred prestige to one in which handling situations effectively in real time is what matters. Future society will chiefly require mathematician-scientists and mathematician-organizers to have imagination.

Relevance-enriched material may therefore be justified both by its 'horizontal' relevance to things in the student's actual or imaginative experience, and by its 'vertical' relevance to the kind of mental equipment needed by the student in adult life. The empirical test whether the continued use of relevance-enriched material does in fact produce mental qualities of the kind predicted is not of course possible until such material has been in continued use for some time. For this reason it has not been included in the terms of the curriculum hypothesis.[7]

THE UNIT OF MATERIAL

The unit of material chosen by the project is the *package*. This comprises a mini-textbook of 20–50 pages for the pupil, i.e. the sixth former; in addition to the pupil text there is also a *Teacher's Guide*, a booklet containing *Hints and Answers*, a *Harder Problem Supplement* and in some cases *Tables* or *Charts*. Although the material embodies a certain number of options, the packages produced so far are not in any significant sense programmed. Trials of the project's material have been trials of single packages, which have generally involved schools in work lasting intermittently from two to five weeks with a single sixth form group.

The reason for adopting this trial pattern has been the difficulty facing a project which produces material of a new kind for sixth form work with examination-committed groups. It is not so difficult to change the syllabus content, provided that texts covering the required work exist; nor to change teaching methods while keeping the content fixed; nor again to change the material style in certain respects, for example from conventional to programmed texts. But it *is* difficult to change the underlying philosophy of the approach: one cannot easily operate a halfway house between an old approach and a new one. Until a great body of the new material has been produced, it is unreasonable to launch an examination; yet one cannot usefully build up such a body of material without testing and developing it step by step under class-room conditions—which at the sixth form stage inevitably means with pupils preparing for existing examinations.

The logic of the situation has therefore led to a pattern of trials in which relatively small fragments of material are tested in a wide range of schools. The material in the early packages has been chosen to be as generally useful as possible in the context of existing examinations, so that teachers who conduct trials of project packages will not feel that they have led their sixth formers too far away from their examination requirements. Everything in the project's first three packages is needed somewhere in A level mathematics examina-tions. On the other hand, discussion of situations, situation-to-mathematics translations and the interpretation of the mathematics, are time-consuming activities. The content of the project's package on *Indices* is covered in two or three pages in almost all the standard textbooks; the content of the package on *Limits* receives at most a paragraph or so. It is the change to a slower rate in covering topics, demanded by the situational approach, which presents prob-lems—the slower rate does not, of course, mean that the work is necessarily less demanding, but that extra effort of various kinds is required in addition to formal mathematics. These problems of adaptation have led the project team to recommend that not more than two packages should be tried with any one examination group in any one academic year.

EVALUATION

The evaluation of the material is concerned broadly with looking to see if it behaves as well under classroom conditions as it was expected to behave: whether it is as effective as the curriculum hypothesis, on which it was based, predicted. Clearly, however, this is not a once-for-all operation. One may re-gard evaluation rather as a continuing process: consisting of (i) a flow of rele-vant feedback information from the classroom to the project team, and (ii) the interpretation of this information. As a result of the interpretation, the project is liable to, and does, modify new material and revise old. The project material should not therefore be regarded as a static product. Its planning, design and production is and ought to be constantly re-examined, so that the lessons learned in the current generation of material can be built into the next. The curriculum hypothesis summarized on p. 49 does not define a single or pre-cise or finite range of treatments for a given topic. It defines rather a kind of material or an area of possible material, within which we may expect to find what is needed to achieve the effects envisaged in section (*f*). The project is in the position of an oil company which believes with good reason that oil is to be found in a certain region, but does not know exactly where the wells should be drilled; *some* success might reasonably be expected with sites chosen at random from within the area defined. Early material produced by a project in accordance with its curriculum hypothesis might be regarded in a similar way.

Some success could be expected with such material, simply because it lay within the area marked out by the curriculum hypothesis. Such material, then, represents here a first attempt to achieve the results envisaged in section (*f*) of the hypothesis. By the same token, one would expect to improve on this early material. As the project team come to understand the effect on the pupil-teacher-material triangle of the change in material, they should begin to discern ways which the material might achieve *more* of each of the effects mentioned in section (*f*). In a word, a continuing process of feedback from the classroom should lead to a gradual improvement in the quality of the material.

Unfortunately, however, this is an unduly simple and optimistic statement of the position. Under present conditions, in which many schools are in an unsettled condition, there can be no guarantee that close attention to feedback will automatically lead to progressive improvement of the material. The feedback contains a great deal of what may be called 'noise', including sentiment generated by random interactions of personalities quite outside the project's control. This is true even after applying the series of filters dscribed in the section on 'Preconditions for Trials'. In addition to a close attention to feedback, therefore, the project team has had to use every theoretical model and insight at hand to identify and detect directions of improvement in the material. What is needed is a clear understanding of the original curriculum hypothesis and a continuing effort to sharpen focus.

EVALUATING THE PROJECT

The evaluation of the project may be distinguished from the evaluation of the project material. The aim of the material is summarized in section (*f*) of the curriculum hypothesis above, and in the discussion of the project material's vertical relevance on pp. 49–50. The aim of the *project*, however, is not merely to answer the academic question whether the curriculum hypothesis is correct; it is to disseminate the answers, at least in some degree. It can be argued that the final measure of a project's success is the extent of this dissemination and its consequent influence on the situation in schools. But it can also be argued that project time and effort is precious, and that these resources should be devoted to obtaining the best possible answers, leaving dissemination and influence to the natural processes of word-of-mouth recommendation, discussion in journals, summer courses run by the Department of Education and Science, etc.

The difference between these answers is the difference between the extensional and the intensional point of view. On the one hand, it can be argued that if a project is not influencing teachers in progressively wider circles, it is hardly justifying its existence. On the other hand, it can be argued that unless a project concentrates a fierce intensity of effort on the quality of its material, it stands little chance of having any influence in the long run. It would surely be a mistake for any project to seek primarily to engineer a 'bandwagon effect' with its material. If the material is good enough to interest a widening circle of the more thoughtful teachers, such promotion will hardly be necessary. If it is not, the promotion is likely to lead to a bubble phenomenon of the kind described by Christopher Booker in his book *The Neophiliacs*—an unnatural rate of growth in interest followed by collapse.

The truth seems to be that there are no easy victories in the curriculum development field. Like products of other kinds, an approach through new material in the classroom demands an extraordinary degree of critical and constructive attention before it stands even a *chance* of long-term success. Even after a great deal of such critical and constructive attention, there is still a risk of failure, if the material is ill-tuned to the true situation in the classroom in any respect. The project must therefore aim to develop a product which is tuned to the true situation in the classroom in all significant respects.[8] If it is necessary to discard twenty draft units of material to achieve one fully-tuned unit, this may seem a poor return, quantitatively, for the effort involved. If the tuning process is a complicated one, it may appear that such a sophisticated product is unlikely to make headway in more than a minority of schools. But history suggests that the long-term success of 'working' products is rarely achieved in any other way. The material may indeed only make headway in a minority of schools; but if long-term success is the aim—as it must surely be—there is no alternative to this approach. When W. H. Carothers first synthesized nylon, the chemical process needed to manufacture it seemed formidable indeed, involving a long sequence of organic derivatives. Obstacles loom large when one is unsure that the end-product is worth while; but once the value of the end-product has been established, perspectives change and the obstacles come to be seen as hurdles to be overcome.

What one must look for in evaluating the material, then, is its general correspondence to the needs of the classroom situation. Such correspondence can be discussed in terms of each of the effects mentioned in (c) to (f) of the curriculum hypothesis. For example, (c) implies a need for material whose justification is clear to schoolboys and girls in the sixth form. The project team must check that justifications which they *think* are likely to possess this clarity really do make sense *for this particular age group*. Similar correspondence needs to be checked in the case of each of the claims made in (d) to (f). Before discussing the situation more closely, however, we must take a more detailed look at the particular kind of material the project is attempting to produce.

Project material

CONTENT

The topics treated in the first three packages are: *Indices* (package 1), *Quadratic Models* (package 2) and *Limits* (package 3). For those who reach the sixth form via an established O level course, the first two packages are essentially revision material, but package 2 does contain new work for those who arrive in the sixth form via some new maths courses. *Limits* offers new work for most sixth formers at the level of logic adopted; but many students reach the sixth form having acquired an imprecise notion of limit as a by-product of their O level work in calculus.

TYPES OF HORIZONTAL RELEVANCE

The project material may be classified as situational, the main difference between it and conventional material (whether traditional or new maths[9]) being that it is introduced by means of situations, illustrated by means of situations, and consolidated by a body of question-problems set in the context of briefly sketched situations. It may be noted that situational problems like those of packages 1, 2 and 3 are almost totally absent from the corresponding sections of standard texts.

Because of this distinct difference between the project material and conventional material, it is quite easy to overlook the effect of changes in secondary characteristics of the project material which may play a surprisingly large part in the classroom situation. There is, for example, a change in style from package 1 to package 3: the material in package 3 is relevant to more fully described and developed situations than in the earlier package. Even more important, however, is the change in the type of relevance involved in the use of the situations, from the *actual* through the *imaginary actual* to the *hypothetical* mode. In the actual mode a situation is described as a fact, i.e. as an existing state of affairs. The ordinary-significant (O-significant)[10] questions we can ask about it could be answered by experience, observation or experiment. In a sense, therefore, a mathematical treatment of such problems is not actually necessary. Experienced people may claim with some justice that expert judgement, data records, photographs, telerecordings, measurements, etc. are more useful guides here than mathematics, since they make us aware of the untidiness, difficulty, unpredictability and awkwardness of the real situation. To prefer mathematical treatments here looks rather like dodging the rough and unpredictable encounter with reality. This is probably the reason why movements towards relevance in mathematics have had such limited success in the past.

In the imaginary actual mode, situations which do not actually exist are described as if they did exist. This makes the use of a pleasing variety of material possible (at some cost in terms of realism), but the basic weakness discussed above still applies. Many of the problems in package 1 and some of those in packages 2 and 3 are in this mode.

In the hypothetical mode, on the other hand, a situation is described as a non-actual possibility, and the properties of this situation can be progressively explored by manipulation of the mathematical model, at least in those respects which the model reflects. Thus the only alternative to the employment of mathematics here is the use of imagination. If the problem material is designed so that the answers are O-significant and hinge on a fine balance of mechanisms, which unaided imagination is unable to penetrate, mathematical thinking and manipulation is placed in a context where its usefulness is most patently visible (the usefulness is essentially one of illumination). Imagination is still important, but it is the combination of using mathematics *with* imagination which is most valuable, and it is this which the material should draw out.

METHOD OF USE

The project has not so far recommended any particular method of using its material. The method of presentation chosen by trial schools has in fact varied from a simple handing out of material to a carefully taught course given in specially timetabled lessons. It should be borne in mind, however, that the project does offer an overall attitude, or way of thinking about mathematics, which was summarized on p. 48. What the project is attempting to develop is not simply material, but a package deal approach through material. The project has recently introduced a diary-type form, which will provide more information about patterns of use of the material in trial schools. This inform-ation should enable the project to interpret the results of trials in a more de-tailed way.

Preconditions for trials

It is clear that in experimental sciences of all kinds experiments can be faultily set up. Such experimental faults may become clear fairly quickly, or they may remain obscure for a time. In both cases, one has to regard the discovery of a degree of faultiness in the experiment as indicating possible invalidity in the results. If an experiment is found to be faulty in a crucial respect, this is regarded as automatically invalidating its results. In these cases, the findings obtained from the work are not regarded as results to be qualified, or results of a special kind, but as non-results. This is an important consideration to bear in mind in examining the results of a curriculum development project prior to analysis. The question is where the line should be drawn between re-sults and non-results. Educational situations are far removed from the relative tidiness of conditions in a research laboratory. This means, among other things, that in important respects it is only possible to give qualitative des-criptions of the conditions under which a trial will provide results rather than non-results. Nevertheless, words do have correct meanings in ordinary language, and qualitative description accurately employed is often sufficiently definite to serve as a basis for legal, political and social decisions.

To identify the preconditions for valid trials, it is necessary first to consider what observable effects the use of the material may be expected to have.

Various combinations of conditions can then be considered, under which such results could not be expected. Such combinations of conditions will clearly be those under which the results will not be valid. It would be absurd to test a hypothesis for effects under conditions in which, for known reasons, they could not be expected to occur.

The teacher's role in the classroom as interpreter of the material is very important. It is clearly necessary, in the interests of valid results, for the teacher to introduce the trial material in a way which does not misrepresent its character and purpose.[11] But it would be unreasonable to expect teachers to appreciate every facet of a new and unfamiliar material approach and all the unformulated assumptions incorporated into its design. There is always likely to be a certain gap between the originator's concept of the material and the interpreter's (c.f. variations between different pianists' interpretations of a concerto). So the important question is at what level a teacher's misinterpretation of the character and purpose of the material will make the crucial difference between obtaining valid and invalid results. The situation may be shown diagrammatically as in Fig. 3.

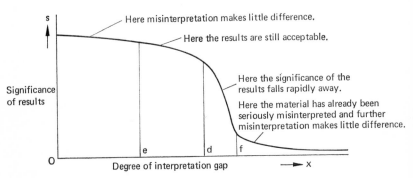

Fig. 3 Sixth Form Mathematics: how teacher misinterpretation affects trial results

For the curve shown, *d* represents the point beyond which the significance of the results rapidly falls away. It would be reasonable in such a case, therefore, to define valid results as those obtained from *x* in the range between O and *d*. Notice that in the case shown, an interpretation gap represented by *x* in the range between O and *e* will make relatively little difference to the significance of the results. The graph is offered as a clarification device showing the *kind* of situation which obtains.[12] (One would expect the graph to exhibit the same general shape as that shown in Fig. 3 under a fairly wide range of different quantifications of *s* and *x*.) This shape may also be expected to appear in the case of each of the main validity-influencing factors listed below:[13]

1   the teacher's interpretation of the nature and purpose of the material, and his effectiveness in conveying this to the class;

2   attitudes to the project held by other teachers in the school;[14]

3   the teacher's comprehension of the class's revision needs, concept readiness, etc.;

4   pupils' attitudes to the teacher and/or the school, in the social context;

5   the class's comprehension ability;

6   the class's background knowledge;

7   the class's confidence in, and ability to perform, non-linear work;[15]

8   the class's awareness of the intrinsic interest of the subject and the importance of clarifying ideas for long-term progress.[16]

In each case, no doubt, quantification could be adopted to represent these factors or competences. In each case too there is a range of values of the quantified factor, beyond which the results obtained will cease to be valid. The attitudes of other teachers to the project (2) and the extent to which these attitudes are communicated to the class by other members of the staff are clearly important considerations. Where a hostile attitude is communicated to the class, one can hardly expect a trial to yield valid results.[17] The teacher's comprehension of a class's revision needs (3) will also have a marked effect. If insufficient revision has been done on topics presupposed by the material, the class will be unprepared for the concepts encountered in the work. If the class's revision needs are over-estimated, the danger will lie on the other side—doing too much revision to the point of tedium. This is connected with the factor of the teacher's interpretation (1) in that teachers may overdo revision work because they have not fully grasped the point of the exercise.

Clearly, too, the teacher-class relationship (4) is important. A class may react badly to material as a result of tensions created by a poor *rapport* between teacher and class. In such cases the reaction of the class to the material may tell us something about the relationship, but it will not tell us very much about the material.

Factors (1) to (4) are general factors likely to affect curriculum development projects of all kinds. Factors (5) to (8) on the other hand, are particularly relevant to projects such as the Sixth Form Mathematics Curriculum Project, which offer material based on the discussion of situations. Comprehension ability (5) is needed by sixth formers when they are offered material from the present project, because this material involves analysing situations, and interpreting results in terms of aspects of those situations. Background knowledge (6) is needed for the same reason. The ability to perform non-linear work (7) is needed by the student for problem material of various kinds,[18] e.g. traditional algebraic problems; it is certainly needed by the student tackling relevance-enriched material. Finally, factor (8) is important in cases where new material which is not directly examinable is injected into an existing course. Some pupils may, consciously or unconsciously, make less of an effort to assimilate this material than they would if it were in the category of directly examinable material. If this reduction of effort is at all marked, the validity of the results will be affected.

FILTERS

If one asks whether the required level of competence obtains for each of the factors (1) to (8), the answer poses a real problem, in that we do not know exactly to what degree such competence is needed, nor exactly how much competence is available in individual schools (see pp. 63–4). In a flourishing school situation, one might hardly have to spend any time on this problem, which is really a consequence of the present unsettled and fluid state of many schools. The eight items may be thought of as filters through which the feedback material has to be passed. Essentially, only schools in which each item proves acceptable are fully suited for the trial of project material. Where the requirements are not all met, the results will carry little significance, either positively or negatively. Attaching significance to results of this kind can be misleading in both directions.

It could be argued that many schools will fail to meet all the requirements involved in the eight items, and that to adjust the material to suit conditions in schools which do fully satisfy these requirements is to aim from the beginning at producing material for 'better' schools. Surely a project such as the present one should aim rather at producing material to suit the needs of schools which do *not* fully satisfy the requirements. One may sympathize with this view, but it is very doubtful whether the problem is soluble in these terms. Certainly, the line of development represented by the present project depends crucially on background knowledge, comprehension ability and the confidence to do non-linear work. These are essential if the project material is to 'go over' in the classroom; there is no room for compromise here, since a compromise would imply a withdrawal of the central message in the curricular hypothesis. We may, however, (i) hope that some schools will progressively 'raise their game' in these respects, and (ii) offer specific material which will be remedial at the particular point where it is needed, e.g. a booklet providing background explanation, in simple language, of the situations used in the material. Here it is best to aim ahead of target.

Assessing results

THE FLOW OF INFORMATION

We have considered the project's aims, the character of the material and the preconditions which need to be satisfied if a trial is to yield valid results. We can now turn to the feedback process—the channels along which information about the response to the material may flow from the classroom to the project team. The information may be divided into three parts:

(i) that which the teacher notices;

(ii) that which the student notices;

(iii) that which neither the teacher nor the student notices.

A channel is provided for (i) in the form of two questionnaires for the teacher, forms A and B. On Form A (Fig. 4) the teacher makes a question-by-question entry which is in effect a comment on the material, first in terms of a series of hurdles to be overcome, and second in terms of the overall interest and impact of the material. The form consists of sheets ruled vertically and horizontally. Each horizontal line corresponds to a problem-question in the

Fig. 4 Sixth Form Mathematics: abridged version of form A

PACKAGE EVALUATION: QUESTION-BY-QUESTION COMMENT

Package no. ... This page relates to questions ...., pp. ....

Trial no. ...   Date ....

For instructions on completing this form, see the attached booklet, *Evaluating the Package*.

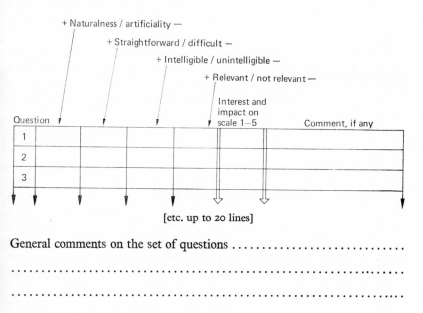

[etc. up to 20 lines]

General comments on the set of questions ....

. . . .

. . . .

. . . .

package concerned. The first four columns represent the hurdles of artificiality, difficulty, unintelligibility, and relevance. The teacher places a negative sign in these columns if he judges that the material failed to surmount these hurdles. For example, a negative sign placed in the first column for question 1 indicates that, in the teacher's judgement, the first question in the set appeared to the class to be artificial. In the fifth column the teacher puts a score in the range 1–5, an attempt to quantify subjectively the interest and impact of the question as experienced by the class. The final part of each line is set aside for particular comment on the question by the trials teacher. All entries on this form indicate the teacher's assessment of the *class's* response, not his private judgement of the material. At the bottom of each page the teacher enters a general comment on the set of questions covered by the sheet.

Form B (Fig. 5) contains the teacher's comments on the overall effects and value of the trial.

A channel is provided for (ii) in the form of an attitude questionnaire, form D (Fig. 6), and three tests, forms CXi, CXii and EXi, which vary for different packages. 'X' denotes an identification letter representing the package concerned; for example, CLi, CLii, ELi are the forms relating to the package on *Limits*. These forms are completed by the students who have used the material, CXi being a pre-test of content, CXii being a post-test for content, and EXi being a delayed post-test given about a month after CXii, designed to assess retention of the material and understanding of its main conceptual themes. The design of CXii is such that it includes a subset of questions in one-to-one correspondence with those of CXi. It is clear that there are many things which the sixth former may be expected to know or be able to do after completing a package, which he could not reasonably be expected to know or be able to do, before. This is particularly true of packages which introduce material which the student is unlikely to have seen previously, such as the project's package on *Limits*. In the case of a revision package such as *Indices*, the corrsepondence extends to all the items of CXii.

The project team provide a channel for (iii) by visiting trial schools after completion of trials, meeting students who have used the material, and talking about the results in some depth with the teacher. One of the questions put to the students is: 'Which bit, or bits, of the package did you find (*a*) most interesting, (*b*) most difficult?' This question could be asked on form D, but it seems better to collect some of the information about students' responses by verbal inquiry; if all the information were collected on form D, there would be no initial *raison d'être* for the conversation with the student. And it is in these conversations that the team have become aware of incongruencies, weak emphases and the desirability of changes in procedure of a kind which could easily have been overlooked.

The information gathered on forms A to E affords many opportunities for statistical analysis and presentation. One should, however, beware of produc-

Fig. 5 Sixth Form Mathematics: form B

PACKAGE EVALUATION SUMMARY AND OVERALL COMMENT

Package no. ...   Trial no. ...   Date ....

For instructions on completing this form, see the booklet *Evaluating the Package*.

Would you comment on:

(A) The interest or lack of interest shown by the class in the questions.

....
....

(B) The degree of consolidation of ideas resulting from the work.

....
....

(C) The degree of manipulative skill resulting from the work.*

....
....

(D) The level of manipulative confidence.

....
....

(E) The effect (if any) of the work on the class's general momentum.

....
....

(F) The effect (if any) on the class's attitude to mathematics.

....
....

* Scores in the mechanical tests should be entered at the bottom of the page.

Some questions (cross out inapplicable answers):

Was the use of the package in general worth while?

Very much/quite useful/not useful.

Would you be interested in using similar material on other topics, assuming that the topics were in your Board or Project's syllabus?   Yes/possibly/no.

Any general comments on the package and/or suggestions for improving it:

....
....
....
....

[etc. 9 lines in all]

Did the trial go as well as you expected?   Less well/as well/better.

Was the class which used the package above, below or about average compared with other classes of the same kind in previous years?

Above/slightly above/average/slightly below.

Average score in the mechanical post-test ....

Average score in the mechanical pre-test ....

Did you hand out the sheets in stages?   Stages/in one bundle.

Fig. 6 Sixth Form Mathematics: form D

Package .... Trial no. ...

Name ....

This is not a test and there are no 'right' or 'wrong' answers. *Would you indicate the degree to which you agree or disagree with the statements in quotation marks on the scale explained on the back on this sheet.* [This is included below.]

1 'The questions were quite interesting'   Agree ☐ ☐ ☐ ☐ ☐ disagree

2 'The questions were difficult to
understand'   Agree ☐ ☐ ☐ ☐ ☐ disagree

3 'I would have preferred straight
exercises without the problems'   Agree ☐ ☐ ☐ ☐ ☐ disagree

4 'I would like to try a package on
another topic'   Agree ☐ ☐ ☐ ☐ ☐ disagree

5 'Looking at mathematics in this way
one can really see what it is getting at'   Agree ☐ ☐ ☐ ☐ ☐ disagree

6 'I could not see the wood for the trees'   Agree ☐ ☐ ☐ ☐ ☐ disagree

Would you tick the appropriate box or delete the inappropriate phrase:

	Yes	No
7 'Mathematics is my favourite sixth form subject'	☐	☐
8 'Mathematics is the sixth form subject I like least'	☐	☐

9 'I worked *very hard/quite hard/not very hard* on the package'

10 'I generally find mathematics *hard going/fairly hard/quite easy*'

Name any other school subjects or topics in current affairs or general skills and knowledge which you find interesting:

....

Would you comment on the following statements:

1 'The package brings out the use of mathematics and makes the subject more
interesting'

....

2 'The package would be improved if there were no "problems" in it but
more concentration on straight algebra'

....

Any other comments on the package:

....

Which subjects beside mathematics are you studying at A level?

1 .... 2 .... 3 ....

Answering code for the questionnaire

To answer the question, one puts a tick in one of the spaces:

Agree ☑ ☐ ☐ ☐ ☐ disagree means 'I agree very much'

Agree ☐ ☑ ☐ ☐ ☐ disagree   'I agree with reservations'

Agree ☐ ☐ ☑ ☐ ☐ disagree   'I neither agree nor disagree'

Agree ☐ ☐ ☐ ☑ ☐ disagree   'I disagree somewhat'

Agree ☐ ☐ ☐ ☐ ☑ disagree   'I disagree strongly'

ing and being content with a conspicuous display of statistics of questionable significance. The logistics of the trial situation make it virtually impossible for the project to obtain statistically significant trials of all the material: for example, in trials planned for the autumn of 1971, a set of thirteen packages required the co-operation of seventy-eight schools, even though each package was to be tried in only *six* schools—six being the minimum number which could be expected to yield any useful information. It is doubtful whether a team of the existing size could handle more while retaining an effective relationship with each school.[19] The important point, therefore, is that all the information collected should have a use: it should be, as it were, a *cog* capable of setting in motion the machinery of correction, revision, reconsideration, redesign and reconstruction. The conflict of aims between the extensional and the intensional point of view makes itself felt here. The project's evaluation methods presuppose the intensional point of view; in the last analysis, their object is to improve the quality of the material. The test of their success will be whether they do result in an improvement in the quality of the material.[20]

INTERPRETING THE INFORMATION

Which parts of the information gathered on forms A to E relate to which of the effects predicted in the curriculum hypothesis? To what evidence on the forms do we apply the filters discussed on page 58? There are two basic problems here.

(i) How does one assess the possession of qualities of a very general kind, such as a sense of purpose?

(ii) To what degree is it legitimate or illegitimate to lower the acceptance levels of the filters? (See note 8.)

Problem (i) arises both in dealing with the bearing of the data on section (*f*) of the curriculum hypothesis (p. 49), and in applying the filters. Problem (ii) arises from the recognition that some form of filter is needed, while in extreme cases it might be argued that the acceptance levels of the filters should be reduced (cf. *d* on Fig. 3 and note 12) until only 'good' results remained (the 'bad' which might be expected in a random mixture having been thus filtered out). Clearly, to lower the acceptance levels would be a misuse of the filtering process, while too little filtering might obscure the valid results to the point where their characteristics were no longer detectable.

Much of the difficulty surrounding (i) stems from the fact that a trial lasting 2–3 weeks hardly provides sufficient involvement to produce very striking changes in qualities of this kind. If trials lasted longer, it might be possible to make an objective judgement based on a fairly large collection of behavioural and subjective evidence. In the present case the team have collected informal subjective evidence from items (E) and (F) on form B and from conversations with the teacher, as well as taking into account sixth formers' comments on form D wherever these have been relevant. Table 5.1. indicates the sources of information for each of the five effects mentioned in section (*f*) of the curriculum hypothesis.

Table 5.1   Sources of information for section (*f*) of the curriculum hypothesis

Effect	Source of information
Does the material develop imagination?	Conversation with trial teacher
Does the material strengthen the sixth former's ability to recognize pattern in situations?	Conversation with trial group; form EXi, question 4
Does the material raise and sustain interest?	Form A scores; form B, item (A); form D, statement 1 and comment 1
Does the material generate a sense of purpose?	Form B, items (E) and (F); form D, statement 4 and comment 1; conversation with trial teacher
Does the material lead to a development of clear thinking?	Conversation with trial group; form CXii discussion questions

The difficulties surrounding problem (ii) are more serious, and the project team are not yet confident that they have found the right way to deal with them. The concept of the characteristic significance curve (Fig. 3) seems to be useful, but the work involved in putting this on a sound factual basis for each of the eight factors on p. 57 would be formidable indeed. The team's approach has been in effect to use high acceptance levels, i.e. to use conservatively high estimates of the value of *d* in each case.[21] It is possible that in at least some cases more would have been learnt from the feedback information if lower estimates had been used. Project policy on this matter is to preserve confidentiality on *which* trials are judged to have met the eight requirements.[22] The full body of material is, after all, available to the project team for further study if it is subsequently decided that revised acceptance levels should be used. Thus the use of filters is a device to enable the project team to obtain a body of valid evaluative information. Misuse of filtering would result in the project not taking notice of defects which were in fact inherent in the material, even when it had been used in the manner envisaged by the writing team. This would lead to retention of unrecognized contradictions in the project material. Because the aim of the kind of on-going evaluation being attempted here is to improve the material, the project has no vested interest in filtering the results too much.[23]

The information on which filtering is based is gathered from the feedback material as shown in Table 5.2.

Table 5.2 Sources of information on which filtering is based

Factor	Source of information
(1) Teacher's interpretation	Conversation with teacher; general comments on forms A and B
(2) Other teachers' attitudes	Conversation with other teachers at trial schools when possible
(3) Comprehension of class's needs	Form CXi; pupils' comments on form D
(4) Pupils' attitudes	Conversation with trial group; pupils' comments on form D
(5) Class's comprehension ability	Form D, statement 2 and comments; form EXi, question 2, first part; form A, column 3
(6) Class's background knowledge	Form A, comments; form D, other subject information and comments
(7) Non-linear working	Form CXii, certain questions; form EXi, certain questions
(8) Intrinsic interest and ideas for long-term progress	Conversation with trial group; form D, comments

In some cases the project may begin to produce material of the kind needed to help schools to reach the required acceptance levels. It seems probable in any case that the project's use of the filtering process will diminish as time goes on, in that it is unlikely that the project will invite schools to conduct new trials if their results have fallen well below the level needed to pass the series of filters.

The problem of recruiting sufficient schools to perform trials of material which embodies a change of underlying philosophy is not essentially a problem of getting volunteers. It is more that all teachers who do trials of the material must understand the general insights on which the approach is based, i.e. they should satisfy the requirements for factor (1). Teachers who see what the project is trying to do are likely also to see the need for sufficient standards in factors (2) to (7).[24]

MACHINERY OF REVISION

It is important that each item of information collected by the project should, under certain circumstances, have a definite part to play in activating the

machinery of revision. The conditional actions to which each questionnaire/
test relates are outlined in Table 5.3. It must be emphasized that this table

Table 5.3 Conditional actions to which each trial questionnaire/test relates

Questionnaire/test	Conditional action
A (teachers' questionnaire)	The question-by-question entries indicate which questions stand in *greatest* and *least* need of revision. The comments on sets of questions suggest possible changes in overall emphasis, weight, length, etc.
B (teachers' questionnaire)	Is a substantial revision needed, or is the package taken as a whole broadly satisfactory? Comments may suggest need for guidance on methods of use.
CXi (pupils' pre-test)	Are the presuppositions of the level of knowledge and competence built into the package valid? Suggested changes at this level.
CXii (pupils' post-test)	Has the content of the package been assimilated uniformly well? Possible changes to achieve uniform effectiveness.
D (pupils' attitude questionnaire)	Is a substantial revision needed, or is the package taken as a whole broadly satisfactory?
EXi (pupils' retention/ understanding post-test)	Have the main themes of the package stuck in the mind of the sixth former? Possible changes of emphasis in cases where this has not occurred.

gives only an outline account of the actual process of package revision which
the project team have used. An additional source of information is provided by
the comments of teachers and others who have seen the material, or who have
worked through it at seminars, etc. In the case of package 1, more radical
changes were thought to be necessary than would have been prompted by
following the above procedure (which was not at that time fully formulated).
This arose from the development of the project's curriculum hypothesis itself,
rather than from the detailed results of the first trials. The early results
showed that some changes were needed, but they did not in themselves provide much guidance as to what they should be. It is clearly important as a
general rule that all negative results of trials should be fully and adequately
explained.[25] In some cases it may be necessary to make additional visits, and
to correspond with the teacher conducting trials at some length, in order to

arrive at the truth. It is also important to remember that evaluation data as such do not generally *solve* any problems. They may tell us when the material is not fully satisfactory, but they provide no substitute for the creative imagination needed to put that material right.

Publisher for the project: Heinemann Educational Books.

Notes and references

1   The project's terms of reference were as follows.
(*a*)   A general review of the content of sixth form mathematics aimed at assessing the value of various topics and especially, perhaps, those of recent introduction, for different categories of pupils.
(*b*)   An investigation into the connection between mathematics and physics. This would consider not only the range of mathematics needed to facilitate the effective teaching of physics, but also whether some topics, notably some of those conventionally included in applied mathematics, would not be better regarded as part of physics.
(*c*)   An investigation of the mathematical needs of pupils taking other subjects, such as biology and economics.
(*d*)   An investigation into the mathematics that can profitably be taught to the non-mathematician (i.e. the pupils whose main interests do not include mathematics or subjects requiring mathematical servicing) in the sixth form.
2   This diversity was brought out by W. L. James in a study made in 1967–8. See *Mathematics Teaching*, 48, 1969, pp. 43–5, also the project's *Newsletter* 1, autumn 1969, pp. 16–17 and p. 23.
3   See Ormell, C. P. 'Mathematics, science of possibility' *Int. J. Math. Educ. Sci. Technol.* 3, 1972, 329–41.
4   See Ormell, C. P. 'Why relevance' *Polymetrics* 6, 1973, 2–11. The general point here is that *meaning* is generated by *use*; we can only generate a robust sense of meaning by showing the use (which is essentially illuminative).
5   An improvement in motivation is not likely to happen for sixth formers who are already very interested in mathematics; but if the hypothesis is correct, the form of the rationality the interested sixth former acquires will be modified.
6   Most of the 'necessity' stems from the cumulative effect of interrelated mathematical work. The sixth former 'needs' high standards of acquired perception inside mathematics in order to sort this out.
7   See note 8, however, where it is pointed out that the teacher's awareness of the vertical relevance of the material does play a considerable part in the situation.
8   The 'truth' involved here is not to be found wholly in the classroom, but in the long-term wisdom of a characteristic pattern of thinking, learning and responding. From this the paradox arises that the best kind of material is likely to differ from material designed merely to fit in well with conditions as they appear on the surface in the average classroom. The long-term (vertical) relevance of the material should be seen by the teacher and hence be inferred by the class through the teacher's implied valuation of it.
9   New maths at the primary level is associated under some schemes (e.g. Nuffield) with situational work, but at the sixth form level the tendency has been towards a more abstract treatment.
10   I.e. aspects of situations which are relevant to the dilemmas of ordinary life, or which might be the object of ordinary curiosity. In conventional problem material, the answers intended frequently reflect mathematical interest rather than interest of an ordinary kind.
11   This is connected with the observation in note 8 that the teacher's valuation of the material is inferred by the class. When a teacher misinterprets the aims of the

material, he is likely to acquire mistaken expectations of it, and hence to be disappointed when it fails to fulfil them. For example, if the teacher interprets the purpose of introducing relevance to be *mainly* that of creating interest and clear-cut learning, he is likely to be disappointed when certain questions in the material fail to generate immediate interest, and when the learning seems to be more difficult than it was under a more conventional treatment.

12   x is a measure of the interpretation gap, i.e. the degree of misinterpretation. d is a value of this below which the results are acceptable, hence d may be called the acceptance level.

There are many ways in which x and s might be quantified, the simplest of which would consist in averaging of marks allocated by judges.

13   For a general discussion of factors, see Malvern, D. D. 'Thoughts about synoptic evaluation', *Polymetrics* **6,** 1973, 32–7.

14   I.e. the attitudes of other teachers to what the trial teacher is doing. See Rudduck, J., & MacDonald, B. 'Curriculum research and development projects: barriers to success' *Brit J. Educ. Psychol.* **41,** June 1971, 148–54.

15   I.e. when the sixth former meets a problem which is expressed in words and contains no definite clue telling him where to begin. The problem has to be, as it were, assimilated whole. In the harder cases this amounts to the need for what Mr de Bono calls 'lateral thinking'. See Holt, J. *How Children Fail* Penguin, 1969, p. 57.

16   I.e. awareness that a sufficient degree of general understanding is desirable, even when A level performance is the only recognized objective.

17   See Rudduck and MacDonald (note 14) on 'Innovation without change'.

18   This might be described as characteristic of sixth form work in mathematics. This is the point at which the need for mathematical thinking arises, and where many pupils who have mastered the drills of pre-O level work, with insufficient reflection on their meaning, find the going difficult.

19   The need for a close relationship at the trial stage stems mainly from the relative novelty and hence vulnerability of the underlying philosophy. When this is more widely appreciated, the need for close contact should disappear.

20   The test is therefore a comparison of the effectiveness (in terms of item (f) of the curriculum hypothesis) of earlier and later material. The project has not attempted the much more difficult problem of a comparison with established or new maths work.

21   The team's method here has been simply to make subjective judgements as to whether, on the evidence available, the trial schools have met the required standards in each of the eight factors; but the team have erred on the side of caution in applying the filters.

22   Each trial school has a number which is known to the teachers involved and to the project. Some sets of comments have been circulated under trial numbers, but not the results of the filtering process.

23   It can be argued that there is still a danger of filtering out too much, as the project team may not be prepared to face the full difficulties inherent in developing a new approach. Itemization of the factors does something to reduce the danger.

24   This does not mean that they are likely to be able to remedy inadequacies in all the factors (2) to (7) but they may be able to go some way towards this.

25   A properly based system of filtering, of course, provides an explanation for some of these, i.e. that certain trials have not met the necessary preconditions.

Papers on curriculum objectives in mathematics

Allanson, J. T. 'Mathematics for the majority' *J. Biol. Educ.* **2,** 1968, 87–94.

Elliott, W. G. M. 'Ideology and school mathematics: a reply' *Proc. Phil. Educ. Soc. Gr. Brit.*, **III,** 1969, 55–64.

Kline, M. 'Intellectuals and the schools: a case history' *Harvard Educational Review* **36,** 1966, 505–11.

Ormell, C. P. 'Ideology and the reform of school mathematics' *Proc. Phil. Educ. Soc. Gr. Brit.,* **III,** 1969, 37–54.

Ormell, C. P. 'Mathematics, applicable versus pure-and-applied' *Int. J. Math. Educ. Sci. Technol.* **3,** 1972, 125–31.

Ormell, C. P. 'Mathematics through the imagination' *Dialogue* (Schools Council newsletter) **9,** autumn 1971, 10–11.

Ormell, C. P. 'Newtonian mechanics and the sixth form syllabus' *Int. J. Math. Educ. Sci. Technol.* **2,** 1971, 233–41.

Watson, F. R. 'Aims in mathematical education' *Int. J. Math. Educ. Sci. Technol.* **2,** 1971, 105–18.

Williams, J. 'Problems and possibilities in the assessment and investigation of mathematics learning' *Educ. Stud. Math.* **4,** 1971, 134–49.

Project papers, including the newsletter *Polymetrics,* can be obtained by writing to: The Secretary, Sixth Form Mathematics Curriculum Project, The School of Education, Reading University, London Road, Reading RG1 5AQ.

6 Integrated studies project

David Jenkins

The evaluation problems faced by the Integrated Studies Project arose from the nature of the project's task and the limited resources available to the team. The following observations, however, may be significant because the difficulties encountered by the project closely reflect those confronting any individual school that attempts a large-scale innovation. Moreover, some of the things originally regarded as limitations later—surprisingly—began to appear as advantages.

General

The Integrated Studies Project was set up at Keele University in 1968 to examine the problems and possibilities of an integrated approach to humanities teaching in secondary schools. Unlike other projects in the humanities with a similar purpose, this was not specifically part of the programme for raising the school leaving age; it covered five years of the secondary school and all ability levels.

The project's first concern was to investigate patterns of curriculum organization that might promote greater interrelation and cross-fertilization between subjects. Teaching therefore centred on themes or issues that crossed subject boundaries. The project team prepared packs of curriculum material around the chosen themes and tested these in thirty-six trial schools, the majority of which were within the region covered by the area training organization of Keele's Institute of Education. The LEAs of Cheshire, Shropshire, Staffordshire and Stoke-on-Trent each appointed a full-time co-ordinator, such officers being full members of the project team but with particular responsibility in their own area.

The most fundamental question to ask about any curriculum project is what precisely is being recommended. The question was especially pressing in a project such as Integrated Studies, which focused on ways of *organizing* the curriculum. An environmental study with eleven-year-olds does not involve the same difficulties and possibilities as a discussion of social problems with school leavers; both cross subject boundaries, but one would argue their usefulness in different terms. It was by no means obvious that the work on integrated studies would suggest a range of objectives, or point to a particular style of teaching.

Several aspects of the situation seemed potentially embarrassing. The project's brief might be interpreted as a commitment to one particular way of organizing learning. At worst, this could make integrated studies appear as an end rather than a means, and inhibit means/ends analysis. Equally, it became increasingly clear that integrated studies had not one, but many growth points in the school. This led the project team to develop a 'family' of packs, planned around different themes, problems or issues and based upon alternative theoretical models, which are explained below (p. 72).

Evaluation targets

A first-generation project may well set itself limited evaluation targets. The Integrated Studies Project did not, therefore, attempt to comment on the relative advantages of integrated curriculum units over other types, but concentrated on the following aims.

(*a*) To analyse features that seem to characterize certain kinds of integrated themes, and to offer a framework for planning units which involved novel combinations of school subjects.

(*b*) To produce curriculum material for trial, in order to seek a consensus on the appropriate objectives, material, organization and teaching methods for the models being explored. Since the team wished their work to remain open to interpretation within individual trial schools (which could not be expected to share all the objectives, use all the material, or have a common organization or a recognizable 'Keele style'), this created a danger for the evaluation: the material might produce no significant results or even have no significant identity.

(*c*) To use the experience of the trial schools in developing and refining packs of curriculum material. This task clearly called for continuous feedback rather than end-of-course testing (military intelligence has little value when the war is over).

(*d*) To comment on the practical problems of collaborative planning and teaching raised by the project team's contention that integrated studies should be organized around themes and issues of human importance, involving several disciplines. Such areas of interest would seem to be best handled by a team of teachers from the contributing subjects, operating a 'blocked' timetable. But how far did the organization of secondary school teaching create a division of labour which conflicted with production of a common strategy by teachers as a group?

Model units

The original proposal which led the Schools Council to set up this project posed a question which the team came to regard as crucial to their work: is it possible to regroup ideas and knowledge between subjects in the secondary school so as to provide new and intellectually reputable curricula?

The team faced an immediate dilemma; if they supported every single growth point which could be claimed to cross subject boundaries, their work would lose any intellectual coherence. On the other hand, they observed a number of viable patterns for integrating themes regarded as worthy of careful consideration—hence their interest in model units and worked examples. The units possessed a broad family resemblance but had a number of vital individual differences.

Within the general framework, six models units or themes were developed; these were not intended to offer a comprehensive course of study, but it was hoped that they would be useful in subsequent thinking towards one. Three were basically for the junior end of the secondary school, three for the senior end. In support of each theme, the project team offered a 'map of inquiry' around which the curriculum material was organized; schools were at liberty to extend, modify or amend, since it has long been obvious that the best humanities courses are sensitive to the enthusiasms of the teacher and the opportunities afforded by the environment.

The project first produced an introductory unit called *Exploration Man*. This was a handbook for teachers which discussed the integrated curriculum and suggested activities drawing on familiar objects in the local environment. It raised the basic question 'What is man?' and investigated both the complexity of human beings and the range of ways of finding out about them. It was seen as an introduction both to subjects and methods of inquiry and to the ways in which different kinds of knowledge interrelate.

The other two junior packs arose from aspects of *Exploration Man*. The first of these, *Communicating with Others*, was linked, at least in its choice of theme, with the open-ended explorations of 'inter-disciplinary inquiry', as defined by the Curriculum Laboratory of Goldsmiths' College, London University. This popular approach is frequently organized around a broad concept like 'expressionism' or 'communication', which has no obvious logic of inquiry to help a school define an appropriate range of activities or degree of open-endedness. The project team was interested in the balance between explorations carried out by an individual school or teacher and the topics they themselves had identified and included in their pack. Compared with units based on a more specific theme, the selection of context and of curriculum material for this kind of unit was somewhat arbitrary. This pack was a useful model unit, as it forced everybody concerned to expose their assumptions early in the exercise.

The remaining junior pack, *Living Together*, operated generally in the social studies area. It dealt with man's social organization and tried to relate an environmental study to a series of carefully chosen cross-cultural comparisons. Each community or culture studied was seen as attempting to solve certain problems of living. Attention was directed to the basic concepts of comparative social studies, including a concern for values, beliefs and world views. However, the pack also showed that integrated units could be based on natural groupings such as the social sciences or the creative arts.

The senior packs were seen as arising to some extent from issues encountered in the junior packs. They stood rather differently in relation to the arguments put forward for integrated studies, being in general a little more concerned with putting knowledge to use and a little less with developing basic inquiry skills, though the distinction is inadequate and one of emphasis only. The fact that knowledge is 'put to use' suggested that it might be useful to look at the role played by different kinds of knowledge within a total culture. Harry Broudy has developed novel groupings of knowledge from this standpoint. At least two of these offer themselves as a possible basis on which knowledge can be organized for instruction and learning.

(*a*)   Societies organize knowledge along routes of social, cultural and historical development. This offers a widely conceived framework for study, although such work may be equally concerned with vital contemporary political, cultural, economic and social issues.

(*b*)   Societies organize knowledge and identify problems in areas of social and moral uncertainty. Social problems are live issues and evoke a genuine passion. They exist at the growing edge of man's quest to control his personal and social world.

These considerations gave rise to the project's packs on *Africa: a developmental study* and *Groups in Society*.

The *Africa* pack was to some extent a natural extension of the view that geography is a field of knowledge. The contributing ideas had been allowed to propagate others. Interest in human experience, for example, was reflected in a sub-theme on the human life-cycle.

Groups in Society focused on a social problem. The pack supported inquiry, reflection and discussion about the nature of human society and the groups (or individuals) within it that have been despised, disvalued, regarded as threatening, or have attracted various sanctions against them. Some of these groups are disturbingly different from the society around them. They may break the law or fail to meet other expectations in a number of ways. What do we know about such groups, and what counts as evidence in trying to understand the social structure that produce them?

The final pack was a rather high-risk unit called *Man Made Man*. It was based on the assumption that any attempt to understand man must usefully focus at some point on the way man represents himself to himself. Man has always been obsessed with his own image, and makes representations of himself in line, metal, stone, paint, prose, verse. He has also developed stereotyped mental images. These man-made men have become embedded in the culture of human societies in a way that modifies our understanding of being human. Whether they are seen as value exemplars or obsessive images, these representations give us our masks and make-up, our heroes and enemies, our clowns and fools. The unit also involved some consideration of technology, since man extends and amplifies his own human capacities by increasing control over the materials of his environment.

The project in the trial schools

There is an interesting choice of procedures available to a curriculum project when first entering its trial schools. An experimental approach would involve a systematic adjustment of the variables within the situation and the setting up of control groups. An analytic or judgemental approach would depend more upon an emerging consensus of judgement; it seeks agreement rather than proof. The Integrated Studies Project was firmly within the second tradition. This had a backwash effect on the project's concept of curriculum design.

Although the conventional thinking on curriculum development includes the notion of 'trial', there is perhaps less awareness than one might expect that trial situations can be set up within a number of alternative design philosophies. The most familiar model, exemplified by the early American projects in the physical sciences, is that of a strictly regulated sequence of numerous discrete objectives. These are laid down as prior guides to action, and are often specified in behavioural terms. This suggests an emphasis on the vertical dimension in the design process (see p. 9). The Integrated Studies Project tended to emphasize the *horizontal* dimension, arising out of a situational analysis and the exploration of a number of part-solutions.

The project took as its starting point two opposing principles: firstly, that teaching is an intentional process, and is typically organized around aims and objectives; secondly, that what seemed to be needed was not a preoccupation with an infinite variety of discrete outcomes, but the re-stating of objectives in a way that provided a realistic framework for organizing teaching behaviour. This is not to deny that the project team would have been grateful for hard evidence based on an 'operational' approach to some of its aims and objectives; but with limited manpower resources it was felt that the firm would be better run by curriculum entrepreneurs than by curriculum accountants.

Objectives as frameworks for organizing teacher behaviour

A useful way into this problem was felt to be a reconsideration of the origins of educational objectives, since these are not produced spontaneously but derive from a number of sources.

(a) *The disciplines of knowledge:* Rather than proliferate specific objectives, the team asked teachers to keep in the forefront of their consciousness the methods of inquiry of the contributing disciplines, and the standards relating to well-tried activities within each. If these inquiry methods were to be taught to pupils as participants rather than spectators, clear demands would be made upon any material that was regarded as suitable. *Groups in Society,* for example, was centrally concerned with problems of finding out about groups with a low social 'visibility'. Some of the material was therefore taken from the field reports of social scientists.

(b) *Instrumental skills:* Quite clearly, any curriculum unit will pay some regard to basic instrumental skills (reading, comprehension, interpretation, representing information, etc.). This would imply, for instance, that the reading level of any suggested material must be looked at critically. Feedback from teachers has indicated that the team was less than successful in this matter.

(c) *The growth towards self-reliance:* This range of objectives was concerned with providing the pupils with certain kinds of opportunity, and required material geared to the situations regarded as appropriate: such situations as individual and small-group study; self-directed work involving the identification of a problem and the construction of a rational plan; creative, exploratory or dramatic follow-up.

The project team believed that these considerations would provide an adequate framework within which schools might refine their particular objectives, and also make possible an evaluation of the material itself. Within this framework, modification of emphasis was allowable in the individual school. (The alternative experimental approach would have been to make each and every trial school formally avow a set of objectives. This might very well have appealed to teachers dedicated to 'rational planning', but the project team were particularly anxious not to frighten off some who—like two of their own members—operated intuitively within a broad framework.) At a later date the team did, however, develop a more detailed set of objectives for each unit, and possible test items for *Living Together,* but this did little more than make explicit what was already implicit, and the analysis was not enthusiastically received except in the half-dozen schools that found it useful.

Some evaluation techniques

The evaluation process, as has been said, was analytic and judgemental. The team took account of the individuality of schools, seeing their work as extending the range of choice available to teachers. The possibility of diverse interpretation was not without its problems: it meant that the team had no experimental control over the significant variables close to the kind of life we can observe in classrooms. Yet somehow the team had to take account of human variables (personality, training, anxiety, conceptual expectations, motivation and methods of teaching) and other situational variables, such as various kinds of team collaboration in a variety of institutional contexts.

This virtually dictated a reliance on *participant observation;* this meant that, as in social anthropology, the observer entered and shared the sub-culture being investigated. Not only did the participant teachers become observers, but the observing project members became participant. The project's peculiar organization, in having four full-time co-ordinators appointed by the contributing LEAs to support and advise the innovating schools, made this approach seem particularly appropriate. Naturally the project members, teachers, and advisers concerned themselves with three kinds of data.

(*a*)   An objective description of the aims, objectives, environments, personnel, methods, content and outcomes, as these were apparent in individual schools. A certain amount of basic data of this kind was collected by questionnaire. It was found useful, for example, to collect precise information about the facilities and equipment made available, and the degree of help sought and obtained from outside agencies.

(*b*)   Personal judgements as to quality, appropriateness, etc.

(*c*)   Process studies of the programme in action.

To call the approach 'consensual' was not to expect an easy agreement. The existence of differences in emphasis or diversity of judgement was not only expected but likely to occur at critical points, thus raising the issue of what criteria ought to be employed. The team hoped to present these issues in a form that encouraged professional judgement.

Observation can be categorized as 'open-ended' or 'closed'. In open-ended observation, the observer is sensitizing himself to the situation, open to all manner of 'hunch' and hypothesis. The focus may be teaching, learning or resources, but the decision on focus is an *ad hoc* one, based on what appears significant at the time. The participant observers were encouraged to keep anecdotal records, formulate 'hunches' and make guesses. The team found that teachers were slow to offer this kind of information, at least in writing, possibly because the team had failed to give the kind of assurance that would legitimize the activity. This was remedied to some extent by weekly contact and informal interviewing, some of which was taped and analysed.

Within the category of observation, however, the most consistent feedback was from closed reports, organized around problems, concepts, issues or models. The team gradually refined the areas in which they most needed information. The first of these areas of interest involved the pupils and their learning situation. What was the mesh of individual and group work, the balance of activities, and the degree of involvement or interest displayed? A typical general conclusion would be that in open learning situations involving four or five teachers there is a clear need for stable discussion groups and for one teacher to have a tutorial or supervisory role over each child's folder of work. Otherwise too much choice in an unstructured situation leads to bitty and disorganized folders, and faulty perceptions about the overall structure of the theme.

The team also felt the need to monitor the process of reinterpretation and adaptation. Here, they aimed at an interpretative description of how trial school teachers actually operated in the integrated studies time. What roles were developed, ascribed or achieved? Minimally the team sought evidence of the use teachers made of time and other scarce resources; how they controlled or managed access to knowledge; what styles they evolved for contact with pupils; and what rules and expectations grew up between them. Finally, the team wanted some indication of teachers' plans for assessment, although typically this question rebounded and was instead asked of the project team!

A third area of concern was the management of innovation. A firm conclusion from the team's experience is that a school facing a large innovation is singularly fortunate if it can avoid a trouble-free first year.

Finally, the team tried to develop ways of describing a group of innovating teachers. Several issues forced themselves to the surface; there were marked variations in autonomy and independence. What kind of control and communication network had been established? How flexible and adaptable was the teaching team in terms of both timetables and personalities? How did the teaching team allocate status or esteem among its members? This proved interesting because the arrangements encountered varied from the extremely formal to the very informal. Teachers prospered because they displayed charismatic qualities, carried formal status, or operated as 'gatekeepers', perhaps having lucid command of the theoretical aspects, or having mastered the intricacies of resources banks.

The innovating teachers also provided a most valuable source of feedback. This on-going reporting back was a central feature of the project team's attempt to monitor and record what was actually happening. Teachers were therefore asked to note how each theme or sub-theme developed. Response was predictably mixed, varying between painstaking and meticulous recording and virtual inactivity.

Independent observers' panel

One whole dimension of the evaluation was entrusted by the project team and its advisory committee to an observers' panel made up of LEA advisers, college of education lecturers and co-opted teachers. The panel's interim comments were fed back to the project team as a contribution to the growing agreement about what the 'problems and possibilities' of integrated studies actually are. At the time of writing, it was planned to present a final report to the advisory committee. This was likely to be a significant document in its own right and of real assistance to the project team in producing their introductory handbook (*Exploration Man*). The independence of the panel usefully balanced the project team's own reliance on participant observation. The panel decided not to duplicate observations on Keele-based schedules, but to evolve their own framework. This crystallized as a number of questions, for example:

How far do the Keele packs help school teams to develop integrated work, or how far do they restrict them?

What deficiences in resources did the use of the project expose?

How are teaching teams composed in relation to the balance sought between creative opportunity and the factual approach?

How do schools envisage the link between the Keele project work and other work going on in the school?

How far does the use of Keele packs help teachers to foster the development of individual children?

Although it would be wrong to offer quick generalizations before the final report, the observers' panel certainly highlighted one or two areas of inadequacy (or at least of failed communication) in the Keele project. Several teachers told panel members that the packs were over-ambitious, even unrealistic. One teacher felt that Keele prompted integration only from 'good' teachers. Another said that the packs had been 'produced by a group of people living in an ivory tower, completely removed from the needs of staff and students, especially the lower ability groups'. Such perceptions are themselves most interesting, and it is not to deny the element of truth that one recognizes it as part of the wider ideological gulf between the 'transit camp' and the 'battlefield'. One of the interim conclusions of the panel put the central dilemma rather succinctly:

The selections from school comments illustrate the dilemma of the pack-making project team. The packs are intended to give opportunities for the development of integrated work but, produced with thoroughness, they can daunt some and irritate others by their imposed themes, or emphasis upon styles of learning. They could easily become textbooks to the faithful. Only the occasional teacher has the confidence to work both within them and from them. Perhaps it is a question of teacher maturity. For the immature, they are firmly parental; for the adolescent, something to rebel against; for the mature, something to relate to and draw from as appropriate. In themselves they do not seem capable of developing new approaches to learning.

Curriculum material

The techniques of evaluation relating to the material were relatively simple. Much of the participant observation reports comprised direct or indirect comments on material. In addition, the team decided to expose the packs to professional readers from the educational or publishing world, and seek judgement based on experience rather than use. (A sociologist looked at *Groups in Society*, a philosopher at *Exploration Man*, an art educator at *Man Made Man*.) The project also sent packs to teachers' centres, the Keele Advanced Diploma curriculum group and college of education lecturers. This allowed regular local feedback meetings involving trial school teachers and informed outsiders. Systematic feedback from trial school teachers was organized to yield information on 'user' assessment of individual items by pupils and staff, in terms of suitability, clarity, interest, level of understanding, cross-linking, value for discussion, etc. as appropriate. The team also asked teachers to consider the organization of the material in relation to teaching/learning strategies, choice, routes, sub-sequences, media, format, relevance and gaps. One or two schools submitted number grids on which groups of pupils had recorded their route through the material.

The process of innovation

Dr Marten Shipman, Lecturer in Sociology in the Keele Department of Education, received support from the Nuffield Foundation in developing his own research interest in the process of curriculum reform by conducting an independent evaluation of the project's organization and the team's relationship with the trial schools. The research will have additional significance in that Dr Shipman has planned a follow-up study beyond the terminal date of the project.

The project team's own interest in innovation has been directed to commenting, in a way that is sensitive to the difficulties faced by schools, on the use actually made of scarce resources of personnel, time and money.

Publisher for the project: Oxford University Press.

7 Humanities curriculum project

Barry MacDonald

All evaluation is concerned with providing information for decision-makers, but not all evaluators agree about who the important decision-makers are, or what information they need. One argument of the present paper is that evaluation, at least in some curriculum areas, should pay more attention to diagnosing and satisfying the needs of decision-making groups other than the programme developers. This is not to question the validity of formative evaluation. Certainly, we must devise sound curriculum offerings, but if they are to be effectively used, we must also understand better the forces that shape their fate in schools.

How is a democracy to handle controversial issues in its schools? That, in a nutshell, is the problem tackled by the Nuffield/Schools Council Humanities Curriculum Project which, following three years of research, is now publishing packs of teaching materials and advising schools on developing teaching skills and insights into the problems of curriculum work in this area.

The project was set up in 1967 as part of the preparation for raising the school leaving age in 1972. The project team was asked to provide stimulus, support and material for schools teaching the humanities to pupils aged 14–16 of average and below average ability. In the team's view, the defining characteristic of the range of subjects labelled 'humanities' was a concern with important human issues, and they decided to focus their research upon the special problems of work in controversial value areas. In this way they felt they could help schools respond to a demand[1] that the curriculum offered to adolescents should be relevant to their needs, and that schools should tackle controversial issues with these pupils in an honest and adult way.

As the team saw it, the central problem faced by schools which tried to meet this demand was how to allow pupils to explore issues responsibly without being restricted by the teacher's bias or subjected to undue pressures from other pupils. They approached this problem by attempting to stimulate and study in classroom settings a pattern of inquiry teaching with a particular style of discussion at its core. Collections of original source material were gathered around inquiry areas and used as evidence[2] for discussion. Teachers, in the role of discussion group chairmen, took responsibility for feeding in evidence that the pupils could study and interpret. They also undertook not to give their own views on the issues, and to protect divergence of view among pupils. This teacher neutrality, although by no means a new idea in this context,[3] has attracted a great deal of public attention during the life of the project, and has been perceived by some to be its defining feature, a judgement which may over-stress what is only one element in the teacher role which the project has been exploring. The project team produced initial collections of material in such areas as *War and Society, Education, The Family, Relations between the Sexes, People and Work,* and *Poverty.* (Collections on *Law and Order* and *Living in Cities* were later added.) During the years 1968–70, these collections were used by some 150 teachers in thirty-six schools throughout England and Wales. The project team put forward hypotheses about teaching strategies, and asked these teachers to test them by adhering to suggested rules. The teachers were also asked to comment on the usefulness of the materials when these rules were followed, to suggest alternative rules or hypotheses, and to develop other inquiry activities that needed to be built up around the discussion.

From Easter 1970 revised packs began to be published commercially, and training schemes for teachers were set up throughout the country to meet the response from individual schools and LEAs. During the academic year 1970/71 some 600 schools bought the materials which were available on the open market. Although most of these schools expressed the intention of adopting the research strategy explored by the project team, fewer than half of them had attended training courses by the middle of 1971.[4]

The first evaluator was appointed in 1968. His job was not closely specified, but it was broadly intended that he should study the work of the project, provide feedback to the project team about the progress of the experiment in the schools, and design a suitable evaluation programme for implementation in 1970–2. During 1970 he was joined by three colleagues, and four people have since been engaged in carrying out that programme.

The problems of evaluation looked formidable when the evaluators began. When a curriculum experiment is mounted in a largely unresearched field, as with this project, information is lacking by which to predict its impact or anticipate the problems it will encounter, although there is, of course, the accumulated wisdom of previous innovation efforts.[5] Measured against this, a gloomy prognosis emerged: the project seemed at first glance to have many of the hallmarks of past innovation failures. It required induction courses for teachers; it was difficult to use; it was costly in terms of school resources; it conflicted with established values. This prognosis assumed that the project should be judged by the amount pupils learned in a given period. This later seemed an inappropriately narrow criterion for judging the merits of a curriculum development of this kind. A closer look at three key features of the project may help to underline this, and will also explain the influence of the project's design upon the development of the evaluation.

The first point concerns the design of the project. The most widely advocated model of curriculum development is that which begins by specifying learning objectives in terms of end-of-course pupil behaviour. The content of the programme and the method by which it is taught are then varied until the desired behaviour is elicited. These programme objectives provide the evaluator with his criteria of success, since his main task is to assess the extent to which they have been achieved. This model is clearly most useful where statements of objectives are easy to make and command wide agreement, where side effects are likely to be insignificant or easily detected and controlled and where strict adherence to the objectives is unlikely to undermine educational values which they do not contain. The Humanities Curriculum Project team, considering that the nature of their experiment precluded such conditions, had reservations about the usefulness of setting objectives, and decided to take a different line.[6] To put it simply, they set out to answer three questions, in the following sequence: what content is worthwhile? what general aim would be appropriate in teaching this content? what kind of learning experience is most conducive to furthering that aim? Answering the last of these questions would involve extensive experimentation in classrooms. Using hypotheses about effects, rather than objectives, the team hoped to develop the general lines of an effective teaching strategy consonant with the attitude they had adopted towards the teaching of controversial issues.[7]

The assumption in this design is that teachers can develop successful teaching strategies from their understanding of a general aim. The emphasis is on the attempt to embody the aim in classroom process. It places a heavy burden on the teacher,who is responsible for seeing that what he does in the classroom is both consistent with the aim and effective. In an approach which is not based on objectives, there is no ready-made niche for the evaluator. He must await events, see what happens, trace the different ways in which the work unfolds, and try to link patterns of effects to patterns of teaching. *Outcome* and *process* alike demand his attention. A particular problem is which effects to study. In an evaluation programme, it is no use providing answers to questions that no one is asking.

The second point concerns the project's aim to develop an understanding of social situations and human acts and of the controversial value issues which they raise. In adopting 'understanding' as their aim, the team expressed their faith in an 'educational' rather than a 'social adjustment' approach to these issues. But the practical implications of this aim, in terms of pupil and teacher roles and relationships, meant setting up in many schools a pattern of behaviour in conflict with established assumptions and habits. Given the likelihood that such a conflict would influence the work of the project, and the certainty that the degree of conflict would differ from school to school, the evaluator had to study the *context* in which the programme was to operate.

The third point concerns the team's general approach to problems of curriculum innovation. Whereas most externally conceived attempts at curriculum reform have been characterized by efforts to minimize their dependence on the individual teacher's judgement, the central assumption of the project's design was that there could be no effective, far-reaching curriculum development without teacher development. To promote this development, the team asked teachers to accept the project as a means of exploring for themselves the problems of teaching controversy rather than as an authoritative solution devised by experts. It was important for the success of the project that teachers should understand this position and see themselves as creators of curriculum change rather than mere spectators. For the evaluator this indicated that some study of the project team's communications and personal contacts with the schools would be called for, in order to gain information about the success or otherwise of this effort. In short, some attention to *input* from the project was necessary.

The evaluation then, had to cope with an attempt at creative curriculum development with variable components, obvious disturbance potential, and a novel approach. The aim at that stage was simply to describe the work of the project in a form which would make it accessible to public and professional judgement. In view of the potential significance of so many aspects of the project, a complete description of its experience was needed initially, as was awareness of a full range of relevant phenomena. Evaluation design, strategies and methods would evolve in response to the project's impact on the educational system and the type of evaluation problems which that impact would throw up.

The project in the experimental schools, 1968–70

The thirty-six schools which mounted the experiment in the autumn of 1968 were not selected by normal sampling methods. They were nominated by their administering authorities, and their variety reflected interesting differences in judgements and priorities among the LEAs. Only in a few cases were the criteria of nomination made explicit: in most cases they had to be elicited or inferred. Pursuing the reasons which lay behind LEA choices was an important evaluation exercise. It helped the evaluators to understand the characteristics of the school sample, to learn something about LEA policies with regard to curriculum development, to assess how well different LEAs knew their schools and by what means they judged them. Clearly, there were a variety of criteria involved in nomination. In some instances, schools were nominated which were likely to reflect well upon the authority concerned, i.e. the showpiece school was chosen, whilst in others the chosen schools were those which were considered to need an injection of new ideas. It appeared that occasionally an old school might be offered participation in an innovation as a compensation for having to put up with very poor material conditions and facilities.

The grounds for nomination might be still more doubtful. In one authority there appeared to be an understanding that the head of the school would not use the project as an excuse to demand an unfair share of resources such as new equipment. Some schools were, of course, self-selected in the sense that the initiative had come from the head or the staff who, having heard about the experiment, pressed their claim upon the authority. On the whole, LEAs seemed to nominate schools which they considered to be good in some not very specific way. Close acquaintance with the experimental schools suggested that some LEA decision-makers did not know their schools very well and tended to make judgements about them on limited criteria, particularly community image. Such comments on LEA choices should not be allowed to disguise the fact that a primary consideration in most nominations was the perceived suitability of the school for the experiment.

During the summer of 1968 the participating teachers had discussions with the project team at regional conferences, where the nature and design of the experiment were explained to them and their task outlined. By all accounts most of them went away from these conferences with some enthusiasm for the task. The experimental schools were distributed throughout England and Wales, and located variously in rural, suburban, urban and conurban environments. Questionnaires completed for the evaluators by each school showed differences in type, size and organization, and in the formal characteristics of their client populations. The project's policy of sharing decision-making meant that this contextual diversity was compounded by differences in the schools' decisions about how to introduce, organize and implement the experiment. For instance, the time allocated to the work came to four periods in one school but fifteen in another, while the number of staff taking part varied from one teacher to ten. Some schools chose to involve their able fifth-year pupils, while others worked with their most limited fourth-year leavers. The situation was further complicated by variables—which became clearer as time went on —in the motivation, understanding and expectations of the people participating in the experiment. Yet another variable was the extent and nature of the support each school received from its local authority.

The immediate impact of the project was on the whole alarming. There was enormous confusion and misunderstanding, leading to a general failure on the part of the schools to respond appropriately to the project specifications. There were many unexpected problems, and widespread misconception of the demands that the project was making. Some elements in this are discussed in (a) to (c) below.

(a) The importance of headmasters in innovation was under-estimated by the team, who did not at first see the scale of the demands they were making on rather inflexible administrative institutions. It was not easy for schools to create the necessary conditions for the experiment, nor for teachers to undertake such difficult and novel work without the head's understanding support.

(*b*) The teachers did not anticipate the extent to which a large number of pupils, in their previous schooling, had been 'trained' into incapacity for this work, nor the depth of alienation from any kind of curricular offering felt by a good many of them. Nor did teachers allow for the degree to which they and their pupils had been moulded into a tradition of teacher dominance and custodial attitudes. They were confounded when pupils, invited to discuss, maintained a sullen or embarrassed silence. Many were surprised by how dependent the pupils appeared to be upon the teacher taking and maintaining the initiative, or by the scepticism with which the proffered invitation to talk freely was received. It would appear that almost all schools and teachers are more authoritarian than they realize. The implications of the project for the school authority structure became increasingly clear. Teachers found themselves locked in role conflicts, or in attempts to bridge an unforeseen credibility gap between themselves and their pupils. Hence the following comment from a teacher: 'I'm very tolerant in the discussion group to what the group wants to say . . . but then at other times when they approach me in an easy, offhand way, I find my adult pride springing up in me and I find I have to sort of take a position over them—you know, authority . . . sort of show my superiority, in a sense, in relation to them and this causes a bit of anguish on my part, inside me.'

(c) It emerged that the project team had failed at the outset to communicate the nature of the enterprise successfully. From the teachers' point of view, the ethos of the project was evangelical rather than exploratory, and the suggested teaching strategies looked like tests of teacher proficiency rather than research hypotheses. Many felt on trial. This both reduced their capacity to profit from the experience and adversely affected their feedback to the centre.

Had the picture from the schools been as uniform as these points suggest, perhaps the evaluation might have developed differently But it was not. Although the programme proved generally to be demanding, difficult and disturbing, there were striking exceptions and many contradictions. While many schools reported severe problems, for example, with the reading level of the materials or the attitudes of the pupils, others expressed surprise at accounts of difficulties which they had not themselves encountered. Limited explanations of perceived failure or success, such as pupil ability, teacher behaviour or institutional ethos, could not readily be generalized. Nor was it easy to reduce through experience the number of theoretically postulated variables. Teachers working in the north-east of England suggested that the difference in the response by boys and girls to small group discussion could only be explained in terms of a powerful sex differential in expectations and aspirations in that region's working class culture, while teachers in a Welsh school claimed only part-jokingly, that the reason they couldn't get discussion going was that there was no such thing as a controversial issue in the Welsh valleys!

During the first year, while the project team grappled with the problems of the schools in an effort to sustain the experiment in a viable research form, the evaluators concentrated on trying to establish precisely what was happening in the schools, and on gathering information that might help to explain differing patterns of action and response. They studied the team's activities and the interaction between the project, the LEAs and the schools; gathered data for each school about the external forces of support and opposition that were mobilized by the introduction of the experiment; produced a checklist of hard and soft data items which added up to an institutional profile of each school; tried to assess, by questionnaires administered at conferences, the participating teachers' understanding of project theory and their attitudes towards it; and organized a feedback system of taped classroom discussions with written supplementary data. Videotape recordings of classroom work were made through the generous co-operation of a number of educational television units throughout the country.[8] The needs of the project team and of the evaluators overlapped sufficiently to form a continuing basis of co-operation, even if the demands of their support roles made it increasingly hard to match priorities.

The evaluators embarked on a series of visits to the schools, intending initially to study all of them at first hand. After visiting about half of them this plan was abandoned in favour of taking a small number as case studies, principally because it was so difficult to understand the causes of the behaviour observed in discussion groups. Why were the differences between schools in this respect so much more marked than the differences within schools? Why was one group of pupils enthusiastic about the work, and a group with similar formal characteristics in another school so hostile? Other questions accumulated as the evaluators began to seek contextual clues. Why did some staff groups support the project, while others were indifferent, still others openly hostile? Why did some schools react in dissimilar ways to apparently similar problems? A host of questions like these arose as the diversity of institutional, teacher and pupil response unfolded.

Towards the end of the first year and throughout the second year of the experiment, clinical field studies of some half-dozen schools were carried out. These schools were selected on multiple criteria, but represented the range of the schools' response to the experiment. Case study strategies included observation of classrooms, interviews with staff, pupils and parents, and gathering detailed information about the various forces and circumstances, both inside and outside the school, that might be exerting an influence on the project. It is not possible here to give an account of these studies, but we can list some of the propositions arising out of them that the evaluators decided to explore.

(*a*) Human behaviour in educational settings is susceptible to a wide range of variable influences. This is a commonplace, yet in curriculum evaluation it is sometimes assumed that what is intended to happen is what actually happens, and that what happens varies little from setting to setting.

(*b*) The impact of an innovation is not a set of discrete effects, but an organically related pattern of acts and consequences. To understand a single act fully, it must be located functionally within that pattern. It follows that innovations have many more unforeseen consequences than is normally assumed in development and evaluation designs.

(*c*) No two schools are so alike in their circumstances that prescribed curricular actions can adequately supplant the judgement of the school staff. Historical evolutionary differences alone make the 'innovation gap' a significant variable for decision-making.

(*d*) The goals and purposes of the programme's developers are not necessarily shared by its users. The project has been used variously as a political resource in an existing power struggle between staff factions, as a way of increasing the effectiveness of a custodial pattern of pupil control, and as a means of garnishing the image of institutions which covet the wrappings, but not the merchandise, of innovation—the phenomenon of 'innovation without change'.

The rationale and framework of the evaluation programme, 1970–72

It must be pointed out that evaluation of the project has not been solely the work of specialized personnel. All members of the development team have devoted much of their time to evaluating their work in order to increase their understanding and improve the quality and appropriateness of their support to schools. Many of the schools have, with the assistance of the team, devised examination syllabuses and forms of pupil assessment. However, what is described here is the work of an independent evaluation unit attached to the project.

Evaluations may be judged by whether they get the right information to the right people at the right time. But who are the right people, what is the right information, and when is it needed? Faced with a project team who were opposed to the setting of objectives, the evaluators had to look elsewhere for a concept of evaluation to guide them. In any case, as they became aware of the complexity and diversity of what was going on in the experimental schools, they became increasingly sceptical of confining evaluation to measuring how far the project's intentions were being achieved. They then explored the possibility of defining their responsibilities in relation to likely readers of their report. The idea of evaluation for consumers attracted them. In time 'consumers' became redefined as decision-makers and four main groups of decision-makers emerged: sponsors, LEAs, schools and examining boards. The task of evaluation was then defined as that of answering the questions that decision-makers ask. This definition was subsequently perceived to be unsatisfactory, principally because it assumed that these groups knew in advance what questions were appropriate—an unjustified assumption when the educational process is so little understood that the effects of intervening in it cannot be fully anticipated.

The evaluators came to see their task as that of feeding the judgement of decision-makers by promoting understanding of the considerations that bear upon curricular action. This definition has two main advantages. In the first place, it greatly increases the number of people for whom the evaluation is potentially useful. Secondly, it goes some way towards meeting the oft-voiced complaint that evaluation data come too late to affect decisions about the programme. Where the evaluation findings have been specifically tied to the programme and have not generalized beyond it, this criticism is a telling one. The findings from the evaluation of the Humanities Curriculum Project had to be relevant to recurring problems of educational choice, and contribute to a cumulative tradition of curriculum study.

With these considerations in mind, the objectives of the evaluation unit could be defined as follows:

(*a*) to ascertain the effects of the project, document the circumstances in which they occurred, and present this information in a form which would help educational decision-makers to evaluate the likely consequences of adopting the programme;

(*b*) to describe the existing situation and operations of the schools being studied so that decision-makers could understand more fully what it was they were trying to change;

(*c*) to describe the work of the project team in terms which would help the sponsors and planners of such ventures to weigh the value of this form of investment, and to determine more precisely the framework of support, guidance and control which were appropriate;

(*d*) to make a contribution to evaluation theory by articulating problems clearly, recording experiences and, perhaps most important, publicizing errors;

(*e*) to contribute to the understanding of the problems of curriculum innovation generally.

Not everyone would agree that these are all defensible objectives for an evaluation unit set up to study one project. But it may be argued, firstly, that objectives are in part a function of opportunities, and secondly, that at a time when curriculum development is becoming increasingly the concern of a number of new and relatively inexperienced agencies, it is incumbent on those involved in the field to contribute what they can towards an understanding of the problems of change.

There still remains the problem of what is the 'right' information. Decision-making groups differ in their data requirements. Teachers may be mainly interested in pupil development, headmasters in teacher development, LEAs in school development, planners in project strategies, boards in the adequacy of examinations for assessing what pupils have learned. Moreover, individuals differ in the degree of confidence they place in different kinds of data, and in the levels of confidence at which they are prepared to act. Faced with such diverse interests and requirements, the evaluators undertook a very broad study of the project, combining both subjective and objective approaches (to use a convenient, if misleading, dichotomy) in the acquisition of relevant information.

The work contains clinical, psychometric and sociometric elements. Basically, information has been sought from two overlapping school samples, one large and one small, the idea being to study in some detail over a period of time the experience of a small number of schools, while gathering sufficient information about what was happening in a large number of schools to permit interpretation from one sample to the other. The evaluation design is as follows.

(a) *In the large sample of schools (c.* 100)

(i) Gathering input, contextual and implementation data by questionnaire.

(ii) Gathering judgement data from teachers and pupils.

(iii) Objective measurement of teacher and pupil change. (At the beginning of 1970, the evaluators carried out pre-tests of pupils by twenty-one objective tests—representing the combined judgements of teachers, pupils, the project team and themselves—of likely dimensions of pupil change. This was a massive operation, but would be justified if it could help establish pupil effects and lead to the employment in the following year of a small but accurate test battery.)

(iv) Tracing variations in teaching practice through the use of specially devised multiple-choice feedback instruments which required minimal effort by the teacher and were monitored by pupils.

(v) Documenting the effect on the school by means of semi-structured teacher diaries.

(b) *In a small sample of schools (c.* 12)

(i) Case studies of patterns in decision-making, communication, training and support in local areas.

(ii) Case studies of individual schools within those areas.

(iii) Study of the dynamics of discussion by tape, videotape and observation.

To sum up, the evaluators now had the job of describing the experience of hundreds of schools embarking on work with the project materials and, moreover, of describing that experience in ways which would be helpful to those who had judgements to make in this field. The evaluators believed that much evaluation work in the past had been over-simplified in its approach, or so subservient to the canons of traditional research that its attention had been too narrowly focused. Perhaps, at this stage of our understanding, bolder

E.C.D.—4

evaluation designs can give us a more adequate view of what it is we are trying to change, and what is involved in changing it. That is why the evaluators of the Humanities Curriculum Project adopted such a comprehensive plan of evaluation. By interweaving the studies outlined above, they hoped to advance understanding of the interplay of forces in this curriculum innovation.

Note: A version of this article is included in E. R. House (ed.) *School Evaluation: Process and Politics* Berkeley, Calif: McCutchan, 1973.

Publisher for the project: Heinemann Educational Books.

Notes and references

1   See Schools Council Working Paper 2, *Raising the School Leaving Age: a Co-operative Programme of Research and Development*, HMSO, 1965.

2   'Evidence', as the word is used by the project, has a judicial or historical connotation. It means merely that the material is relevant to the matter under discussion.

3   See, for instance, John Adams, *Errors in School*, University of London Press, 1927, pp. 227–9.

4   The evaluation unit, which has been attempting to document the overall pattern of adoption and use of the materials, arranged to be notified by the publishers of all sales, and has asked all purchasers for information about how they intend to use the materials.

5   See, for instance, M. B. Miles (ed.), *Innovation and Education*, New York: Teachers College, Columbia University, 1964.

6   For a full account of these reservations, see L. A. Stenhouse 'Some limitations of the use of objectives in curriculum research and planning', *Paedagogica Europaea*, 1970/1, pp. 73–83.

7   'The work of the Project has been based upon five major premises:

   1   that controversial issues should be handled in the classroom with adolescents;
   2   that the teacher accepts the need to submit his teaching in controversial areas to the criterion of neutrality at this stage of education, i.e. that he regards it as part of his responsibility not to promote his own view;
   3   that the mode of enquiry in controversial areas should have discussion, rather than instruction, as its core;
   4   that the discussion should protect divergence of view among participants, rather than attempt to achieve consensus;
   5   that the teacher as chairman of the discussion should have responsibility for quality and standards in learning.'

Reproduced from Schools Council/Nuffield Foundation, *The Humanities Project: an Introduction*, Heinemann Educational Books, 1970, p. 1.

8   These recordings have now been edited into a master tape of excerpts supplemented by contextual and interview data. This visual report is currently being used in project induction courses and is available on hire or sale from the Centre for Applied Research in Education, University of East Anglia.

8 Nuffield A level biological science project

Peter J. Kelly

It was the responsibility of this project, which was set up in 1965, to determine the needs of sixth form biological education, to attempt to meet these needs by introducing relevant and effective innovations, and to provide the framework for successful implementation. Evaluation was geared to decision-making throughout this work, being concerned in the broadest sense with the collection of data on which reliable judgements could be based. In essence, the evaluation strategy consisted of establishing the issues on which decisions had to be made and asking seven questions about each of them.

(*a*) What is the nature of the issue?
(*b*) What data have to be collected for evaluating it?
(*c*) How are the data to be collected?
(*d*) Who is to collect them?
(*e*) How are the data to be judged?
(*f*) Who is to do the judging?
(*g*) What may be the use and influence of the evaluation?

The answers to these questions provided the guidelines for evaluating each issue.

The work of evaluation commenced with the first activity of the project and then unfolded into a series of interrelated phases, each depending on those preceding it and to some extent on those that were to follow. Fig. 7 shows the main phases of evaluation and their relation to the stages in the project's work.

It was contended that, in the final analysis, evaluation rested on human judgement, however objective the techniques employed might be, and thus an evaluation strategy has to be focused on people, not on the techniques they use. Hence it was considered important that, within the limits imposed by time and administration, a range of people concerned with the products of development should play a part in as many stages of the evaluation process as possible. They included the project's development team, teachers and students, and those with an interest in A level biology who were not participating directly in the project's work, e.g. biologists, examiners, HM inspectors and LEA advisers. Reasonable consensus of opinion obtained from such people, based on adequate data, could be used as acceptable criteria for judging the

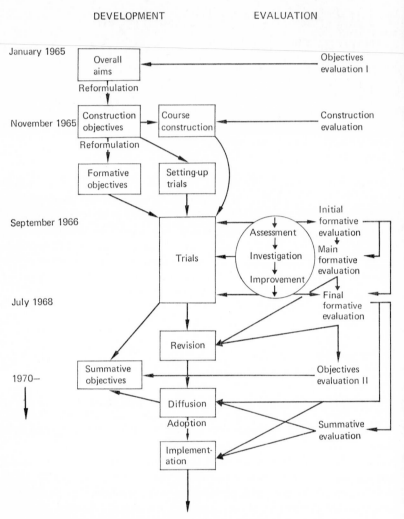

DEVELOPMENT   EVALUATION

January 1965

Overall aims

Objectives evaluation I

Reformulation

November 1965   Construction objectives   Course construction

Construction evaluation

Reformulation

Formative objectives   Setting-up trials

September 1966

Trials

Assessment
Investigation
Improvement

Initial formative evaluation

Main formative evaluation

July 1968

Final formative evaluation

Revision

1970—   Summative objectives

Objectives evaluation II

Diffusion

Adoption

Summative evaluation

Implement-ation

Fig. 7 Nuffield A Level Biological Science: relations between evaluation and the development and post-development stages of the project

level and quality of achievement. In turn, these criteria were likely to be acceptable to the wider groups from which these people came. Teachers were seen as the focal group; it was recognized that the validity and acceptability of the work must depend on their professional judgement.

A policy of limiting the influence of individual commitment on evaluation by changing and redeploying personnel was also adopted. This was done in three ways. The first, which has already been referred to, involved employing a variety of people to make judgements on data. The second way was to involve a variety of people in preparing and using data-collecting techniques. For example, in the construction of examinations, items were obtained from teachers conducting trials, members of the development team, and teachers and biologists not taking part in the project. These were then moderated by a committee including both item writers and people with similar backgrounds, or with particular expertise in devising examinations, who had not written the items.

Thirdly, an effort was made to blend the work of developers and evaluators, allowing their separate expertise and motivation to be expressed without polarizing into a position of antagonism. This was achieved not by employing an evaluator simply as an external observer and analyst but by planning an evaluation strategy within the total project strategy. Here people with specific skills were employed. Some were concerned with the construction and use of examination and assessment procedures, others with observations in the schools of a particular area (area co-ordinators) or nationally (the trials co-ordinator). Some scrutinized the curriculum materials in preparation (the editorial team) and for content validity and consistency after preparation (biologists and teachers outside the development team). And teachers, of course, evaluated the use of the materials and teaching and learning strategies through feedback based on classroom experience with them. There was some overlap of people taking part in each of these activities, for participation or consultation, so that an interchange of experience was possible. Working parties, each dealing with a specific evaluation issue, were set up from time to time and included people providing appropriate experience. The evaluation work as a whole was monitored by a committee consisting of three evaluation specialists not otherwise connected with the project, one person (the co-organizer) representing the writing team, two people concerned with the production of the examination and assessment procedures used in the project, and the project organizer (the present author) as chairman.

Objectives

To satisfy the project's terms of reference, it was necessary to define what was meant by a suitable education in biology at the sixth form level. This involved considering the nature of the subject and its relationship to the sixth form curriculum as a whole; to the needs of students in terms of their backgrounds, abilities and aspirations; and to constraints, such as limited facilities, that might be imposed on their studies.

A review of current and possible future trends in the biological sciences and their importance to education was undertaken; in addition, a series of working parties including members of the development team, subject specialists and teachers were set up. Most of the working parties were concerned with specific topics, for example, applied biology. They worked out the objectives in teaching these topics, the basic concepts underlying the topics, outline teaching schemes, connections with other topics, types of curriculum materials that might be used, and the type of trials and evaluation required. Some working parties were not specifically concerned with subject content and dealt with matters such as project work and examinations. Meetings were also held with people from the Association for Science Education, colleges and university departments of education, colleges of advanced technology (as they were in 1965), medical and dental schools, industrial organizations, as well as with university biologists to gain some insight into their views of the shape sixth form biology should take. In addition, the project co-operated with a survey conducted by the Royal Society/Institute of Biology's Biological Education Committee,[1] covering some relevant aspects of biology teaching in sixth forms, including teachers' opinions about its requirements, analyses of the backgrounds, ability and aspirations of students taking A level biology, the suitability of facilities, and the probable effects of changes in the curriculum.

The data obtained from these sources were presented independently to meetings of the project's development team and consultative committee. Verbatim minutes of these meetings provided further data and the whole was then analysed by the project organizer; a document, intended to represent a consensus of their judgement, with a draft statement of objectives and an outline scheme of the content, activities and materials to be developed, was presented to the development team separately and then jointly with the consultative committee. At the same time, feedback on it was sought from members of the various working parties. The document was modified and the development team approved a statement of objectives some eleven months after the project commenced.[2]

This evaluation stage, geared to the formulation of objectives, was considered central to the whole evaluation strategy. Quality of achievement in curriculum development is mirrored in the quality of intention. This does not mean that achievement necessarily will—or should—reflect objectives precisely. However, as the process of development is a continuity in which each stage guides those that follow, the ideas that initate the process will inevitably dictate its general direction. For this reason it was considered of paramount importance to base judgements concerned with the formulation of objectives on as careful an evaluation of relevant data as was possible.

The role of objectives

The initial objectives were seen as providing the guidelines for development but nevertheless open to eventual modification. A new curriculum establishes a new situation and, as such, is likely to have characteristics which cannot be predetermined. In establishing objectives for developing a new curriculum, this new situation has been prejudged and possibly with incomplete information. For this reason the project's objectives were seen more as hypotheses than as absolutes, bearing a similar relation to the trials as a hypothesis to an experiment, so that they might be proved, disproved or modified. It was, in fact, a deliberate policy to emphasize that the objectives were mutable, so as not to restrict the exploratory and creative aspects of development, in which new ideas and new approaches are sought continually—it cannot be assumed that they were all thought up before the work started.

This policy was justified in practice. It was found that discussions of objectives invariably reflected a tension between arguments about what could be achieved and what was desired. When, however, it was possible to redefine or discard objectives and include others not previously considered, people were more willing to try to achieve the desirable, and this led to unexpected successes. To take an example, at the beginning of the project, when teachers were asked to rate the extent they considered the objectives were desirable and achievable, the development of the ability 'to handle quantitative information and to assess the error and degree of significance involved' (student objective 2 (d), see p. 97) was strongly suggested as desirable but only a minority opinion thought it could be achieved. After the trials the high rating for the desirability of the objective was now approached by that for its achievement. This was due to an extensive analysis and development of those aspects of the work involving mathematics, in which, as will be seen later, the teachers played a major part. There seems little doubt that this was aided by the atmosphere of experiment that pervaded the trials, which was in turn encouraged by the use of objectives as hypotheses. The success of individual project work was another example of the achievement of objectives that was contrary to many people's original views.

These positive outcomes were matched by negative ones of equal significance. Some were concerned with the nature of some of the objectives. From replies to questionnaires and discussions with teachers and students, it was found that some of the objectives were obscure to the point of appearing to contain inherent contradictions—as in the confusion between the course objectives 'to expect students to gain a sound body of knowledge' based on inquiry and understanding and 'to discourage the uncritical memorization of facts', which referred to rote learning of inconsequential minutiae. Other objectives were interpreted in a variety of ways, depending on a person's background. Even terms such as 'variety of life' and 'whole organism', accepted widely as common parlance among biology teachers, were variously interpreted.

Although such errors seem obvious in hindsight, the fact was that, despite extensive efforts to establish well thought-out objectives, these problems did not come to light until the trials were well under way. Such an experience underlines the importance of clear communication and the value of having an open mind towards the validity of initial objectives. Paradoxically, it also points to the importance of having objectives because clearly without them the problems (which were of fundamental importance to many aspects of the project's work—not just to evaluation) might not have been detected.

As the development progressed, some objectives were abandoned. At the start of the trials it was intended to include short optional courses in the overall 2-year scheme.[3] After about a year the experience of the main courses suggested that this was unwise on the grounds, for example, that optional courses would increase the teacher's administrative load and lead to greater rigidity in the scheme by encouraging excessive class teaching and decreasing the possibility of meeting the needs of individual students. In this case, then, the objective was rejected before it was tested. An objective which was rejected after testing was that 'to increase the depth and pace of work gradually through the two years of the scheme'. Teachers gave a consistently low rating to the achievement of this objective. Students had similar opinions. Biologists who studied the content of the scheme considered the objective unattainable because separate biological topics, e.g. genetics and ecology, contain their own hierarchies of difficulty in their conceptual structure but there was no hierarchy between the topics: genetics, for example, was no less, nor more, difficult than ecology. As a result of this combined evaluation, the objective was discarded.

Coverage of evaluation

The extent and concern of the project's evaluation programme can be gathered from Fig. 7 on p. 92. The objectives were of 3 main types: those related to the achievements of the students *per se* (student objectives), those concerned with the form and activities of the courses (course objectives), and major issues seen as implications of the scheme (implicatory objectives).

STUDENT OBJECTIVES

Information derived from studies of the nature of the biological sciences and their educational relevance was set against the question 'What abilities would a person need to understand and participate in biological studies and to be able to evaluate them in terms of their credibility and their implications to society?' This produced a set of nine abilities.

(*a*) Acquiring information, terminology and conventions related to study of living systems.

(b) Classifying and synthesizing biological data.

(c) Making relevant observations and asking relevant questions about them.

(d) Handling quantitative information and assessing the error and degree of significance involved.

(e) Assessing hypothetical statements critically with regard to their origin and implications.

(f) Evaluating implications of biological knowledge for human society.

(g) Analysing observations and/or acquired biological knowledge; using these for identifying and solving problems with unfamiliar materials.

(h) Contributing creatively to investigatory and problem-solving studies.

(i) Recording and communicating adequately and relevantly.

To determine the subject-matter of the scheme, key questions that are pursued in biological studies were identified and formed a framework for the major concepts to be covered. Units were constructed on 'The Living Community', 'The Maintenance of the Individual Organism', 'The Organism in relation to its Environment' and 'The Developing Organism'. Within this structure the subject-matter gave a balanced and integrated coverage of the main fields of biological science, both pure and applied, and including human biology. Major principles, e.g. adaptation, homeostasis, evolution and variety of life, were built in to all units, as were features of biological investigation and social, aesthetic and humanitarian aspects.

The expression of students' abilities occurs through the use of subject-matter but is also influenced by the type of activity undertaken. This may, for example, be theoretical or practical, involve reading prose and extensive writing or the mathematical analysis of data. The expression of a student's ability may also involve a variety of modes of thought, e.g. when the ability to recall knowledge involves 'pure' recall, selection from alternatives or understanding relationships. Hence achievement was seen as a complex of four major components: a student's *abilities* expressed in context of varied *subject-matter* and *activities* and involving different *modes of thought*. Student objectives were seen as aspects of achievement related to different combinations of the components, corresponding to the types of activity undertaken by the students in the scheme:

(a) recalling a wide range of biological knowledge involving a choice of alternatives and an understanding of relationships;

(b) writing essay accounts of designs for investigations and explanatory descriptions of biological topics;

(c) solving written problems involving biological data;

(d) acquiring, understanding and applying information from reading;

(e) undertaking practical work and recording and handling the results;

(f) undertaking a project with these operational divisions: (i) statement and consideration of problems in the area of interest, (ii) selection of a limited

E.C.D.—4*

topic for practical investigation, (iii) background research, (iv) planning the investigation, (v) recording data, (vi) interpreting data, (vii) relating interpretation of data to background knowledge and suggesting further investigations, (viii) compiling bibliography and acknowledgements.

Analyses of achievement in these six major categories, and also in those related more specifically to individual abilities and different areas of subject matter, contributed to the evaluation of the scheme.

The course and implicatory objectives provided the guidelines for evaluating the quality of the students' experience in the scheme and its influence on their achievements.

COURSE OBJECTIVES

1 *Content*

(*a*) To expect students to gain a sound body of knowledge but to discourage the uncritical memorization of facts.

(*b*) To cover all levels of biological organization but with the focus on the whole organism.

(*c*) To start topics with questions about function rather than form.

(*d*) To provide a balanced and integrated coverage of the main fields of biology.

(*e*) To consider the biological principles that apply to particular living things but at the same time to provide an adequate appreciation of the wide variety of life.

(*f*) To ensure that pure and applied biology, together with biological technology, are adequately integrated.

(*g*) To deal with aspects of the physical sciences and mathematics in the context of relevant biological topics.

(*h*) To encourage students to appreciate the aesthetic aspects of biological study.

2 *Approach*

(*a*) To focus the work of the scheme on investigations, either of a practical nature or based on second-hand evidence.

(*b*) To allow teachers to use their own initiative and, within reasonable limits, permit the teaching materials to be adapted to meet the aptitude of a wide range of students.

(*c*) To require students to undertake studies on their own and be responsible for the organization of their work, especially in the later stages of the scheme.

(*d*) To increase the depth and pace of work gradually through the two years of the scheme.

3 *Feasibility of materials and circumstances*
   (*a*) To be able to undertake the work adequately in the time available.
   (*b*) To be able to undertake the practical work without undue difficulty.
   (*c*) To be able to use the publications effectively in respect of accuracy of information, level of treatment, clarity of exposition, illustration and layout, and ease of reading and cross-reference.
   (*d*) To be able to provide materials at a cost acceptable to school financing authorities.

IMPLICATORY OBJECTIVES

   1 To enable the scheme to be undertaken satisfactorily in different types of school.
   2 To enable students with a variety of O level backgrounds to undertake the work adequately.
   3 To enable students also taking a variety of other subjects in the sixth form to cope with the demands of the scheme adequately.
   4 To provide a satisfactory basis for the students' studies or occupations after leaving the sixth form.
   5 To ensure that the course can be used within the examination and college and university selection systems.
   6 To ensure that supply agencies and other services can provide, in the long term, for the requirements of the scheme.
   7 To ensure that the scheme can be fitted into a strategy of future curriculum development.

Setting up school trials

This involved public relations as much as obtaining a suitable sample of schools for evaluation. In order to persuade schools to participate, they had to be assured particularly that their students would not be adversely affected when applying for places in higher education. At the same time it was necessary to site the trial schools so that they could eventually be effective in helping other schools wishing to participate in the scheme after the trials. The sample of trial schools was the result of a compromise between these requirements.

   The paper *Aims and Outline Scheme*[2], setting out the project's intentions, served as the major instrument of negotiation in arranging the school trials. It was distributed to heads of biology, pharmacy and other departments in universities and colleges of advanced technology, to deans of medical and dental schools and to principals of colleges of education, who were asked to give an assurance that, on the basis of the document, students applying for places in their institutions would not be at any disadvantage. Some 70 per cent replied, all in the affirmative.

Through information received from various contacts, a sample of schools was selected on the basis of the following criteria.

(*a*) The sample had to have a wide geographical distribution. Where possible, four or five schools were selected in each area, the areas being distributed throughout Britain and among rural, suburban and city localities. The intention was to include a variety of circumstances in the sample, but at the same time to have a system by which teachers from small groups of schools could meet together regularly and thus provide both mutual assistance in administering the trials and a regular source of evaluation through discussion. Someone who was familiar with the work of the project, and occasionally a contributor, who had the personality to act as chairman to a group and was willing to help with the administration, was appointed as a co-ordinator for each area.

(*b*) The distribution in the sample of schools with different status (e.g. maintained, direct grant) and different ability ranges (e.g. grammar, comprehensive), and of boys', girls' and co-educational types, had to be comparable to the distributions in the national population.

(*c*) Although the sample was not intended to be statistically representative, it was designed to include schools within and containing a variety of circumstances that mirrored, in their kind but not necessarily in proportion, the range of circumstances which existed nationally, particularly with regard to facilities.

(*d*) Sufficient students had to be available to allow statistical analyses of examinations and assessment results, and of comparative performances of sub-samples. As the average number of students in sixth form biology classes was relatively low (12–13) and the range of class size considerable, a larger number of schools (48) was used than was necessary to obtain a sufficient range of circumstances, in order to provide the number of students required for these analyses.

(*e*) The area groups were intended to be used as foci for diffusing information about the development, and to assist with in-service training of teachers after the trial period. A wide distribution of these groups was needed to cover the country adequately for this purpose.[4]

The heads of biology departments in the schools were first approached, often in person; when they consented to participate in the trials, an official request was made by the Nuffield Foundation to the LEAs and headteachers concerned. When a school could not participate (this happened in five cases), further inquiries were made, usually with the LEA in which the school was situated, in an effort to find an equivalent school. In these inquiries the *Aims and Outline Scheme* was used extensively.

After the sample had been set up, detailed data about the schools and their teachers and students were obtained by postal questionnaires, and a survey of facilities undertaken through visits, mainly by the trials co-ordinator.

Data were collected for the following characteristics of the school sample:

(*a*) students: sex, O level experiences (subjects taken and attainment in them), other subjects taken in the sixth form, attitudes towards A level biology (reasons for taking the subject, career aspirations);

(*b*) teachers' attitudes towards the objectives of the scheme;

(*c*) type of school: organization, sex of students;

(*d*) geographical distribution: part of country, type of area;

(*e*) sizes of school, sixth form, A level biology class;

(*f*) facilities: laboratory space, project work space, library, fieldwork arrangements, greenhouse and animal accommodation, garden, laboratory assistance;

(*g*) time available for A level biology: total classwork, practical work, homework (or preparation);

(*h*) achievement of previous students in A level biological subjects in 1965 and 1966;

(*i*) careers of students leaving in 1965 and 1966.

In general terms, the data obtained showed that the range of circumstances in the sample was extensive but that the previous A level performance of the schools and the students' O level performance were of a slightly higher standard in some respects than those of the national population. The teachers affirmed that they considered the objectives of the scheme desirable, although on the whole they were less certain—sometimes considerably so—whether these objectives could be achieved.

The teachers participating in the trials were briefed on the overall objectives and the details of work for the first two terms at a one-week residential conference in July 1966; they had already received some copies of the early trial publications and the requirements for practical work. LEAs had also been given this information. The teachers, usually in association with LEAs, were responsible for acquiring the materials (other than publications) needed for the work and the administration of the scheme in their own schools.

Sources of evaluation data

During the trials, data for evaluation were obtained from nine sources.

(*a*) Examinations held in March and July 1967 and July 1968.[5-6]

(*b*) Teacher assessments of course practical work at intervals during the two years,[7] and of students' individual project work.[8] These items were also moderated externally.

(*c*) Feedback by teachers through postal questionnaires on the details of the work of each chapter (a chapter covered about 2–3 weeks' work of the scheme).

(*d*) Teacher assessments of how far objectives had been achieved. These were supplied through postal questionnaires at the end of the first and third terms and after the scheme was completed.

(*e*) Comments by students through discussions and questionnaires.

(*f*) Evaluation working parties of teachers at national meetings in April and July 1967. All the trial teachers attended these meetings, together with teachers and others not taking part in the project.

(*g*) Reports by area co-ordinators of discussions at area meetings.

(*h*) Visits to schools by external observers, particularly the area co-ordinators, the trials co-ordinator and the project organizer.

(*i*) Content analysis of the publications and other materials by people (as individuals or through organizations) outside the project. These included teachers, biologists and specialists in allied fields, research educationists, members of HM inspectorate, suppliers, medical and legal experts (concerned with the feasibility of experiments using human beings and other animals), and experts on the maintenance of living organisms.

Initial evaluation

Towards the end of the first term of the trials, an evaluation was undertaken which was concerned as much with logistics as with quality of performance. In effect, it was part of the commencement of the trials, providing the information needed to smooth out initial problems encountered by the schools. The data were obtained from the facilities survey mentioned above, observations by visitors to schools, reports from area co-ordinators and an analysis of teachers' replies to a detailed version of the chapter feedback questionnaire; these replies covered the time taken by the work, the different activities undertaken by a class (both those suggested by the development team and extra or alternative ones introduced by teachers or students), the success or otherwise of the activities, and the reactions of both teachers and students to the work. An evaluation report was compiled and discussed by the development team, the consultative committee, area co-ordinators and the evaluation committee. As a result, steps were taken to remedy the deficiencies it exposed.

It was found, for example, that work was being seriously impaired by the pressure of time felt by the teachers. They tended to spend more than the estimated time on practical work, which limited the time available for discussion, further reading and other non-practical activities. This was partly caused by the development team's inaccuracy in estimating the time needed for teaching certain topics. However, the teachers had clearly assumed that practical work was more significant than was intended. There was also a wide variation in the time taken by schools to deal with topics. To help relieve this problem, a document suggesting more specifically than before how activities could be planned was distributed to the schools. At the same time, area co-ordinators were alerted to advise teachers not to be concerned about the time factor.

The supply of materials to schools was also found to be a problem, and an arrangement was made for the project's headquarters staff to alert suppliers about the future demands of individual schools, not just the estimated overall needs of the sample.

The initial evaluation pinpointed the need to make the project objectives clear to teachers and the importance of informing their students. To help with this, meetings of all the area groups were arranged at which the project organizer discussed the objectives with the teachers as well as dealing with other problems that had arisen. This evaluation also assisted with the production of the publications and other materials. The manuscripts of trial courses not yet published were revised before distribution. The load of work per chapter and assessments of time were both reduced. An attempt was made to shift the emphasis away from practical work towards the non-practical by suggestions in the *Teachers' Guides* and by increasing the amount of theoretical work available in a book of problems designed to balance the *Laboratory Guides*. More careful consideration was given to establishing the preliminary knowledge necessary for understanding topics and, where possible, introducing exercises that could cover potential deficiencies. Finally, an effort was made to state the aims of each chapter of work more clearly.

Formative evaluation

Evaluation during the trials (formative evaluation) was seen as a means of developing the materials and strategies of the scheme, not as an end in itself; and as a continuing process in which assessment, investigation and the introduction of improvements were intimately and repeatedly linked.

The objectives listed on pp. 96–9 provided most of the 'issues' on which formative evaluation was based and the evaluation of one of these can be used to illustrate the processes involved. Similar accounts could be written for many of the other objectives, particularly those for the student and the course. However, with some objectives, and especially the implicatory ones, although the overall process of evaluation was similar, the techniques used were somewhat different.

The objective considered below is item (*d*) in the upper list on p. 97, 'handling quantitative information and assessing the error and degree of significance involved': put in easier but less accurate terms, the ability to do the mathematics included in the scheme.

At the commencement of the trials, as previously mentioned, teachers rated this objective as highly desirable but were clearly sceptical about its achievement; in fact, biology students had built up an image of being traditionally non-mathematical. At the end of the first year of the trials, these views appeared justified. In the examinations after the second and third terms the students' performance (measured as facility values) in items devised to test the achievement of the objective tended to be average or low compared with their performance in a whole examination. Moreover, on two occasions during the year, the teachers had rated the achievement of this objective sixth in a list of eight ability objectives, most of them considering it to be inadequately or no more than adequately fostered, while very few rated it as very adequate. It had to be accepted that the achievement of this objective was unsatisfactory and the reasons for this were investigated.

The first step was to discuss the problem at local area meetings with teachers conducting trials and with various people who might shed light on the issue. Some teachers argued that students taking up biology tended to have low mathematical ability, others held the view that the mathematics included in the scheme was too difficult. To test the first claim, the O level mathematics results of students in twenty-six trial schools taking the physical sciences and mathematics (not biology) were compared with those of students taking biology (with or without physical sciences or mathematics), the assumption being that if the claim was true, the physical scientists would have higher O level results than the biologists.

There was, in fact, a statistically significant difference (at the 1 per cent level) between the mean grades of the two groups. However, the disparity between the groups was predominantly at the extremes of the scale of grades. While 63 per cent of the biologists and 60 per cent of the physical scientists had grades 2–5 inclusive, 24 per cent of the physical scientists had grade 1, compared with 9 per cent of the biologists, and 28 per cent of the biologists had a grade 6 or below, compared with 16 per cent of the physical scientists. If grade 5 was taken as a clear O level standard (grade 6 is the pass), 72 per cent of the biologists had an acceptable background. Thus it appeared that a minority of students was influencing the opinion of the teachers.

A related suggestion put forward by the teachers was that the girls taking A level biology were less able at mathematics than the boys. Data obtained from the total sample of trial schools showed the difference to be of borderline statistical significance (at the 5 per cent level) but that again a minority of students appeared to be influencing opinions. It was found that 78 per cent of the boys and 73 per cent of the girls had grade 5 or above but 27 per cent of the boys and 14 per cent of the girls had grades 1 or 2.

The correlation between the O level mathematics and biology grades of the students was positive but extremely low. For the boys $r = +0.0968$ and for the girls $r = +0.0956$. Teachers' reports that some students who were expected to do well, as judged by their performance in biology, found the course difficult because of its mathematical content, were no doubt reflecting a lack of ability, background or interest already apparent at O level. On the other hand, students with lesser biological backgrounds, who would be expected to flourish, apparently did not make such a great impression.

Judgements may therefore have been influenced, in part at least, by the lack of correlation between achievement in mathematics and biology and by the presence of relatively few very mathematically able students taking biology. These influences appear to have disguised the fact that the great majority of students had a reasonable O level background in mathematics.

The next stage in the process was to look carefully at the mathematics content in the scheme. Virtually all of it was found to be included in O level mathematics syllabuses, although not all of these contained statistics. However, the statistics was used only as a manipulative tool, and students were not expected to pursue a mathematical understanding of any but the most elementary aspects. The background of the students would have been thought sufficient for the mathematics in the scheme.

The matter was finally discussed by groups of teachers at a national conference in July 1967. They concluded that the problem was related not so much to the level of difficulty of the mathematics or the ability of the students as to the learning strategies employed. They pointed out that students were not necessarily antagonistic towards mathematics, and indeed this was shown by the large number of students who maintained that they did not consider 'biology does not include much mathematics' was a reason for taking up A level biology when they were questioned before they knew what was in the Nuffield scheme (see p. 101). However, teachers reported that there was a 'tendency for students to grumble that the biology lessons were turning into maths lessons'. They found it 'difficult to prove to the student the necessity for the use of quantitative thinking in some cases, as the practical experiments did not produce enough results to do, say, a standard deviation'. They pointed out that mathematical topics occurred spasmodically through the course and lacked continuity; there was a need for exercises by which mathematical topics could be revised in different biological contexts, even when they were not part of current studies. Such exercises would need to be suitable for individual use because of the diversity of relationships between students' mathematical and biological interests, abilities and backgrounds.

This advice was borne in mind in compiling the work for the second year of the trials. Exercises were introduced to reinforce the learning of mathematical topics at regular intervals.[9] Small booklets reviewing the mathematics in the scheme were also produced.[10] In the July 1968 examination performance in mathematical items tended to be comparatively high or average; teachers rated the achievement of this objective much higher than previously, in fact second of the ability objectives. These ratings were similar, incidentally, to those of the students at the end of the scheme. The improvements introduced by the evaluation were now judged successful.

This example is of a reasonably straightforward evaluation. Others were less so, as when teachers' assessments contradicted examination results, for instance. Such conflicts might then require visits to schools by outside observers as well as discussions with teachers and their students. Usually the discussions were of greatest value; there was no lack of self-criticism or criticism of the scheme, and an exchange of views often provided insights that formal testing or observing did not (or could not) reveal.

Other problematical situations arose when the effort put into improving achievement for one objective resulted in a decline for another. All in all, the team learned that evaluation required a very flexible approach in which techniques needed to be matched not only to the specific issue concerned but also to the context in which that issue was being evaluated.

Examinations, evaluation and standards

One of the major tasks of the project was to devise new forms of A level biology examinations, including the assessment of course practical work and of students' individual project work.[5-8] These examinations were also used as evaluation tests because it was maintained that examinations should be closely related to the scheme and equally that they provided the means by which to measure the achievement of objectives related to the abilities of students and the content and activities of the scheme.[11] There were difficulties in this, particularly as it was not always possible to obtain a full coverage of objectives in each examination and the number of items for an objective was sometimes too small to be of real use for evaluating its achievement. However, the examinations did provide a means of judging the overall standard of achievement.

It is frequently asserted that achievement in a new course should be measured relative to achievement in the course being replaced, in order to find out whether it is better. This proposition becomes difficult to support when, as with the Nuffield A Level Biological Science Project, the replacement is so different that adequate common criteria and standards for comparison are hard to determine. In such cases the question 'Is it better?' is effectively answered by judgements when the new objectives are established and the new materials prepared, and thus evaluation related to these activities requires as much attention as evaluation of the students' achievements. This is one of the reasons why it was a major component of the project's evaluation programme.

The alternative to judging the standard of the scheme by comparison was to judge it by acceptability. Was the achievement of the students acceptable to those who normally make judgements on A level biology? Four procedures were used in an attempt to obtain a fair answer to this question.

First, the objectives of the scheme and the overall design of the examinations were considered and finally accepted by a wide range of people, including members of examining boards. Each examination was then scrutinized by a preparatory committee of some twelve members, constituted as described on page 93. The preparatory committees were charged with improving the structure and content of items, assessing the validity of the items, discarding the least suitable ones, and agreeing on an examination they considered to be of A level standard with the distribution of marks usually applied to A level examinations.

The second task was to provide guidelines for judging the standard of the scheme. These were based on data from the schools sample, particularly performance in A level biology of previous students from these schools and O level results of students in the trials. Compared with national statistics these results were slightly high and this fact was borne in mind when assessing standards.

As a third step, after each examination teachers and students were asked to estimate its difficulty. Invariably the examinations were considered more difficult than results warranted, and this was seen as a reasonable indicator of an adequate standard. The examiners also assessed the overall standard of the results in the light of their considerable previous experience of A level marking, and considered it satisfactory.

Fourthly, a further assessment of standard was made possible through a Special paper, which included questions common to both Nuffield and normal A level biology candidates. Of the Nuffield A level students, 22·2 per cent took the Special paper; this was high compared with 10·3 per cent of the normal candidates, some of whom were from third-year sixth courses. Even allowing for the slightly above-average attainment of the schools in the sample, it was a reasonable assumption that within those schools the Nuffield Special paper candidates would have the same basic calibre as the normal candidates; they might even be of lower ability. Yet on six of the seven common questions the performance of the Nuffield students was, on average, higher than that of the others. Candidates for the Special paper were expected to have studied widely and to produce continuous prose answers of a superior type to those for A level. This is the kind of item on which the Nuffield candidates did least well at A level. The ability of the Nuffield students to do better than the others on the Special paper suggests that their overall A level standards were at least no lower than normal A level standards.

These procedures were combined to provide the data by which those associated with the project were able to judge whether the performance of students taking the Nuffield scheme was acceptable.

Continuity of evaluation

The evaluation processes outlined above produced a mass of evidence, which was applied to the reformulation of objectives and the final redesigning and rewriting of the scheme prior to the commercial production of the books, visual aids and equipment.[12] At the same time, information concerning details of such matters as items of practical work and the illustrations and layout of the books was obtained mainly from the chapter feedback forms, visits to schools and small-scale trials of items in the course. The latter were necessary in the later stages of the course to offset the decline in the amount of feedback from the teachers. This information was of incidental value in drawing up the overall scheme for revision, but of major practical value in the task of rewriting.

The logic of curriculum development, however, is one of decreasing deficiency. At any stage in the evolution of a curriculum, it is only possible to say that a course is likely to be improved, never that it is better. Even if a course has been through several trials and has been modified after each, there is no absolute guarantee that its objectives will be achieved perfectly because no one has tried out the latest modification. A curriculum development project is thus only a beginning, and one that inevitably has an element of imprecision about it.

Imprecision is also assured by the changing circumstances in which a course has to operate. Even during the development life of this project, there was continual debate about the nature of the sixth form curriculum, and changes seem likely to occur in the future. Developments in biological research and the influence of the growing social significance of biological studies are also contributing to the uncertainty of the future.

This factor of continually changing influences on the curriculum had to be taken into consideration together with the results of formative evaluation, in redesigning the scheme for publication, and led to the blending of the formative evaluation studies of the project with those which have subsequently been undertaken in the post-development stages. So far this work has been devoted to studying factors affecting high and low achievement, diffusion, adoption and implementation of the scheme in schools other than those in the trials, follow-up studies of students when they enter higher education or occupations, and the development of ancillary facilities.[13-14]

Publishers for the project:
texts—Penguin Education;
film loops—Penguin Education, Rank Audio Visual, Macmillan Education, Gateway Educational Films;
film—Rank Audio Visual.

Notes and references

1   Royal Society/Institute of Biology, Biological Education Committee *Biological Sciences in Sixth Forms and at Universities in the United Kingdom* Institute of Biology, 1966.
2   Nuffield A-level Biology Project *A-level Biology: Aims and Outline Scheme* Nuffield Foundation, 1965.
3   The term 'scheme' is preferred to 'course' in order to emphasize its flexibility. There are several units of work which in the trials were called courses; teachers and students can use them in a variety of ways.
4   Lists of the trial schools are given in the *Teachers' Guides* of the Nuffield Advanced Biological Science series (Penguin Education, 1970-1).

5 Nuffield A-level Biology Project *Report on the Trial Examinations, March and July 1967* Nuffield Foundation, 1968.

6 Lister, R. E. 'The aims of questions in A-level biology examinations' *School Science Review* **50**, 172, 1969, 514–27.

7 Kelly, P. J. and Lister, R. E. 'Assessing practical ability in Nuffield A-level biology' in *Studies in Assessment* ed. J. F. Eggleston and J. F. Kerr, EUP, 1969.

8 Eggleston, J. F. and Kelly, P. J. 'The assessment of project work in A-level biology' *Educational Research* **12**, 3, June 1970, 225–9.

9 Kelly, P. J. (general ed.) Nuffield Advanced Biological Science *Study Guide: Evidence and Deduction in Biological Science* Penguin Education, 1970.

10 Eggleston J. F. Nuffield Advanced Biological Science *Topic Reviews: Thinking Quantitatively I, Descriptions and Models; Thinking Quantitatively II, Statistics and Experimental Design* Penguin Education, 1971.

11 Kelly, P. J. 'A reappraisal of examinations' *J. Curriculum Studies* **3**, 2, 1971, 119–27.

12 Nuffield A-level Biology Project *Major Criticisms and Proposed Remedies: an Outline Scheme for Rewriting* Nuffield Foundation, 1967.

13 Kelly, P. J. 'Evaluation studies of the Nuffield A-level biology trials' parts 1–5 *J. Biological Education* **5**, 1971, 315–27; **6**, 1972, 29–40; **6**, 1972, 99–107; **6**, 1972, 197–205; **6**, 1972, 259–66.

14 Kelly, P. J. 'Implications of Nuffield A-level biological science' *School Science Review* **52**, 179, 1970, 272–85.

Acknowledgements

It will be clear from this account that acknowledgement is due to many people for their contribution to the evaluation of this project. However, it is also appropriate for me to express my particular gratitude to R. E. Lister, the project's trials and examinations co-ordinator, and to W. H. Dowdeswell, J. F. Eggleston and the Joint Matriculation Board for their invaluable work and advice.

9 Programme in linguistics and English teaching: language in use project

John Pearce

The Language in Use Project originated as the secondary section of the Programme in Linguistics and English Teaching, set up in 1964 by the Nuffield Foundation and supported from 1967 by the Schools Council. The project team were given a wide brief and great freedom to interpret it. Nothing could illustrate more nicely the problems facing the team than the existence, outside their own ranks, of a wide variety of hopes and expectations about their output: everyone seemed to have his own idea of what the brief was or of how it should be viewed.

The project was, however, placed quite firmly within the domain of the academic discipline of general linguistics, and it was in this domain that the team's brief had to be defined. At its most general, a definition was provided by J. R. Firth, for whom linguistics was the study of 'how we use language to live'. To pose that definition as a question, and ask just how language and living interact, might seem to be asking a simple sort of question. It was Noam Chomsky who showed that one aspect of the matter was rather more complicated: 'What is it about language,' he asked, 'that enables a native speaker of a language, from a very early age, to speak many sentences he has never heard before, and understand many others he has also never heard before?' This is primarily a question about language, and only secondarily about the brain or memory or any of the things that have interested psychologists; Chomsky was pointing to the enormous wealth inherent in a native speaker's mastery of his own language, and this is something that a project working for native speakers could not begin to evade. But Firth's definition, while also primarily concerned with language, is about society as well—about variation between place and region and social class and the other things that have interested sociologists. Psychology is beginning to discover the complexity of language, because between experimental psychology and general linguistics there have been some decades of interacting thought and argument and research. Sociology is still, on the whole, in process of this discovery.

It is necessary to start on this somewhat defensive note, and lay claim to the independence of linguistics as a field of study, because it is linguistic study which has revealed much more about language than the two associated fields seem at times to appreciate. It is necessary to stress from the beginning the very advanced attainment, in terms of skills, which being a native speaker represents. For in a collection of papers on curriculum evaluation we are in the broad domain of educational psychology, and psychology and linguistics have until now operated from sharply different notions of what language *is*. Experimental psychology, particularly in the field of measuring intelligence and studying attention, is accustomed to using items of language as test material. The assumption behind this custom, for most workers, has been that when items of language are removed from their linguistic context, they are for practical purposes inert, having a determinate semantic content and a self-evident grammatical status. This custom, as far as psychologists follow it for their own purposes, is not here in question, though the accepted psychology view of language has been steadily undermined from within.[1] But the assumptions about language which are embedded in the routines of applied educational psychology are wholly different from those required by the linguist or by the teacher. Much the same may be said of the use of language items in testing, in survey research, and even in most published writing, within the domain of sociology. The precise relationship between sociology and linguistics is still the subject of widespread confusion.

Language, as something which we all use all the time, varies in response to a very large number of constraining factors. The social setting of the linguistic act, the medium employed, the nature of the audience, the speaker's relation to his audience, the nature of the language task being undertaken, the roles being adopted by and ascribed to the participants—all of these and many more are variables in the use of language. In any given language-using situation, change a single variable and the language used will change also. The change may be so slight as to be scarcely perceptible, but it is the linguist's business to concern himself with minimal contrasts. But these apparently quite insignificant differences in language may be critical for the act of communication.

To communicate, we must know, choose, or accurately assess whom we are addressing, whether we are speaking or writing, or writing to be read aloud, what our status is in relation to our audience, whether we are speaking face-to-face or at a distance—the list can be made very long. A realistic view of linguistic activity has to take cognizance, not only of the operation of all these and many more variables, but also of their simultaneity. It is not helpful to say that psychology 'ought' to be able to devise ways of measuring these as variables, just as it is not helpful to suggest that linguistics ought to be measuring them in some sense. There are too many specialists in one field telling other specialists what they ought to be doing in their field. The relations between psychology and linguistics are becoming clearer; when a similar clarity emerges from a great deal of research into the borderland between linguistics and sociology, the ways in which all three disciplines have a bearing on language as we use it may begin to cohere. But this is not to be hoped for at present.

What we can do at present is to recognize that linguistics has some very powerful insights to offer into language, not as grist to the mill of physiologists or psychologists, nor as categories for the analysis of sociological data, but as an analysis of a human phenomenon with extraordinary flexibility and freedom of choice. These insights can be trivialized, and linguistics is no more free from trivializers than are other fields. We can say quite firmly that measuring verbal ability, whatever that may be, by sampling lexical information is a very dubious procedure linguistically. We can say that it trivializes linguistic insights into grammar to suppose that subordination is a meaningful idea when based on schoolbook notions of what constitutes a clause. We can say too that treating grammatical transformations as subject-matter for lessons to boys of eleven trivializes transformational grammar on the one hand and the boys on the other. But if linguistics, in the hands of its serious specialists, often seems concerned partly to throw stones at its abusers, the record of linguistic misconception exhibited by many otherwise intelligent scholars may account for it.

The rigour which obtains in conventional evaluation work is not to be had if the subject-matter involved is language, for two reasons. First, if the educational knowledge transmitted has to do with how language is used in a real situation, there is no known way of measuring that use, whether before or after the classroom work which is being evaluated. Secondly, if the measuring instrument is itself a user of language, there is no known way of measuring the effects on any test results of the language-use of the tests themselves. The latter objection applies, of course, to many kinds of evaluation procedure, and to support this objection would require more space than is available here.[2] But whatever evaluation procedures can be adopted within the context of a language-use project will certainly be very different from anything else described in this collection of papers.

The Language in Use Project: its nature, design and aims

The team's brief was to try to help English teachers in the broad run of secondary schools. This gave a context of diverse, often conflicting, conceptions of what 'English' in the curriculum might be. Sustained debate in the profession over the previous decade still continues, about the nature of the subject, its role in the curriculum, and how it should be approached. Schools of thought are not clearly defined, often appear to argue at cross purposes, and are nowhere more at variance than over the part played by the study of language. The only widespread agreement is on the futility of conventional instruction in grammar or usage—where specialists generally have abandoned what stands out all the more sharply as a too-frequent support of the non-specialist.

'Knowledge about' language has failed in the past to improve the language performance of pupils who have received it—and teachers have mostly been unable to conceive of this knowledge as having any other value. Research evidence on the failure of one characteristic part of such work has been taken, perhaps rightly, as discrediting all formal language teaching.[3]

A more positive concensus has emerged in recent years: the view that English is not a subject as is history or mathematics. It is at once less than these, in lacking a definable body of facts to be learned, and more than these, in powerfully affecting the life-chances of young people. English has come to be seen as the pupil's opportunity to explore his world and his relation to it. An influential book because it embodies this consensus, John Dixon's *Growth Through English*[4] makes imposing demands on the classroom teacher. A very similar outlook, although with more social emphasis, is shown by the related *Language and Education* by F. D. Flower[5] and the passages on English in the Newsom Report.[6] All three documents appeal to the widest common feature of English teachers: their training in literature and their belief in its humanizing power. Many English teachers would go further, claiming great literature not merely as *the* subject-matter of English, but as the one civilizing and sensitizing instrument in the whole curriculum.

These debates have scarcely affected those who handle more than half the secondary teaching of English—those qualified in other subjects or in none who are drafted in to assist with English. The magnitude of this problem, first publicly stressed in 1965,[7] is now a cause for official concern.[8] At no time since 1960, on the available figures,[9] have as many as half our secondary classes had specialist teaching in English, and most of those have naturally been the upper school ones. The non-specialist remainder, baffled by debate among the specialists, have often relied on course book and textbook, supposing the public examinations to propound the one acceptable model of the subject-matter of English. It is these teachers, in all their natural diversity, as well as the specialists, that the Language in Use Project set out to help.

The team accepted the view that English is not ordinary subject-matter. What it is must depend in some degree on the pupil being taught. His attitudes, dispositions, capabilities, as they are when the teacher faces him—these the teacher must meet and exploit. So any help offered to teachers must meet this diversity, or enable the teacher to do so. There is no way of doing this without building the diversity into the material itself, by making the pupil a participant in the English class. The pupil changes his role: he ceases to be merely the receptacle of knowledge. The teacher changes role also, in the way common to many projects, becoming the organizer of situations and activities which give rise to learning. But whether the activities are talk or writing or improvised drama or the study of literature will be for the teacher to choose, in the light of the subject-matter and the class. The teacher will come to abandon the supposition that there is only one way to study a particular novel or write an essay. If this is a demanding view of the job, that is true of most other serious approaches to it. Where it is most demanding, however, is not in maintaining a ceaseless supply of 'great moments', but in seeing just where the work is going.

These considerations dictated the design of *Language in Use*. It would be for the teacher, not the pupil. It would not be geared to age, partly to avoid the unmerited *cachet* of authority that such a product might bear. There would have to be quite a lot of material to cater for the diversity of need. It had to be organized so that teachers could make coherent choices between its parts. These choices would have to be related to a principled basis of language study, and would have to offer some likelihood of meeting the needs of classes. And since the study of modern English on descriptive lines is not normally part of the training of teachers, it would have to contribute to the teacher's own education as he went along.

The material is accordingly arranged as a store of units. Here, a unit is a plan for a sequence of lessons, nominally four or five sessions of some forty minutes each. Each unit is a set of organized suggestions about classroom activities which relate to a particular content (i.e. an area of subject-matter in the use of the language), such as regional speech, making speeches, or sports reporting. The unit is not a rigid prescription. The notes deal quite closely with practical details of the sessions, but they are recommendations, with alternatives offered at many points and built into other units. The user is intended to find out quite early on that if there is no unit on a topic he wants to explore, several existing units offer ways of doing it. In each case, a unit suggests how an aspect of language in use can be brought into focus, so that the activities pursued by the class lead to greater awareness or insight about the topic. The level of the work, its difficulty, is determined by the teacher, mainly through what he asks of a class in formulating its findings. Each of the 110 units is independent—that is, no unit requires any other to have been done first. This autonomy is symbolized in the physical layout: every unit occupies a single sheet in a loose-leaf binder.

The objectives of *Language in Use* are twofold:

(*a*) to help teachers to generate in their pupils an awareness of the nature and function of language, and of the part it plays in their own lives and in the life of the community;

(*b*) to help in developing pupils' ability to use spoken and written English in the wide variety of situations where, in a complex industrial society, they may be expected to use language.

If there is an emphasis within these objectives, it is on giving the student not information about language, but insight into it. In particular, a developed insight is a necessary objective because it alone can enable the native speaker to reflect upon, and hence modify, his own use of language in adult life. The delicacy and subtlety of messages which he both sends and receives through language, the range of meanings to which he has access, whether as speaker or as audience, are closely related to his linguistic awareness—which in this case is also a social awareness.

The evaluation problems

Summative evaluation was out of the question for the Language in Use Project, and formative evaluation was subject to very severe limitations. The evaluation work that was undertaken was limited for four main reasons: manpower, the design of the material, the nature of its objectives, and the nature of language itself.

MANPOWER

Language in Use was written as a co-operative effort by a small team; material was not assigned for individual authorship. The material itself often suggested a process of group writing, for use in schools, and the members of the group themselves accepted that discipline. This has meant that the group was unusually close-knit. There was no separate evaluation officer, and none of the team could be spared to work as one. So evaluation became a secondary concern for one of the team of writers. Where questions arose which, in other circumstances, might have created tension between writers and evaluators, they were settled in the interests of preserving the cohesion of the writing team—without which the originality of the material's design could not have been achieved.

DESIGN OF THE MATERIAL

The design of *Language in Use* was intended to provide teachers not merely with a wide choice of material, but also with a very wide freedom to interpret whatever parts they chose. The purpose of the trials was essentially to test this. It was thus not possible to ask any teacher to try out a particular unit; the team could notify participants which units were as yet untried, and did so, but for this to lead to pressure on teachers would have altered the whole basis of the trials. Similarly, it was not possible to ask teachers to try out particular groups of units in any particular way.

The material rests on the consonance between its objectives and those of the teacher. The trials revealed the extent of this dependence in an unexpected way. While the material sought to make clear that the units existed to serve the needs of teachers, some participants chose to see their role in the trials as serving the needs of the units; they 'tried them out' in an almost consciously experimental sense, stating their aim as being 'to see what happened'. The team were well aware that this approach would communicate itself to the class. And the usual result of this treatment was for class and teacher alike to wonder what the work had achieved. In many more cases, where teachers began on units without fully knowing their objectives, the work brought a specific objective to the teacher's attention and gave the unit the focus intended by the team. There could be no way of planning this, or even of monitoring it through evaluative instruments, which accounts in part for the very heavy programme of visiting during the trials.

The other main consequence of the design is that to secure trial use of every single unit without constraining the teacher's freedom of choice would have meant a very large-scale trials indeed. The team settled for a more modest affair, on the basis that trials in which some units were not used at all would reveal a great deal about the units as a whole.

THE MATERIAL'S OBJECTIVES

The objectives of *Language in Use* are quite specific, but necessarily very general. They postulate awareness and competence, in that order, and imply a connection between them. The evidence of the trials is quite clear, but not of course conclusive, that there is a causal relationship between awareness and competence in language use. The term 'awareness' in this context is much more than the psychologist's notion of attention, just as 'competence' is much more than efficiency in performing test operations (see p. 118). The difference is not just one of scale; it is one of diversity and perspective. The teachers whose reports on awareness as a source of competence had such force and unanimity were looking at the full range of their students' performances, and at the changes in those performances over time. It is precisely in the nature of awareness and competence that a sampling procedure cannot adequately test them. We can never know whether a person has the language for a situation until the situation occurs, and in language activity we have to define 'situation' realistically, which in turn excludes test situations. It follows that it is not practicable to *measure* a student's awareness of, or competence in, the diversity of situations which life presents and which make a specifically linguistic demand on him.

THE NATURE OF LANGUAGE

As has been said, language is quite extraordinarily complex. The particular contexts in which it occurs each have their own history and social structure. Language is spoken or written by particular speakers to particular audiences. Each of its messages is characterized by the immense diversity of the lexicon available to a speaker in selecting words to use, and by one or more of an enormous variety of syntactic forms into which a speaker orders these items. We know a great deal about these patterns, and about the organization of language as a system. A great deal is known, too, about the way the nervous system works when a speaker is engaged in linguistic activity. The interface between these two systems constitutes a steadily narrowing gap in our under-

standing. But what we do know is enough to make evaluation of language performance inconceivably more difficult than non-linguists may realize. It is
as though excellent judges of efficiency in riding tricycles expected their
technique to apply just as readily to the control of a spacecraft. Those readers
to whom this is labouring the obvious will already possess their own version of
the next few paragraphs.

The complexity of a text, a string of words in speech, lies not only in its
internal syntactic and lexical patterning, but also in the way or ways in which
it is uttered. Variations in what the linguist calls intonation are of great
subtlety, and of great importance for the content of messages. If we consider a
speech situation as having its own history, one of the parts of this history is
the set of known or remembered or recently-used intonations to which a given
utterance may refer. The allusions, repetitions and implicit references of a
given text to earliers parts of the same text are essential parts of its meaning.
This is obviously true of a Shakespeare giving unity to a play by using
thematic imagery, but it is no less true of the gas fitter saying 'Right, Joe:
female!' By looking at the way spoken language refers outward from itself
(technically, by studying exophoric features), we can learn a great deal about
the intricacy of language. The fact that these intricacies do not often appear in
written prose does not mean that they are somehow not language. The same
applies to the linguistic variation which reflects status-relationships between
speaker and audience—variations which are summarized as changes in
formality, but which include vocabulary, grammar, intonation and speech-
sound itself.

Competence, as the project team have used the term, embraces the ability
to use language in those ways, with that flexibility and freedom of variation (in
all the aspects mentioned above and many more), which may be appropriate
to whatever situation the speaker is in. Awareness, similarly, means not the
scholarly condition of being well informed about language, but the possession
of a developed insight into these things and how they affect the self. It is not
necessary to be master of a technical notation dealing with pitch in order to be
aware of the possibilities for meaning that our intonation system can carry.
Expertise in the study of cohesion (textual connectedness) is not necessary for
awareness of the role of allusion in imaginative literature, historical writing or
intimate talk. There is no evidence whatever that instruction in the formal
properties of the linguistic system is of any benefit to its pupils in terms of their
later competence, and there is clear evidence that such instruction is of no
greater benefit than other elements in good English teaching.

An example can illustrate this. We are accustomed to use a wide variety of
forms of address in speaking to other people. We know whom to address by
first name, who has to be addressed by title and surname, which relatives can
be nicknamed face to face, and so on. Linguists have described this pattern
and formalized their description as a linguistic rule. (It also happens to be a

social rule as well, but that is not a necessary property of a linguistic rule.) But the rule is not an account of how our minds work when faced with social situations. The most expert linguist will not be helped by his expertise when he has to decide if a relative he has never met before is to be called Aunt Edna or just plain Edna. What may help a student is to know that everyone has the same basic problem (of placing strangers in the naming system), and that the solutions people produce to this problem convey information about themselves as well as about the persons to be named. Such solutions will influence the social distance maintained within the group and will guide others in their behaviour. When this kind of awareness becomes practised, which takes time, the student will become more competent himself. To the extent that his competence is improved, his value as a social being is improved, and with it his life-chances and the quality of his living.

We may reasonably doubt whether this kind of change is measurable. Existing ways of testing language performance fail to take the complexity of language into account and are not always free of linguistic error themselves. Closed-schedule tests of all kinds are the most obvious instance of tests withdrawing language from context and supplying another context (that of the test situation). The results tell us nothing of the subject's ability to use language outside the test situation—apart, of course, from pathological conditions. Tests of lexical resource again cannot indicate a subject's lexical competence outside the area sampled. Tests which ask the subject to generalize a lexical set, or to derive new words from given stems, may tell us a good deal about the intellectual eligibility of children under twelve for a curriculum heavily biased towards the verbal transmission of knowledge, but they are of little general relevance. From a linguistic viewpoint, most native speakers can (and do) acquire the vocabulary they want to acquire. Before-and-after tests of vocabulary have to assume that the role of motivation in language-learning is either random or invariant. The very fact of differential success in education shows that it is neither. Similar objections would apply to tests seeking to work at the syntactic level. If the test explores the power to organize sets of clauses and phrases into more complex units, the test is not one of linguistic competence, but of the subject's ability to learn to play that particular linguistic 'game'. If the test items are taken from the subject's own utterances, we then discover that syntactic complexity does not correlate with age in a manner which can be distinguished from education. Very similar considerations apply to public examinations in English Language: they represent a social demand, which on general educational grounds is of importance to society and to schools, but they are not in any meaningful sense linguistically valid.

There is a further difficulty: very little is known about the linguistic development of young people beyond infancy. We cannot even be certain that what occurs should be called development at all, if by that we mean a spontaneous and continuous process. We have no norms of linguistic development, and it could be very dangerous educationally if we had. (Even the notion of elaborated code, which Basil Bernstein intended to *describe* the *speech* of children under seven, is being used by some teachers to prescribe the writing of children over twelve.) It is not even possible to suggest a sequence of stages in how the language of young people changes. Such stages as are observable are stages not in language change but in education. What appears to happen is that young people adjust to the linguistic demands placed on them, and do so with varying speed and to varying degrees. The speed and scope of this adjustment does not appear to be related in any simple way to social class (Bernstein's studies deal with childhood well before the secondary stage). It does appear to be related to teacher expectation, and particularly to the very powerful symbolic language of streaming and school position. But in any study of language change in secondary children would have to assume a *terminus a quo* from which to work, and no such agreed or agreeable starting-point exists. The studies of early language acquisition[10] have shown that this is intricately bound up with socialization. We are as yet only at the beginning of an adequate sociology of the secondary school which would enable us to look at how language relates to it, but there is no reason to suppose language change among secondary pupils to be any less related to socialization patterns than it is with infants.

Even if we grant the existence of linguistic development in secondary children, within the terms of a meaningful definition of development, its time-scale is not a simple linear one. Leaving aside the problem of defining the 'learned' or 'acquired' in a language context, it makes a difference (to the linguist a very big difference) whether the test is written or spoken. If the test is of written language, how does the test procedure cater for the time-lag between the arrival of a new influence in a child's language-learning and its emergence in the child's written competence? This is a very wide and very variable period. Any summative evaluation of language performance faces this dilemma: internalizing the content of a language-learning experience must take time; rehearsing and refining its accurate use in written language must take still more time; and these time lapses expose the test population to uncontrollable sources of other language-learning which could and would obtrude on the test procedure.

Evaluation by testing pupils, in the team's view, would have been a waste of time for the project's limited manpower. This opinion has been reinforced by recent findings about the influence of uncontrolled factors in test situations, which suggest that the methodology of current evaluative techniques is questionable in many hitherto unsuspected ways.[11] The team believed that useful progress in evaluation could be made on the basis of observation. Instruments need to be developed for this, not so much on the lines of the interaction-analysis school, but in the directions suggested by studies of therapy groups and one-to-one dialogue situations such as telephone conversations.[12] These studies suggest that teacher-class interaction is strongly role-marked and therefore strongly rule-bound in its language. But the basic research from which evaluative instruments might emerge is yet to be done, and even then this type of evaluative work is very expensive in manpower.

The logical alternative requires evaluation by careful attitude-testing of the participating teachers. This was considered, and rejected on simple practical grounds, that it would not prove anything. It was already clear that teachers taking part in the trials would require an open mind or a positive commitment to innovation, and that material could not be written which rested on any lesser co-operation. The changes in teacher attitude which might be measured would at best be from neutral to positive; teachers with initially negative attitudes would be either unwilling to try the material or suspect. Attitude measurement would need to be applied on a very detailed and sophisticated scale to show the kind of change which was predicted, and in cost-benefit terms was not justifiable.

Evaluation procedures adopted

The evaluation of the Language in Use Project was entirely formative. Without the manpower, instruments or time for systematic evaluation of pupil performance or even of teacher attitudes, the team were compelled to concentrate their very limited activity on the work calling most urgently for it—the design of the material itself. The chief pressure on the team in this decision was the time-scale involved: if the material was to be given an adequate trial in the academic year 1969–70, only one academic year remained in which to rewrite it and see it through the press. At the time of writing this report, *Language in Use* was in course of being rewritten, with a view to publication in the autumn of 1971. This rewriting was a more searching and structured version of a process which took place between the pilot trials and the main trials. In both cases, the resulting material was a fuller and more explicit realization of the intentions of the design than anything that went before, while the design itself has been significantly improved also.

The design of *Language in Use* has the following formal features.

(*a*) It is written for the teacher, not the pupil.

(*b*) The material is divided into units of given nominal length.

(*c*) Each unit is divided into sessions of given nominal length.

(*d*) Subject-matter, procedures and activities are formulated in such a manner that the teacher evolves his own lessons from the text of the units.

(*e*) Provision is made for the teacher to control the degree of explicitness achieved by the class.

(*f*) The preparation required of the teacher is clearly specified.

(*g*) The aims to be served by each unit are formulated.

(*h*) There are connections between units which relate to an explicit underlying theory of language.

(*i*) The individual unit is autonomous.

The material's flexibility of use with a wide range of age and ability inheres chiefly in (*d*) and (*e*), while the teacher's freedom of choice inheres chiefly in (*a*), (*b*), and (*i*).

Not all of these items are susceptible of evaluation by any procedure which arouses the attention of the respondent, since a number of them are intended to operate at a level below that of conscious attention. The features of the design were a carefully articulated set, intended to reinforce one another. The loose-leaf format was only the most obvious of these; it symbolized the autonomy of the unit but enabled the user to select his units in any order, both by abstracting pages and by so arranging his teaching work. The flexibility this was intended to provide could not be canvassed without appearing to make unacceptably exalted claims. The flexibility of substance, whereby the user developed his own particular sequences of lessons on the basis of the units, was similarly intended to operate with as little obtrusiveness as possible. The trial version of the material also included units which varied greatly in the extent to which they achieved the intentions of the design, and the only satisfactory way of evaluating the relative success of the units was to ask users to report on their use of units rather than of the design. The design features which were intended to work unobtrusively had to be evaluated without recourse to questionnaires.

The heavy programme of visiting trial schools undertaken by the team was planned to make possible a widespread monitoring of users' responses to the material's layout and physical features generally, and to design features which very few users spoke of in general terms. The responses were given very openly and freely, for reasons to be discussed below. The format was given unanimous and forceful approval by the users; the team was able to contact more than three-quarters of the participants in the trials, and their welcome for the material's division into units, and the division of units into sessions, was very striking. This approval was equally clear whether the teachers were using the units with fairly close adherence to the suggestions or were departing from them quite widely.

The usage patterns of the units would be the acid test of the design. It was important to know whether the user was as free to select and combine them as the design intended him to be. It was also important to know whether this freedom continued to operate regardless of the age or ability of the class. The team judged it sufficient for these purposes to arrange trials in some sixty to seventy institutions (including schools of all kinds, colleges of further education, and colleges and departments of education). The number of schools was raised to the maximum that the team felt able to visit with reasonable frequency, and all schools participating in the trials were visited, except for those in the group organized through a teachers' centre. In all, *c.*180 teachers were involved and the team was at some pains to establish direct personal contact with most of them. The number of questionnaires issued is irrelevant, since there was also a wider, less formal trial, in which the teachers were free to respond or not as they wished, and questionnaires were distributed to both groups. Some trouble was taken to establish what proportion of the work was covered by the questionnaires received. The number of users replying was not a clear guide to this, any more than the number of schools they represented; the best guide to the amount of work done was the number of units used with a class. The team's estimate was that the written evidence received in the evaluation procedures related to 65 per cent of the use actually made of the material. There were gaps in this total, especially from certain types of schools, and these were made good by drawing on the wider trials, which also filled the gaps caused by illness and the difficulties that school life is heir to.

It would seem that 65 per cent is a very high response rate for a trial of this kind. There were two explanations for this. One was that the material was designed to do as little violence as possible to the existing patterns of a teacher's work. It made neither obvious nor covert demands on timetabling. It did not seek to be brought into the classroom with public announcements and fuss—indeed, many classes which did fine work in the trials were unaware of any trial element throughout. Secondly, in their search for trial institutions, the team avoided approaching those local authorities who were not known to be strongly interested. The trials were planned in regions (to save travelling), and in each group the schools approached were selected in consultation with a local adviser, or a local college of education lecturer, who himself understood the material and the kind of trials sought. Induction conferences before the trials catered for at least one teacher from every trial institution, and the only questionnaire reports for which one of the team could not supply further information about the school or the teacher concerned were those from college students involved in teaching practice. The trial participants also received five regular newsletters, giving accounts of exciting uses of the material, discussing common problems, and seeking to reduce the level of formality on which the trials were conducted.

The team's prediction before the trials was that the participating teachers could reasonably be expected to contribute an average of twenty teaching periods to unit work over the year. As a crude average this was an accurate prediction. The team received written reports of about 1000 uses of the units, and the amount of class time taken up by these and the unreported units together amounted to just over 5000 periods. The variation between teachers was striking, however: a score or more reported conscientiously on only one or two uses, while in contrast a teacher in special circumstances devoted a whole timetable to the work and reported over eighty uses in the full year. The closer sampling of some participants in the trials showed that most of them reported carefully on work done with the class which, for them, was the main focus of trial work, but were unable to report on units used with other classes. Of the teachers who were known to have done a great deal of unit work in the trials, only six omitted to report through the questionnaires.

The questionnaires were drawn up with the knowledge that teachers are in general very strongly resistant to questionnaires of all kinds. The questions were set up to be answerable in twenty minutes, and each of the three terminal questionnaires followed the same broad pattern. They asked for basic data about the class, and for a list of the units used, in order. For each unit there was a set of pointed yes/no questions covering every aspect which could be handled in questionnaire form. Were the predictions about time borne out in practice? Did the work follow the suggestions given? Did the class carry out the activities suggested? Was there too much preparation for the teacher? Was the unit's stated goal achieved? So many answers to this last question in the first term read 'No, but it was well worth while' or words to that effect that a separate question was subsequently included to cater for this.

The questionnaire responses in respect of the design features listed above were so uniformly positive that it would be tedious to enumerate them. The feedback enabled the team to identify those characteristics which made a unit usable over the full secondary age-range, and to build them into the rewritten version of all the units. Of the total of unit-uses, 2 per cent reported both failure to achieve the goal and failure to produce worthwhile classroom activity. A further 3 per cent reported failure to achieve the goal but worthwhile work nonetheless. A further 8 per cent showed some doubt about the goal or its formulation. Otherwise all the responses in these respects were positive. A similar pattern appeared for the suggested activities; about 15 per cent reported that they did not implement the suggested activities but that the work was worth while. There is some tendency for respondents to indicate a 'Yes' reply to all questions as a quick way of conveying approval, but the questions were so worded as to reveal such a reaction and allow any 'blanket' responses to be set aside.

No indications emerged that the design was faulty. If teachers had chosen units from a narrow range within the store, the underlying structure would have been suspect. If the units chosen with certain age groups had been similarly restricted in range, the intended flexibility would have been called in question. If the use made of the units had frequently departed from the material's general intentions, the formulation of aims would have been shown as defective. In practice, more than thirty units were used with every age-group in the secondary range, and more than eighty units were used with a class over sixteen *and* with a class under fourteen. If the amount of class time taken up with each unit had shown a steady decline, the material's claim to be exploiting the existing knowledge of native speakers would have been exposed as faulty. In practice, the trend was quite the reverse: the longer a teacher had had with the material, the more use he made of each unit.

While the field trials were being conducted, the theoretical basis of the material underwent a rigorous evaluation at the academic level, being tested against the immediately current thinking of several distinguished scholars. The underlying structure of the material is an explicit theory of language and how to it is used. This theory underwent a number of improvements, and each one was exposed to the kind of criticism which would immediately have shown any serious defects. The theory is not, of course, a comprehensive theory of language in general, although it can be so interpreted. It is intended to show how the abstract field of general linguistics bears on the study of language in English teaching. In doing this, it serves two purposes: it forestalls the risk that students may learn things which, at a higher level of study in the same field, they may later have to unlearn; and it provides a principled basis for language study which can make it independent of academic linguistics.[13]

This underlying structure was not fully explicit in the trial version of the material. It was perhaps for this reason that the only considered objections which the material encountered were ideological rather than pragmatic: objections not to the material's way of pursuing its aims, but to the aims themselves. Very few such objections were received. It would have been very odd, however, if all teachers offered the material showed an equal readiness to use it. Some 25 per cent of them in fact made no use of it, but a rising proportion of these have come to make use of it as they have had time to assimilate it and discuss it with colleagues. It was toward the development of active groups of users that much of the team's efforts in the field were directed in later months; active participants in the trials found such meetings of great value.

Beyond the particular use of specific units, however, *Language in Use* was designed to be capable of a wide variety of additional uses:

(*a*) as a shelf-book or store of good practice;

(*b*) as a set of approaches to isolated parts of a teacher's normal pattern of work;

(*c*) as a resource from which the teacher could systematically build a year's or a term's course;

(*d*) as a set of procedures and activities to be applicable to a teacher's own subject-matter;

(*e*) as a guide to teachers in adjusting their approaches to a wide variety of situations and types of class.

The evidence of the trials showed that this flexibility was fully realized. Indeed, many users commented that the material seemed suited to their own teaching situation to a unique degree—quite unaware that the same was being said by users in quite different situations. It was from the trial experience in diverse situations that the team put together the users' papers, designed to make more widely available the experience teachers gained in using the units with younger pupils (i.e. 9–13), slower learners, public examination forms, in further education and among college of education students.

The material has built into it a strong element of enabling a teacher to educate himself about language as he goes along. This arises because many of the inquiries suggested for classes are into aspects of language about which no authoritative or formalized factual statement exists. The teacher is thus in the same position as the class in trying both to make sense of the facts and to accommodate his preconceptions to them. The purposes of the trials would not have been served by trying to explore this matter in detail, but there has been a telling frequency with which teachers have brought forward both new areas of subject-matter, which they have discovered, and quite new interpretations of subject-matter offered in the units.

The material also asks the user to stand back, to inspect his classroom activity, and evaluate it in the light of the principled basis on which it rests. It also seeks to supply a set of technical terms in which teachers can formulate their observations about what happens in classrooms. It is peculiarly attractive to think that, because many of the users have taken up this aspect of the material eagerly, the substance of lessons has changed in lasting or important ways. To set up a classical before-and-after study of *attitudinal* shift would have been to fall prey to this temptation; the real change, bringing the teacher further and further from expository instruction, and closer to organizing learning situations, is bound to take time. While the trials yielded repeated testimony to the occurrence of this shift, often from sixth formers, the team would not wish the project to be judged on the extent of this shift over a mere nine months.

Of the additional uses which the material is intended to have, the questionnaire evidence is clear about all except the first. If the material is used as a shelf-book, this will not appear in questionnaires. In practice, the project team have been increasingly drawn into the ferment of debate about curriculum in colleges of education. Many lecturers seeking improvements have cited *Language in Use* to exemplify what they sought and to show that serious language study could be achieved on a better basis than traditional school grammar on the one hand, or formal academic linguistics on the other.

This extension into colleges and departments of education is not accidental: it derives from the theoretical basis of the work. The units rest on assumptions about the nature of language, the needs of learners, and the nature and function of language in relation to learning. These assumptions relate to all educational practice where the transmission of educational knowledge involves the use of the mother tongue. Even in the secondary school, for which the material was most directly written, the teacher has to do a good deal for himself: his professional judgement is repeatedly called into play. That teachers in other kinds of institution should have found value in the material is therefore natural. This has happened, not by the team's endeavours, in primary schools, approved schools, ESN schools and postgraduate courses in education.

Much of the evidence for the statements in the last four paragraphs comes from the reports sent in by users near the end of the trial year. Many of the teachers found the yes/no pattern of the formal questionnaires restricting, but did not find the questionnaires long enough to tire them. Many wrote about their experience of the units at length, with unusual frankness and perceptiveness. These reports amounted to a third body of feedback, comparable in status with that derived from visiting. The consonance between all three sources of evidence was striking. They told the team much that was already clear, confirmed much that they suspected, and combined to form a pattern of evidence greatly encouraging to the team in their design, choice of procedure and planning of the trials.

There was one clear area of failure, which is significant for other projects. The material set out to match the aims and practice of the best in current English teaching. Some users chose to believe that it was much more distinctive, much more strikingly novel than this, and introduced the work into their classes on a self-consciously experimental basis. This approach was almost always disastrous: it led class and teacher to feel nothing had been gained. The reason in each case was that the work had not been related to any existing objectives of the teacher; it seemed purposeless because it was purposeless. This implies that trying out curriculum material in the classroom is intrinsically a purposeless activity. In a sense, it must be: material gains purpose according to how far it matches the aims of those who are to use it. If the match is not a close one, the teachers concerned need re-training, as several projects have found. In the case of *Language in Use*, the match was close but not always immediately obvious. This is why the trial proved so markedly cumulative: the users found more and more in the volume as their experience grew. One headmaster spoke for most of the participants in saying, 'It's too big a book to get to know quickly, but the more I use it, the more I find there is to use.'

Finally, the team believe that their policy of making the trial participants into a network was an excellent investment. It took time and care to organize the trials so that the participants were a body of users known to each other in differing degrees. The briefing conferences, newsletters, emergence of groups, the team's visiting, their participation in local group sessions, and the mountain of correspondence were more than an insurance against the pigeon-holing of questionnaires, though they were clearly that. They were also part of the policy, stated in the first Schools Council working paper on English,[14] of enlisting local support and fostering local activity that might go on after the brief life of the project itself. One of the team's abiding memories is of how readily doors opened and faces began to lose their anxious look, when they established that their purpose was not simply educational research.

Publisher for the project: Edward Arnold.

References

1   See Miller, G. A. *The Psychology of Communication* Allen Lane, 1968, new ed. Penguin, 1970, chapter 5.

2   The subject is dealt with at length in Cicourel, A. V. *Method and Measurement in Sociology* Collier-Macmillan, 1964; new imp. New York: Free Press, 1967.

3   Harris, R. J. 'An experimental inquiry into the functions and value of formal grammar in the teaching of English, with special reference to the teaching of correct written English to children aged twelve to fourteen' University of London, 1962 (unpublished Ph.D. thesis).

4   Dixon, J. *Growth Through English: a Report Based on the Dartmouth Seminar* Reading: National Association for the Teaching of English, 1967; 2nd ed. Oxford University Press, 1972.

5   Flower, F. D. *Language and Education* 5th imp. Longman, 1968.

6   Central Advisory Council for Education (England) *Half Our Future* [Newsom Report] HMSO, 1963.

7   Ford, B. Chairman's address to the National Association for the Teaching of English, 'Who teaches English?' NATE *Bulletin* **2**, 2, 1965

8   Wilkinson, E. 'Coherence in practice: a look at the field' *English in Education* **4**, (2), summer 1970, 35–48.

9   *Statistics of Education* HMSO (now published annually for the Department of Education and Science).

10   See the summary of B. B. Bernstein's work in D. Lawton *Social Class, Language and Education*, new ed. Routledge, 1970.

11   Cf. for example Cicourel (see note 2); also Katz, I. 'Factors influencing Negro performance in the desegregated school', in Deutsch, M., Katz, I., & Jensen, A. R. *Social Class, Race, and Psychological Development* Holt, Rinehart, 1968. The work of Katz is lucidly summarized in Watson, P. 'How race affects IQ' *New Society* 16 July 1970, p. 103.

12   See the papers by E. A. Schegloff and by H. Sacks in *Directions in Sociolinguistics*, ed. J. Gumperz and D. Hymes, new ed. Holt, Rinehart, 1972.

13   This material was subsequently issued as a separate work: Doughty, P., Pearce, J., & Thornton, G. *Exploring Language* Edward Arnold, 1972.

14   Schools Council Working Paper 3, *English: a Programme for Research and Development in English Teaching* HMSO, 1965.

10 Mathematics for the majority project

Peter Kaner

This project was established at the University of Exeter in 1967 as part of the Schools Council's contribution to preparation for raising the school leaving age. A study of mathematics in secondary schools, undertaken by the project director in 1965–6, showed that the mathematical education provided for children of average and below average ability was very patchy indeed.[1] There were some areas of the country where results with these children far exceeded the best expectations in other areas. The evidence of the Newsom Report[2] also pointed to the poor standards in mathematical education of a vast number of early school leavers, the largest single group when GCE and CSE candidates are considered separately.

The project set up in the light of these findings was financed initially for three years to the extent of £63 000 and then for a further two years with an additional grant of £24 000. The director appointed a team of two full-time and three half-time writers and undertook to prepare a series of teachers' guides which would be thoroughly tested through a group of trial schools. These guides were intended to lead teachers into reassessing their work in mathematics with the young school leaver, and to provide source materials and ideas from which the teachers could make up their courses. The expressed aims of the project team, as far as the pupils were concerned, were:

(*a*) to provide pupils with experiences of mathematical situations, thus encouraging their powers of judgement and imagination;

(*b*) to remove barriers isolating mathematics from other areas of the curriculum and from the pupils' other interests;

(*c*) to give pupils some understanding of the mathematical concepts which underlie the numeracy required for everyday affairs;

(*d*) to enable pupils to appreciate in some measure the order and pattern of their environment.

The director allocated various sections of the writing scheme to each member of the team. The main work plan is shown in Fig. 8 opposite. It was emphasized at every stage by the director that he was not attempting to produce a course of pupil material; that would be left in the hands of local

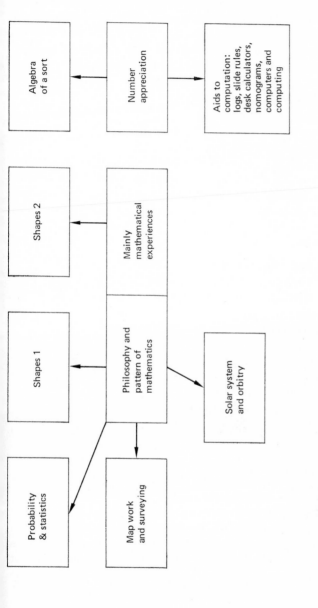

Interweaving the items above:

Fig. 8 Mathematics for the Majority: work plan for production of teachers' guides

mathematics advisers. Nevertheless, the writing was based on the firm belief that teachers should reconsider the material customarily presented to average and below average children in mathematics. A second and perhaps even more important theme underlying much of the material was that these children should learn mathematics through practical and individual work, and that formal class teaching was bound to fail. The project team initially produced ten teachers' guides with the following titles:

Mathematical Experience
Machines, Mechanisms and Mathematics
Assignment Systems
Luck and Judgement
Mathematical Pattern
Number Appreciation
Mathematics from Outdoors
From Counting to Calculating
Algebra of a Sort
Some Simple Functions

Four more topics later completed the set. The books vary from about 50 to 200 pages in length and cover many aspects of mathematical thinking. They attempt to provide a basis from which teachers can develop courses for the less able pupils, more extensive material for brighter young school leavers, and additional background mathematical knowledge which non-specialist teachers need in order to understand the purpose of the proposed courses. The director set up two series of trial schools (known as pre-pilot and pilot schools) and, for reasons explained later, a third tier of nearly four hundred schools were associated with the project:

	No of schools	FROM	No of LEAs
Pre-pilot schools	27		6
Pilot schools	87		23
Associated schools	378		80

The pre-pilot schools consisted of a sample of secondary schools situated close to the project headquarters. The heads of mathematics departments of these schools were asked to give a critical opinion of the first draft of each guide as it was written. These opinions were based on reading of the text rather than working through it with a class, the intention being to make essential alterations *before* the guides went out for large-scale trials in the pilot schools.

After drafts had been reviewed in the light of comments from teachers in the pre-pilot schools, they were printed in loose-leaf form and then sent to pilot schools for trial. Material was selected and adapted by teachers in the pilot schools and used for up to two terms, after which a report was made to the project team to help in preparing for publication. Teachers met in groups to discuss the final form of their criticisms and to make proposals as to how the guides should be changed, edited and augmented. Conferences were a notable feature of the work. Two or three were held each year, giving teachers the opportunity of meeting others from different regions of the country. Lectures, workshops and discussion groups formed the main part of the conferences, which were intended to help plan for the future and to pool ideas and resources.

The class of associated schools was established following the Schools Council's appeal for pilot schools for this project, which met with an enormous response. The need for help was so urgent that the director decided to supply associated schools with the draft guides (at cost price) while they were still undergoing trials in the pilot schools, rather than wait till the final versions were published. No help was offered to these associated schools except that they were grouped by area under a university institute of education and encouraged to develop regional programmes. Liaison officers were appointed with the task of fostering the project in associated areas, and one member of the project team had special responsibility for looking after this vast number of associated schools.

Before discussing evaluation methods, it is worth pointing out some of the problems which arose out of the design of the project itself. The team were tackling three distinct requirements.

(a) The need to improve the mathematical learning of children who had failed in this for many years and whose attainment level was very low. This low attainment was often accompanied by a very poor standard in reading and by a poor attitude (see pp. 138–9), as well as a below-average IQ.

(b) The need to design attractive and valuable mathematics courses for young school leavers of average ability, who might ultimately be persuaded (or compelled) to stay on for a fifth year.

(c) The need to provide a mathematical background for non-specialist teachers, so that they could see the significance of the mathematical ideas they were asked to teach. Many of these teachers taught mathematics only intermittently and often had no more than a superficial knowledge of the subject.

The major problem in evaluating the project's published materials lay in the existence of an intermediary, the teacher, between the project's material and the children's output, on which value judgements had to be made. To add to the difficulty, it was not considered politic—or even desirable—to measure the teachers' mathematical attainment level or teaching skill, though their skill in adapting the teachers' guides could be ascertained by inspecting work cards or pupil output.

Yet another problem arose from the large number of pilot schools involved.

These were scattered across the length and breadth of England, and it was hardly possible to visit any school more than twice a year. Some were not visited at all. This situation was further complicated by the project's time schedule. Writing the first guides and passing the drafts through the pre-pilot schools took longer than was anticipated, so that the pilot schools had to wait over two years before they could begin trials. By then the classes of young school leavers allocated for trial were dispersed; some of the teachers who had prepared for the trials had left that school before material arrived. In any case, trials in pilot schools cannot provide an entirely reliable basis for predicting what will happen when materials are published and used without the support of the project team and the special interest of the LEAs. Pilot schools are not typical nor are they randomly selected.

Evaluation procedures

In order to overcome some of these inherent difficulties, the evaluation work was divided into four main activities.

(*a*) Clarifying and enlarging on the project objectives. This included:

(i) identifying different aspects of the curriculum problem which the project was trying to tackle;

(ii) establishing the aims of teaching mathematics to the average and below average child;

(iii) finding out as much as possible about the educational standards of the children concerned and other related factors.

(*b*) Editing trial versions of the guides and ensuring that essential changes were made before the guides reached their final published form.

(*c*) Measuring the effect of the project's material on the pupils involved, both as regards the declared objectives of the project and in relation to other aspects of pupil behaviour.

(*d*) Work leading to the publication of a descriptive report on the project and its impact on education in general.

Each section is dealt with separately below.

CLARIFYING AND ENLARGING ON THE PROJECT OBJECTIVES

A major objective was to provide material for non-specialists teaching mathematics to older secondary children of average and below average ability. It was important to investigate this situation further. How many such teachers were in action; what were their specialities; what help did they need most urgently? The following example illustrates the attempt to answer these questions.

Allocation of specialist mathematics teachers to third and fourth year pupils
To check the numbers of non-specialists involved and the time they spent in teaching, the evaluator carried out a survey of approximately 100 schools

drawn at random from the *Education Authorities Directory*. Each school was asked to provide its mathematics timetable for the third and fourth years and to classify the teachers in one of the following four categories:

(*a*) mathematics specialist (i.e. a teacher who has, as a minimum qualification, studied mathematics as a main subject in a college of education);

(*b*) other specialist teaching full-time in a mathematics department;

(*c*) other specialist teaching part-time in a mathematics department;

(*d*) other teachers (sometimes headteacher, sometimes remedial).

The geographical distribution of the teachers in categories (*a*) to (*d*) is shown in Table 10.1, and the number of teachers from other subjects who were also teaching mathematics are shown in Table 10.2 (p. 134).

Table 10.1   Teachers of mathematics: by area and category

Area	No. of teachers per category				No. of schools
	(*a*)	(*b*)	(*c*)	(*d*)	
Southwest	15	2	14	3	6
London & home counties	87	11	48	27	25
South Midlands	31	5	24	4	10
Wales	13	1	11	3	4
East Anglia	13	6	21	2	5
North Midlands	44	4	30	8	14
Northeast	34	7	31	16	13
Northwest	44	11	61	28	18
TOTALS	181	47	240	91	95

The pupils were graded according to the ability level of the stream they were in, as follows:

grade 1: academic;
grade 2: average;
grade 3: below average.

These grades were assigned as in Table 10.3 (*a*) and (*b*) (p. 134), the allocation of grades being related to the total number of streams at that age level in the school. Thus, if a comprehensive school had eight streams (Table 10.3 (*a*)), three would be considered to be academic (grade 1), three average (grade 2) and two below average (grade 3).

The timetables also provided information about the length and number of lessons, so that it was possible to compute the time spent on mathematics by each stream. The details are given in Table 10.4 (p. 135).

Table 10.2 Numbers of non-specialist teachers of mathematics: by subject

Subject	No.	Subject	No.
Art	3	Literature	1
Biology	8	Mechanical engineering	1
Careers	1	Metalwork	$1\frac{1}{2}$
Chemistry	4	Modern languages	1
Civics	1	Music	$13\frac{1}{2}$
Cookery	1	Needlework	6
Commerce	4	PE	36
Divinity/RI	10	Physics	6
Economics	2	Practical subjects	2
Education guidance	1	Psychology	1
Engineering drawing	2	Remedial	34
English	13	Retarded/ESN	3
French	4	Science	40
Geography	24	Social science	2
Geology	1	Special education	1
General subjects	10	Speech and drama	1
German	1	Technical drawing	4
Handicraft	4	Welsh	1
Heavy craft	1	Woodwork	4
History	7	Other subjects not specified	126
Jewellery	1		

Table 10.3 Allocation of pupils to grades in comprehensive and secondary modern schools

(a) COMPREHENSIVE SCHOOLS

No. of streams	1	2	3	4	5	6	7	8	9	10	11	12
Grade:												
1 (academic)	0	1	1	2	2	2	2	3	3	3	4	4
2 (average)	1	1	1	1	1	2	3	3	3	4	4	4
3 (below average)	0	0	1	1	1	2	2	2	3	3	3	4

(b) SECONDARY MODERN SCHOOLS

No. of streams	2	3	4	5	6	7	8
Grade:							
1 (academic)	0	1	1	1	2	2	2
2 (average)	1	1	2	2	2	3	3
3 (below average)	1	1	1	2	2	2	3

Table 10.4   Time spent on mathematics, in minutes per week: by pupil grade

| | (a) THIRD YEAR | | | (b) FOURTH YEAR | | |
| | Pupil grade | | | Pupil grade | | |
	1	2	3	1	2	3
Time (minutes):						
mean	195	196	194	201	196	177
least	140	140	115	135	40	40
most	270	280	280	290	280	250
No. of classes	146	172	155	144	145	150

The results of the above survey are also presented in matrix form in Fig. 9, so that streams can be compared for teacher category and for time spent on mathematics (see p. 136).

Conclusions: There was a marked variation in different parts of the country regarding both the number of specialists available and the way in which their time was used (Fig. 9). In the fourth year the slower pupils received less teaching time than more academic pupils, though this was not true of the third year (Table 10.4 (*a*)); in many cases the third year lower streams spent a good deal more time on mathematics. Was this a final attempt to bring them up to standard or was the curriculum limited to fewer subjects for the less able, giving them more time for those subjects they did follow? Some fourth year lower streams spent as little as forty minutes per week on mathematics, which might mean that mathematics appeared in some 'integrated' form elsewhere in the curriculum or perhaps that pupils were taking a special leavers' course in preparation for work. Over half the students in grade 3 were taught mathematics by non-specialist teachers (Fig. 9), and it was clear that improvements in the standard of mathematical education for these students would be largely dependent on the training and assistance given to such non-specialist teachers. This fact was vitally relevant to the Mathematics for the Majority project.

*

The second of the project objectives, establishing the aims of teaching mathematics to less able pupils, was tackled by meetings of the project team. One team member, who was writing a guide on computation, invited teachers to submit their views on the standard of achievement in computation which they regarded as a satisfactory minimum. The teachers held such widely differing opinions that the team wondered if it was possible to agree on these objectives. A fairly general collection of objectives was, however, reached through team discussion; it was not published, as the team did not feel sufficiently confident to wish to impose their patterns of thought on teachers. It was agreed that a

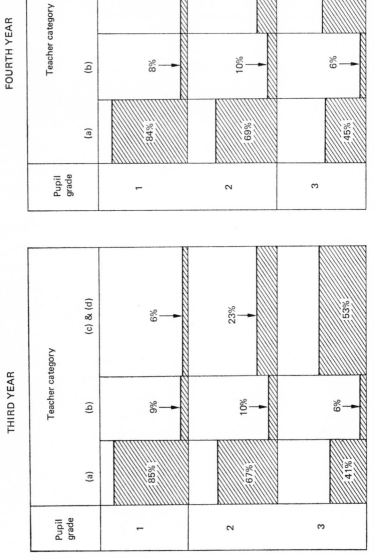

Fig. 9 Mathematics for the Majority: teacher categories and mathematics time compared by stream

leaving pupil who showed the following qualities could be regarded as having had a successful experience of mathematics at school.

Number

(a) He would understand the notational system of numbers and the operations in this system.

(b) He would be able to make a reasonable attempt at a computational problem even if it was in an unfamiliar form.

(c) He would have no fear of numbers and feel himself to be in control when dealing with them.

(d) He would be aware of the development of human skill at computing and also of the part played by this skill and by number in a modern society.

(e) He would have had considerable experience of numerical patterns and of investigations to find the causal relationships behind such patterns.

Shape

(a) He would have discovered a number of important basic geometrical concepts and have had the opportunity to develop his understanding of geometry.

(b) He would be aware of the part played by shapes in the environment and would have had the opportunity of designing shapes for specified purposes.

(c) He would have had experience of spatial patterns and of investigations to find the causal relationships behind such patterns.

Reasoning

He would have had ample opportunity for developing his intuitive powers of reasoning in mathematical situations, numerical and spatial. *Note:* It was not considered important that he should experience and understand more rigid forms of mathematical proof, i.e. axiomatic systems and deductive reasoning within these systems.

Aesthetics

He would have had ample opportunity to exercise his imaginative and creative powers within his mathematical experiences, and would have developed aesthetic awareness in mathematical situations.

Language

He would have an adequate knowledge of mathematical terminology, so that he could communicate mathematical ideas where necessary and not be inhibited from further study in the subject or related subjects.

*

The third of the project objectives involved providing a careful description of the children that the project was concerned to help. The team needed to know the levels of attainment, attitude, and other factors such as reading skill and

IQ, in order to write materials that were on target as far as the children were concerned. This information was collected from a group of the pilot schools known as case study schools. Thirty-six out of the eighty-seven pilot schools volunteered to feed back detailed information on their pupils. This extra information involved devising and giving tests, making subjective assessments and submitting pupil work and regular reports to the evaluation office. College of education lecturers were enlisted to help in setting and marking the tests and in providing a second set of assessments on pupil achievement and attitudes. Initially a college lecturer was allocated to each class, so that a case study unit of class plus teacher plus lecturer could be formed. There were seventy-two such units, two at each case study school. Thus it was feasible to collect data on some 1500 pupils, who were typical of the pupils for whose benefit the project was originally set up. It should be constantly emphasized, however, that this sample of 1500 pupils was not randomly selected. The teachers concerned voluntarily committed themselves to a great deal of extra work and preparation, and the results could therefore be expected to show a strongly positive bias. It would be far from safe to make inferences about a population of school children on the evidence collected here.

Pupil attitudes to mathematics
The following summary of pupil attitudes to mathematics (Tables 10.5–10.7) is an example of the initial information collected and of the form in which it was reported to pilot school teachers and other interested people.

Table 10.5 Pupil attitudes from questionnaire, measured on the scale prepared by the University of Southampton Institute of Education

Category*	Third year non-academic	Third year lowest stream	Fourth year leavers
0	0	0	0
1	34	30	50
2	89	86	145
3	143	126	216
4	166	139	165
5	47	56	26
TOTALS	479	437	602
Mean	3·22	3·24	2·95
Standard deviation	1·06	1·11	1·02

* Key to attitude categories:
0 = test not taken
1 = very poor (score 0–16)
2 = poor (score 17–32)
3 = average (score 33–48)
4 = above average (score 49–64)
5 = good (score 65–80)

Table 10.6 Pupil attitudes from questionnaire: scores in individual schools (maximum score 80)

School no.	Third year non-academic			Third year lowest stream			Fourth year leavers		
	Lowest	Best	Mean	Lowest	Best	Mean	Lowest	Best	Mean
1	28	70	49·9				15	70	45·7
2				11	75	48·8	12	65	41·3
3	13	68	37·6				11	55	40·6
4				24	69	52·3	34	62	42·5
5				13	67	51·3	11	69	34·8
6	{ 13	71	29·5 }						
	{ 12	60	35·5 }						
7	19	69	42·7						
8	13	68	48·3						
9	23	68	46·2	20	72	47·5			
10	25	78	53·9				9	75	49·6
11	19	62	43·1	12	64	43·4			
12				19	73	47·8	17	63	39·3
13				14	53	33·5	11	63	38·0
14				12	67	46·5	14	63	37·9
15				17	69	48·4	6	70	38·3
16				14	61	39·4			
17	12	67	46·5				12	63	40·0
18				18	76	44·6	17	61	36·6
19	18	70	45·7				15	58	38·2
20							{ 9	60	37·4 }
							{ 8	69	45·2 }
21				7	70	40·4			
22							21	63	41·9
23							13	60	28·7
24	10	69	51·3				31	74	43·5
25	{ 37	73	56·0 }						
	{ 27	67	45·9 }						
26							11	70	44·3
27	21	65	41·1						
28				{ 18	69	51·2 }			
				{ 15	75	48·8 }			
29	18	79	56·3				17	54	39·1
30				14	79	48·6			
31							11	62	42·6
32				18	80	47·8	18	59	40·4
33				23	75	54·5	26	70	46·2
34	{ 17	75	44·5 }						
	{ 24	70	45·2 }						
35	11	64	33·7	14	69	43·1			
36							{ 17	59	39·9 }
							{ 22	55	41·8 }
OVERALL	10	79	44·9	7	80	46·5	6	75	40·55

Table 10.7   Pupil attitudes from teacher assessment

Category*	Third year non-academic	Third year lowest stream	Fourth year leavers
0	15	12	0
1	21	22	38
2	73	104	105
3	179	184	258
4	153	93	147
5	38	22	54
TOTALS	479	437	602
Mean	3·24	2·87	3·12
Standard deviation	0·98	0·74	1·00

* Key to attitude categories:
0 = not assessed	3 = average
1 = very poor	4 = above average
2 = poor	5 = good

Comments on pupil attitudes: The questionnaire revealed very little differ-ence in attitude between the two third-year groups (Table 10.5) but indicated a significantly poorer attitude in the fourth-year group. In contrast, the teachers' assessment (Table 10.7) did not show this deterioration. The teach-ers also reported a poorer attitude to mathematics on the part of the less able third-year group. This conflicted with pupils' own reports as shown on their questionnaire responses. The poorer attitude to mathematics admitted by the fourth-year leavers (Table 10.5) may be partly the result of a general decline in the attitude of all fourth-year leavers towards school, and partly due to the inclusion in this group of pupils previously classified as remedial.

Other pupil characteristics assessed
These included non-verbal intelligence, reading ability, general personality and mathematics attainment. In spite of the non-randomness of the sample, the pupil data did throw a good deal of light on the attainment levels of the pupils the project was trying to help. Most noticeable of all was the very wide range of abilities to be found in the non-academic streams, many pupils having an above-average score on non-verbal intelligence tests. This underlined the correctness of the project team's policy of encouraging individual and group work rather than class teaching with these pupils.

*

During the evaluation it became clear that schools and colleges of education were rarely able to maintain a continuous feedback over a long period of time. In this respect, colleges gave up before the schools, but in the later stages of the work it became plain that schools were finding it extremely difficult to keep up with the monthly reports and assessment requested by the evaluator. In addition to the surveys and measurements described above, the need for some pure research on methods of teaching mathematics and on the learning characteristics of slow-learning pupils became very pressing. Various research students presented themselves and asked the evaluator to indicate lines of research which would be valuable to the evaluation of the project. As no funds had been allocated to the evaluation for pure research, these students were very welcome. Studies were undertaken on such areas as the ability of less able children to retain taught facts and programmes of action; the ability of various children to understand linked chains of logical deduction; the limits on the length of such chains of deduction; the degree to which the children could transfer simple concepts from one situation to others; and the behaviour patterns of such children during practical work.

EDITING TRIAL VERSIONS OF THE GUIDES

The traditional curriculum development project relies on its system of trial schools to ensure that its written materials fit teachers' needs and are in accord with such factors as school organization, programmes, syllabuses and examinations. In this project, two sets of pilot schools were used: a cluster around the project headquarters (pre-pilot schools) and a widely scattered collection of small groups of schools (pilot schools proper). The schools were not always clear as to their function but it was evident that the pre-pilot schools were to be used as a first check on the written material.

This work was organized through the LEAs, who arranged meetings of teachers in the pre-pilot schools. The teachers also read the first draft of each guide and sent in written comments on it to project headquarters. The evaluator used these opinions as the basis for a first questionnaire to be sent out with all trial versions of each guide. Points raised at the pre-pilot meetings led to the incorporation of items in the questionnaire, especially if the evaluator felt that a very wide response was needed before the team could be sure of the correct changes to make in their material. For example, most pre-pilot school teachers felt that one guide would be much more useful if a number of sample work cards were included. Some teachers opposed this. The questionnaire going to all users of trial versions asked whether they agreed with the statement 'This guide would be improved if sample work cards were added.' In fact, agreement was so strong that the team had no hesitation in adding the required cards.

The evaluator came to the conclusion that there were too many pre-pilot schools and that they delayed production of the material. However, they occasionally came up with a point of view different from that expected, and quite often they strongly supported material which had seemed dubious to some members of the team. The passage of a guide from draft to publication

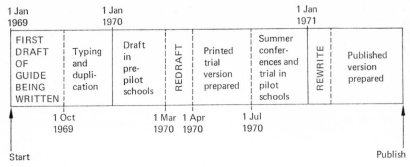

Fig. 10   Mathematics for the Majority: typical schedule for producing a guide

is illustrated in Fig. 10. This schedule vividly illustrates some major difficulties for the project.

(*a*) With this system of pilot trials, a guide took $2\frac{1}{4}$ years from inception to publication.

(*b*) Owing to school holidays, a guide would normally receive just one term's trial in pilot schools.

(*c*) The time for rewriting in the light of trials was very short indeed, yet the rewriting had to be very carefully carried through if the material was to benefit fully from the trials system.

(*d*) Team members were normally contracted for two years; thus, by the time their written material had passed through the system they would have left the project.

(*e*) If a project runs for only three years, it is not possible to embark on new writing after about the first year has passed. This means that the writing team cannot benefit from experience individually.

Groups of teachers from the pilot schools met at regular intervals and discussed the results of attempting to follow the teachers' guides with classes. The discussions were often critical but in every case the teachers became more aware of the problems and benefited accordingly. After one term's trial of each guide, the teachers fed back a considered opinion of that guide to the project headquarters and to the evaluation office. In most cases, the written comments were submitted by an LEA inspector or adviser, occasionally they came from a teachers' centre warden or leader. These are key people in a curriculum development of this sort.

Case study schools were supplied with test material to match the guide they were trying out and asked to return monthly summaries of children's scores on the test items. This work was not altogether satisfactory as the children's results were extremely difficult to assess. With slow children there is no absolute standard, and the teacher is therefore most interested in the child's performance within a limited expectation. A piece of work might be scored A for a child with an IQ of 70–80 while work of the same level would earn E for a brighter child. The problems of assessment caused the teachers a lot of head-aches, and eventually the evaluator gave up this particular attempt to follow children's progress.

This stage of the evaluation involved attending as many teachers' meetings as possible, in addition to visiting the pilot schools, which involved long hours of travelling, as the pilot schools were situated throughout the country. Nevertheless, in some ways this was among the most valuable parts of the work, since the evaluator could report to the team on the sort of response generated all over the country. Such feelings could never have been deduced from the written reports and returned questionnaires alone.

MEASURING THE EFFECT OF THE PROJECT MATERIAL ON THE PUPILS INVOLVED

Although the project material was not directly related to elementary mathe-matical techniques, it was important to preserve the children's current level of mathematical competence while the teachers' guides were being used. This was checked in the case study schools by giving the main elementary mathe-matics test (NFER, C3) to all the children in project classes at the beginning and end of the year. The test carried 50 marks altogether, and the later results showed a mean improvement of between 2 and 3 marks. This improvement was significant at the 0·1 per cent level, but it is impossible to give the project material the credit for the improvement. All attempts to relate the improve-ment to other factors such as reading ability and intelligence failed, and this failure underlines the paradoxical nature of curriculum evaluation. A similar exercise on attitude, using an attitude scale, indicated an improvement of atti-tude which was significant at the 5 per cent level. Although this result was welcome, it was even more difficult to relate to other factors; nevertheless, it drew attention to some interesting points: for example, a case study school with a very high proportion of Pakistani pupils gave an atypical fall in attitude over the year. Could their English have improved over the year so that they understood the questions better, or had their attitude to everything deterior-ated during their last year at school?

The case study schools collected many examples of pupil work; it was poss-ible to use these examples to identify the parts of the material which had been most successful *in the hands of a particular teacher*. In order to collect further evidence of pupil response, a number of booklets of test items relating directly to the teachers' guides were prepared. The children attempted to answer the items at the beginning of the year. The teacher then returned the used book-lets to the evaluation office and received a second booklet for each child (con-taining the same items). The child was allowed to answer the items in his second booklet when he chose, provided that he had attempted all the items by the end of the year. The second set of booklets returned and each child's first and second efforts compared. The analysis of these results was not yet complete at the time of writing; it was hoped that these tests would highlight areas of mathematics where the less able child can really be expected to make progress and also show up where the developers and teachers might be wasting their time.

It is well known that many children cannot convey a true picture of their ability through written work; this is why, in many cases, they find themselves in low streams and classified as less able. However, they may still be able to demonstrate a grasp of a problem if asked verbally. To measure this, as well as to find out more about pupil attitudes, a series of pupil interviews was tried by college of education students. A college lecturer accompanied by ten of his students went into a practical lesson in mathematics in a case study school. Each student interviewed three children, one at a time, while the work of the class was going on, and wrote down on a standard form a summary of their verbal answers to these questions.

(*a*) What is the problem about?

(*b*) How are you working on it?

(*c*) How do you plan to use your results in your attempt to solve the problem?

(*d*) Do you like this sort of work?

(*e*) Is this work hard?

(*f*) Do you enjoy working in a group, or do you prefer to work on your own?

(*g*) Do you think this sort of mathematics will help you when you leave school?

These were children used to visitors and peculiar goings on. Each student also observed his three children for half the lesson, recording their activities in the form of a checklist (Table 10.8). The interview forms and checklists were returned to the evaluation office, together with the pupils' work that was being

Table 10.8 Checklist for recording children's activities

CHECK AT FIVE-MINUTE INTERVALS FOR EACH CHILD

School Pupil's names	College Activity	Talking	Application to problem	Recording	Contribution to group	Use of equipment

done at the time. In addition, the college lecturer interviewed the teacher and recorded the answers on another standard form.

This work was an attempt to find out what actually went on during practical mathematics lessons with non-academic children, in the hope of identifying which material produced the most satisfactory patterns of behaviour, as well as increasing knowledge of these patterns. At the time of writing, the results had not all been collected. The support of colleges of education was invaluable, as the project could not have financed research on this scale alone. The colleges found the experience very useful and lecturers commented that the students had gained a great deal from taking part in the interviews and testing. In fact, some lecturers now see this sort of activity as a permanent part of their students' training. It has, of course, been extremely difficult to reach clear-cut conclusions from this part of the evaluation programme; indeed, basic ignorance of the learning processes of these non-academic children is the greatest barrier to preparing successful teaching material.

WORK LEADING TO A REPORT ON THE IMPACT OF THE PROJECT

The evaluation of a project raises large questions of purpose and motive which are quite distinct from the declared objectives of the project itself. One responsibility of the evaluator is to provide a description which will inform a headteacher or adviser of the sort of outcome he can expect if he encourages the adoption of project methods and material. The evaluator's task could be regarded as establishing the project's true identity—setting up a counter-image to that set up by the project. His description should include the project's declared objectives as identified by the external world, as well as the external view of the original curriculum problem. (There may be more than one such view). The evaluator should measure the impact of the project, in both favourable and unfavourable circumstances, with regard to both published material and other activities such as conferences, meetings and in-service courses.

This activity of the evaluator is more artistic than scientific; it can be compared with literary criticism of the work of a poet or writer, who would be placed within a historical and philosophical context, his techniques discussed and analysed, his conclusions weighed, and his impact assessed. Before the evaluator can carry out this part of the work, he needs a very wide experience of the material, its use and its effect. The present writer formed impressions by visiting schools and teachers' centres, and attending meetings in associated areas; he collected reports from teachers, college lecturers, LEA advisers and Schools Council field officers; and he analysed the pattern of meetings and in-service courses and the production of material which arose as a result of the project. Even so, long-term studies are necessary if we are to know how much of the project effort has had a lasting effect. Perhaps the most significant result of this side of the evaluation has been the setting up of a continuation project[3] with the brief of providing further help where the original project has proved inadequate. The continuation project is providing a wide variety of direct teaching material, including audio and visual resources, and the evaluation of this later work will clearly add to the overall description of the eight-year exercise.

Publisher for the project: Rupert Hart-Davis Educational Publications (formerly Chatto & Windus (Educational)).

References

1 See Schools Council Working Paper 14, *Mathematics for the Majority: a Programme in Mathematics for the Young School Leaver* HMSO, 1967.

2 Central Advisory Council for Education (England) *Half Our Future* [Newsom Report] HMSO, 1963.

3 Mathematics for the Majority Continuation Project, established by the Schools Council to run from 1971 to 1974.   The project is located at 3 The Cloisters, Cathedral Close, Exeter, and directed by the present author.

11 English for immigrant children project

Michael Feeley

The Schools Council project in English for Immigrant Children was established at Leeds University in 1966. Its work differed notably from that of other Schools Council projects, and this difference influenced the project team's approach to evaluation and emphasized the importance of developing an evaluation programme for the specific needs of each individual project.

In many areas of the curriculum, a number of favourable growth points can be identified. An established body of teaching expertise, a substantial literature and systematic provision for teacher training are all growth points which the teams of many development projects can take for granted; it is because they seek to widen teacher choice within these areas by offering new approaches and techniques that they are active. Such projects may be regarded as reforming rather than innovative, and this is the essential distinction between them and English for Immigrant Children.

In the 1960s large numbers of immigrant children made their appearance in English schools. Since there had been no tradition of teaching English as a second language, few teachers were equipped by training to cater for the needs of their non-English-speaking children. Virtually no materials were available, and local support in the form of advisers or in-service training was also significantly absent. From the beginning, therefore, the Leeds project operated in a curriculum vacuum, which restricted the form that its evaluation programme could take.

A major consequence of the distinction between reforming and innovative projects is the different balance that each type of project must strike between evaluating materials and disseminating ideas. Where the object is to improve an area of the curriculum by providing a wider range of choice of teachers, the need to refine the materials is usually more urgent in the first instance than the need to spread the new curriculum message. The function of evaluation here is clearly a justificatory one: without a fairly elaborate assessment, how is the teacher to know whether the new materials or methods are better or worse than established ones? In the case of English for Immigrant Children, however, the major aim of the project was to spread the curriculum initiative rather than refine it, and so the task of dissemination, or making the general body of teachers aware of the new ideas, was regarded as more valuable than a detailed evaluation. The heavy commitment to dissemination meant that the project team spent a great deal of time talking to teachers and students about their work, and about the possible approaches that could be adopted in teaching English to immigrant children.

It may be a useful exercise to consider whether innovative projects generally need to be relatively light on evaluation and heavy on dissemination whilst reforming projects tend to tilt the balance the other way.

Background to the project

During the 1960s teachers in English schools were doing their best, in the absence of suitable training, to cope with the language problems posed by immigrant children from Asia and southern Europe. A Schools Council survey in 1965, reported in Schools Council Working Paper 13, *English for the Children of Immigrants* (HMSO, 1967), identified about 44 000 children who were unable to make normal progress at school because they lacked sufficient English:

> In present circumstances, many teachers of immigrants—whether in primary or secondary schools—have not been prepared either by their original training or by any later training to do this particular job. Many do not know enough about the English language and cannot identify the difficulties the immigrant pupil has to master, and they may know little of the techniques, some comparatively recently developed, that may be employed in this teaching situation. Training facilities are still limited, although some of the larger education authorities now arrange short courses . . . But the very teachers who might wish to attend such courses are often in key positions in their schools and cannot easily be released.

A development project was established at Leeds University Institute of Education; the project team, led by June Derrick as organizer, consisted of four teachers, a linguist, a sociologist and an artist. Their initial objectives were defined in Working Paper 13 as 'the provision of teaching materials to help teachers enable pupils, whose first language is not English, to achieve an adequate command of English, so that they can play as full a part as possible in school and society'. Working Paper 13 went on to observe:

> There are two main strands in curriculum development of this kind: the preparation of teaching materials for use in the classroom by teacher or pupil; and the supporting provision of in-service training to explain the purpose of the new materials to teachers, and to give them the opportunity to criticise them in their trial stages, and to contribute to their further development.

From the outset the team experienced considerable pressure from teachers, who were in the main desperately anxious for help and guidance in a task for which they realized they lacked both training and experience. Nor were there any materials directly relevant to the teaching of English as a second language in England. In this sense the team were working in an ideal situation; from the very beginning, teachers welcomed the help that was directed towards them, and the task of persuasion that other project teams have had to face had little relevance for the Leeds project. On the other hand, the difficulties that had to be faced in the schools were enormous. Teachers were often working under the greatest professional handicaps, and the strain upon them was considerable.

Working Paper 13 had described the special provisions that various local authorities had evolved for teaching English to the new immigrant children. These ranged from establishing full-time reception centres to part-time withdrawal of pupils from normal classes for periods as short as half an hour per day. Clearly, such arrangements had implications for the design and content of the project material. Many of the teaching situations were bizarre: school stages, church halls, staff rooms and, in one case, a deserted house awaiting demolition were all examples of physical difficulties faced by the teachers which had to be borne in mind in planning the material. Moreover, it was the language teachers who proved most vulnerable to staff absences, their class usually being the first to close if a replacement teacher was needed elsewhere in the school. In addition pressure of new arrivals persistently created instability within classes, and often the task of language teaching was left to younger, less experienced or part-time teachers.

With all those indications of urgency, quite apart from the pressing needs of the children themselves, the project had little time to develop on other than pragmatic lines. There was no place for a classical development design with a sophisticated evaluation programme to lay the foundations of the development. The children were in the schools; the teachers were looking to the Leeds project for help that was relevant, practical and above all, immediate.

Development stages

WRITING

Throughout 1966–7 the project team was preparing draft materials suitable for children in the age group 8–13 who were non-English-speakers. A panel of local teachers acted as advisers. By June 1967 the drafts were in an acceptable form for trial. They consisted of a *Teacher's Book* with a basic language scheme, together with suggestions about language teaching methods. Visual and introductory reading materials were also prepared. The language developed through these materials was linked to fourteen teaching units based on themes such as the classroom, the street, shopping, the doctor's surgery, etc. This introductory course, later published under the series title *Scope*, stage 1. was envisaged to take about a year to work through (although this would be related to the amount of special teaching the children received, to age and to ability). A specially difficult feature of the work was the lack of any precise quantum of beginners' language; there was no simple linguistic objective at which the team could aim. Tests of language competence that could have identified levels of attainment did not exist, nor could they have been developed in time to be useful.

ORGANIZATION OF TRIALS

From information received from the Schools Council's survey thirty-eight LEAs were selected to take part in trials of *Scope*, stage 1. This number included nearly all the LEAs with immigrant children in substantial numbers although, because of the need to cluster LEAs for feedback purposes, outlying authorities were not among them. Each authority selected was asked to nominate secondary or junior classes, or both, to take part in the trials; LEAs were asked specifically to nominate classes of immigrant children at the beginner stage. Because of the diversity of educational provision, trials were planned for over 100 classes, and it was hoped that the teachers involved in the trials would be able to help other teachers within the local authority area. A conference was held to explain to LEA representatives what the project hoped to achieve, and for most authorities this was their first introduction to the work of a project team organizing field trials of materials. From the outset, English for Immigrant Children was ahead of other projects and had to 'feel its way' as it went along. Apart from the Nuffield project in French, there was little experience to lean upon.

Although the LEAs had been briefed about the project's requirements, these were not necessarily the people effectively responsible for teaching immigrant children. In 1967 there were only half a dozen authorities which had identified the immigrant education sector by appointing someone with specific responsibility for this. This person was sometimes of adviser or organizer status but more often a teacher with a special allowance. Where such personnel existed, communication between the project and its teachers was greatly facilitated, and LEA support was strongly evident in teachers' morale. Where there were no personnel with overall responsibility for immigrant education, communication was difficult and extension work by teacher groups was less common. Teachers in such circumstances lacked any support outside school and often felt their work was undervalued, considering the difficulties of their task.

By July 1967 the LEAs had nominated 131 teachers (some of whom had been members of the teachers' panel mentioned above) to take part in trials of the materials developed in Leeds. All these teachers were invited to one of two residential briefing conferences lasting three days. Representatives of colleges of education were also invited to attend the briefing conferences. Several did so and maintained that contact with the project throughout its life. At the briefing some basic training was given. Teachers were introduced to the materials and to the thinking of the team, and were able to discuss the materials in relation to their own needs and those of their children, thus influencing the team's work thereafter. For various reasons, however, twenty of the 131 teachers were unable to attend the briefings and were therefore not well informed about the project when they started work in September.

Since the local authorities had been given a fairly precise brief as to the requirements of the project, it was to be expected that nominated classes would conform fairly closely to the criteria laid down, i.e. that they should be classes of immigrant children at the beginner stage. It later turned out that many of the classes nominated were inappropriate for the trials, being linguistically or organizationally unsuitable. One or two authorities had not asked their teachers whether they wished to participate in the trials; indeed, the team heard of two teachers who only found out that they were taking part from a local newspaper two months after the start of term! Thus fifteen classes withdrew from the trials during the first term, either because their children were not beginners, or because there was no chance of providing any special teaching for them, or sometimes because the teacher nominated had moved on. In twenty-six other cases, adjustments thad to be made within schools, with the result that materials were passed on to other teachers or to other classes. Late and desperate pleas for trial materials from new schools meant it was easy to replace schools that withdrew in the early stages; indeed, sometimes the new classes had a more realistic understanding of what the project required than the original ones.

Undoubtedly, timing was a factor which complicated the setting up of the trial classes. The project had, unwisely as it turned out, asked for nominations in June, i.e. before the schools knew details of their new intake of pupils. This is a further indication of how the immigrant sector of education presented local authorities with unique problems, since they were unable to predict the likely composition of new school intakes. The timing of project trials is critical, and the start of a new school year may not be the best time to begin, since new classes take some time to settle down. Trials of materials are therefore unlikely to be systematic before October is well advanced. This was true of English for immigrants: schools were slow in starting work with the trial materials, and delays were not always reported to the team immediately, sometimes only being discovered as the result of a visit.

These were early days for curriculum development, and teachers were unsure of what was important about participation in trials. They were also uncertain of their relationship with the project team, and considerable effort and thought went into the establishment of a good working partnership. Reluctant to add further difficulties to those already hampering the schools, the project members felt they could not insist that teachers started at a particular time or specify how they ought to organize the teaching of English within the school. From the beginning, however, it was clear that the trials could only be an approximation of the classic development programmes characteristic of curriculum development in the United States; the whole field was dynamic and lacking in organizational or procedural stability.

The work of evaluation

TRIALS

Any understanding of the work of English for Immigrant Children must be related to the timetable that was envisaged. It has been pointed out that the role of evaluation in this programme was secondary to diffusion and was therefore restricted to the formative approach only. Even so, the physical conditions faced by teachers in the schools, with the stresses from which the schools were suffering, meant that even the formative element was necessarily limited by all sorts of problems and difficulties.

At the outset, teacher-members of the team saw themselves without distinct activities. Writing and evaluation were seen as complementary roles, instead of a special provision being made for evaluation. It was hoped that, once the writing of the course was completed, the team could together assess what the trials teachers thought of the materials from what they said on the questionnaires which they were supposed to return after using each of the fourteen units; this information was supplemented by two other sources of feedback: area meetings of teachers (see p. 153) each half-term, and visits to schools by team members. The whole team was to be involved in these activities, so that each member was to fulfil a variety of roles at different times. A timetable of team activity appears in Fig. 11 (p. 158).

QUESTIONNAIRES

Questionnaires were open-ended and asked for criticism and suggestions about specific parts of the language scheme, about alternative suggestions for teaching language points, and about the suitability of the visual materials, etc. relating to each unit. Had the questionnaires elicited a high response, they would have given over 2000 feedback items which would have produced a very clear picture of the trial materials in use, with their strengths and weaknesses. However, the return rate of these questionnaires was disappointingly low. The highest returns were from the earlier units, where 50 per cent was the highest return achieved.

The quality of information on the questionnaires also varied greatly. Teachers were reluctant to confine their reactions to the questionnaire framework, which would have facilitated a simple method of analysis by the various team members interested in one aspect or another which they covered. There was an equal tendency to ignore the question framework altogether and to use the blank reverse side of the paper to write an essay covering quite separate issues from those on which data were sought, but with no insight at all into specific points about which the team wanted information! Nevertheless, a great many of these comments proved useful to the team, who were conscious that a highly structured questionnaire may exclude other useful data. In spite of the low returns, much detailed criticism was obtained from the questionnaires, especially relating to the earlier units. Later modifications to the layout of the open-ended questions failed to provide teachers with a more suitable form and thus did not influence the nature of the responses; nor did the use of a brilliant purple colour, so that questionnaires could not be 'overlooked', succeed in increasing the return rate which, despite exhortations, continued to dwindle throughout the trials.

It was clear from the outset that although teachers were unwilling to return written information to the project, they were anxious to meet the team and discuss issues raised by the materials with them in considerable depth. In retrospect, the team could have been even more insistent on the return of questionnaires; it might have been useful if the initial distribution of materials had been more restricted and the dispatch of subsequent materials made dependent upon the return of questionnaires relating to earlier sections. But it was felt that any such pressure or restraint would inhibit the very close relationships the team was trying to build with the teachers conducting trials. It was probably unrealistic to have begun by placing so much emphasis on postal rather than personal feedback. It cannot be taken for granted that teachers anxious to collaborate in trials are equally anxious to devote the considerable amount of time required to completing feedback questionnaires. The team failed to allow for the fact that teachers had already been required to do a great deal in coming to terms with a new methodology and a complex set of materials at the same time.

AREA MEETINGS

Each half-term the team met small groups of 15–20 teachers from trial schools in their own local areas. The contact established at the training sessions and through visits to the schools meant that team members were on good personal terms with most of them; as a result, the area meetings were generally appreciated by the teachers, as well as being very productive from the team's point of view. Whilst the questionnaires dealt with some of the minutiae of detail, at the area meetings teachers were able to concentrate on broader matters of principle or on major points of difficulty.

It is a pity that team members were not able to make better records of the discussion at area meetings; it would have been useful to have taped the sessions or to have had them recorded by shorthand. Instead only general records of the discussion at some of these meetings were retained. The value of the meetings to the team was obvious, but the value to the teachers themselves was not foreseen. For them, the opportunity to meet the team and to gain reassurance from the other teachers present who were facing the same problems was very important. Simply being away from the pressures within their schools was also generally welcomed.

SCHOOL VISITS

One member of the team was given the task of making the bulk of the initial visits to schools, whilst the rest of the team devoted themselves largely, though not exclusively, to preparing further draft materials. These initial visits gave a real insight into the teaching situations within the schools. They illuminated the problems faced by local authorities too, and highlighted the wisdom of those authorities who were centrally influencing the work of their teachers through advisers and teacher leaders.

There was such a wide range of problems that the team realized it would be necessary to spend a great deal of time observing the materials in use with a variety of teachers before the information feedback could be assessed: it was essential to consider what teachers had to say about using the materials within their own peculiar teaching circumstances. As was pointed out earlier, considerable organizational problems were faced by teachers from the beginning of the trials. In some cases, the teachers were bewildered by the expectations of the Leeds team; in a few cases too, teachers were still using materials with children for whom they were totally inappropriate. Only a systematic series of school visits was likely to clear up these difficulties. As the term progressed, there were instances of teachers not really using the materials as they had been requested to do, and yet feeding back data of an apparently significant nature. It was obvious that there was 'feedback' and 'feedback'. Any attempt to treat such a mass of information on a purely statistical basis would have made nonsense of the materials. Where the teachers' evidence might show a fifty/fifty break of opinion, it was important to know exactly who was giving the evidence for each position. The task of visiting schools as a necessary prelude to evaluation was thus seen to be absolutely essential. From this point onwards, liaison and evaluation were regarded as complementary activities.

The conditions under which teachers were working in some schools severely limited the level of their achievement; this meant that the feedback had to be treated qualitatively—in respect of a particular teacher, in a specific class, with a given group of children. Because of the variety of teaching situations, the differing periods of time available for special teaching, and the varied needs of the pupils across the age range (8–13), the materials were designed to be adapted to individual circumstances. Clearly, certain combinations of circumstances were more favourable to the materials than others; this had to be taken into account when assessing the feedback. There were many modifications, extensions and selective treatments of the materials which further complicated the evaluation. Yet these were the kinds of real situations in which the materials had eventually to be used.

Throughout the course of the trials there was an erosion of the classes which had started work in September. The trials took place at a time when a new Immigration Bill was under discussion and when new restrictions on the entry of immigrant adults, and possibly children, were expected. There was a consequent surge of children entering the country in time to miss the expected ban. In schools this meant that the numbers of children requiring language help increased quickly without an equivalent increase in places for them. Newcomers prematurely squeezed out children who had themselves only just begun to learn English. Many classes were changing their composition weekly, and teachers were sometimes torn between meeting the needs of the beginners, by going back to the start of the course, and meeting the needs of the project team and the established children, by progressing through the materials. To some extent this problem was accommodated in the materials, which were so designed that teachers could work at several levels within a single theme, but those teachers with little time available, or with recurring classes of beginners, found it very difficult to make steady progress and several had to drop out. Some teachers never reached the middle units, and even three years after the trials had begun, there was a teacher still striving to reach the elusive 'end' of the materials! Inevitably, the operating conditions in the schools severely limited the value of the trials as an objective exercise in curriculum development; for many classes the only stable factor throughout the year was the project itself! Strain among teachers was readily apparent and was reflected in the high turnover rates. By Easter only eighty-one out of the 131 teachers who attended the briefings were still continuing with immigrant language work within their original schools.

For the teachers who did continue in this field, the opportunity to take part in trials generated an encouragement that they sadly lacked from other sources. Many teachers were coming to terms with the methodology of second language work as the project itself developed, and became leaders of initiatives within their own local areas. Such teachers were able to set up working groups, sometimes in association with the growing Associations of Teachers of English to Pupils from Overseas, with which the project was closely linked. Here again, support within an LEA from someone with advisory responsbility was a very favourable factor. Local groups were able to elaborate and supplement the common core materials produced in Leeds; in this way taped materials were made and broadcast on local radio; a film was produced; and a mass of reading, writing and other supplementary visual materials were produced. These teachers, meeting informally in workshop sessions which were also attended by team members, gave the team insight into the materials in use which might otherwise have been missed.

There was a tendency for teachers to think that, however much their criticisms were requested, it was less than fair to make them of a scheme which was generally of great value. One teacher summarized his feelings on this point later when he said, 'To criticize the scheme or the materials would have been like cutting off the branch on which I was sitting.' This, needless to say, was a form of gallantry the project team would have preferred to do without. Among some teachers there was a temptation to imbue the development team with an authority which the team strongly refuted, since this worked against the ideal of the teacher-cooperative which the team saw as their model. In addition, whilst the links with Leeds University were extremely useful in the team's relationships with local authorities and with some head-teachers, they were sometimes a handicap which had to be actively overcome through direct and personal contact where school visits played a vital part. There was a suspicion that, because the team was based at a university, its approach would be academic and therefore impractical in classroom situations.

From this necessarily patchy feedback information, expanded and qualified by close familiarity with the teachers, an evaluation was made of the materials in use. The picture obtained showed how teachers regarded the materials supplied to them, since the evaluation instruments were not objective tests of pupil behaviour but subjective tests of teacher opinion collected and interpreted through questionnaires, meetings and visits. The disturbances and upheavals among teachers and pupils during the trials phase, though extremely difficul to accommodate at the time, ensured that the materials were tested under the kind of conditions in which they would eventually be used. As it turned out, one of the most fortunate decisions was to conduct large trials. This not only injected the new thinking into the profession quickly, thus meeting the team's commitment to the rapid dissemination of its materials and its approaches to the wider body of teachers; it also accommodated the substantial drop-out rate, the serious interruption to the publication timetable and the low response to questionnaires.

The second source of information, area meetings, proved equally valuable to both team and teachers. Here, inadequacies of feedback were made good, and the direct supportive link between the teachers and the team maintained. Throughout the trials the area meetings were very well attended and highly valued by teachers. It would not have been possible to chart the shifting sands within a large number of trial schools without a considerable programme of school visits, which often kept teachers going and which were essential for the interpretation of the feedback of those teachers who were more meticulous in their questionnaire responses and area meeting contributions. Without the support of visits, the participation of many schools would have foundered, whereas they were able to contribute through to the end of the trials.

A retrospective view of this phase of *Scope*, stage 1 tempts one to identify the difficulties that were encountered without balancing them with the many more positive aspects. It is tempting also to speculate whether, in an area where growth points are so few, it would have been realistic to have expected teachers to engage in either a more thorough or a more sophisticated evaluation programme. These teachers were generally overworked, already facing very great problems within their schools, and ill-prepared to cope with these, let alone with their added responsibilities to the project. The entire focus was on first stage evaluation. Could the work have been of greater educational value if it had shown the long-term second stage impact of the materials in use. A better foundation of teacher experience and training would have been needed to preface any more elaborate assessment. Certainly, closer familiarity with the systems of the language would have been essential, as well as testing instruments which are still totally lacking in the language field. Would a shift in the balance of the project effort from dissemination to evaluation, with the consequent delay in propagating the thinking of the project, have encouraged rather than diminished the extent of teacher participation?

As it happened, nearly half the trial classes were casualties, and the effective contribution of many of the others was reduced. In spite of this, the publication schedules were maintained and the basis of this area of curriculum has been widened as a result. This was the principal purpose of the project.

Conclusions

There are two major reasons for the Schools Council's involvement in development activity. The first is to widen the range of choices that teachers have available to them; such involvement is therefore reforming. The majority of projects are of this type and build upon existing materials, organization, teacher skill and training. In a limited number of circumstances, novel situations arise which teachers are ill prepared for. The teaching of English to immigrants was such a situation. The involvement of the Council in such areas is innovative rather than reforming. The Council hopes to originate solutions which would not be available to teachers without its participation. In such areas there is not the teacher experience, teaching materials, or training available to build upon, and a necessary adjunct of development is to provide these during trials.

Evaluation must be considered in relation to what is necessary and possible within the development phase, rather than to what is ideal. Each development programme has its own balance to establish between development, evaluation and dissemination. In the case of English for Immigrant Children, the emphasis was on development and dissemination, and such evaluation as was done was severely limited by circumstances. A more elaborate evaluation would have possibly been unjustified if it had delayed or interfered with development.

It must therefore be the concern of all projects to decide not *whether* evaluation is necessary but *how much* evaluation is necessary. In established curriculum areas teachers need to know whether a new approach or set of materials is better than existing ones. Such comparison requires a rather sharp evaluation tool. In innovative areas, where there may be a pressing demand from teachers, there will be no alternative materials or approaches available for comparison. The task of evaluation here is not to ascertain how well the approaches or materials fulfil their objectives but whether they fulfil them at all.

The above description deals with an evaluation encompassed within general development and dissemination activities. It illustrates the problems this project had to face and endeavours to show that limitations were imposed by the pressure of time and the overall inadequacy of educational provision in the immigrant sector. Whether general conclusions can be derived from the work of the Leeds project, which can be applied to similar innovative projects, remains to be seen. Clearly, however, the distinction between evaluation for reforming projects and evaluation for innovative projects must indicate there is no ideal; each project must determine for itself the extent to which it must validate its involvement in curriculum change.

Publisher for the project: Longman (formerly Books for Schools).

Acknowledgement

The passages on p. 148 from Schools Council Working Paper 13, *English for the Children of Immigrants* HMSO, 1967, are reproduced by permission of the Controller of HM Stationery Office.

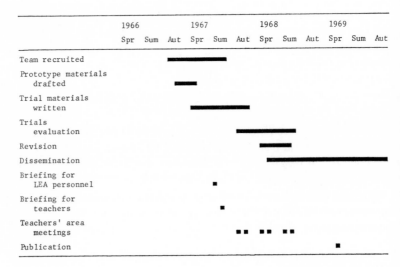

Fig. 11 English for Immigrant Children: timetable of team activity

12 Project technology

David Tawney

Background to the project

Project technology was established by the Schools Council in 1967, following a pilot study in 1966, with an initial grant of £180 000 to finance three years' work. Its overall aim was to help children get to grips with technology as a major influence in modern society and, as a result, to help more of them to lead effective and satisfying lives. Thus the project involved all ages, all abilities and all relevant subjects, including science, mathematics, craft, history and geography. It was believed that the project's aim could be attained by carrying out two functions simultaneously:

(*a*) preparing teaching materials;

(*b*) attacking the restraints which effectively determined the nature and cope of the teacher's work.

The project was based at Loughborough College of Education; the central team there from 1967 to 1970 consisted of four full-time and two part-time members, supported by a varying number of development leaders. These were mainly teachers on part-time secondment, who produced material based on a particular theme, e.g. the applications of photocells, and tried this out in a small group of trial schools; the revised material was then submitted to the central team for wider secondary trials. The project was extended from 1970 to 1972 on the understanding that its work should be specifically directed:

(*a*) to the development of teaching materials;

(*b*) to achieving an increased commitment to technological activities in schools on the part of those involved in teacher training and retraining.

With these ends in view, the central team was reconstituted with seven full-time members and one part-time, in addition to the director, now acting in an honorary capacity.

Aims of the project

It cannot be sufficiently emphasized that the efforts of this project were not devoted to providing a single course of the kind exemplified by the Nuffield

Science Teaching Project's schemes for the 11–16 age group, or even to producing a single set of materials from which a teacher could construct his own
course, like the Nuffield Combined Science Project. The emphasis was much
more on the autonomy of the individual teacher. Although technology is not a
well-established subject in the school timetable and is rarely examined as such,
its concepts have a place in many traditional school subjects; furthermore, it
can be regarded as providing a structure to link together elements of the curriculum which have too long appeared separate. In providing this important
integration, technology is also able to direct the attention of teachers and
pupils away from purely classroom preoccupations towards the outside world.
Ironically, while it occupies this vital place in the school curriculum, technology is in practice regarded very differently, even in those schools which
recognize the importance of fostering an awareness of it in their pupils. There
is no single way of introducing technology; the project team could only en-
deavour to help the individual teacher find his own way, through the three
main means described below.

(a)   TEACHING MATERIALS

Although the team developed one or two courses leading to CSE Mode III,
much of their output was of a kind to stimulate the teacher to develop his own
courses. It was noticeable from the feedback obtained in the secondary trials
of the project material on *Photocell Applications* that many of the schools using
this most successfully had incorporated its ideas into courses or sets of work-
cards of their own. Materials which can be adapted by the teacher to fit a
variety of situations must take a very different form from those designed to be
used without modification in a narrow range of situations. They can be less
structured and, since they are intended for adaptation, the significance of
pre-publication school trials changes.

The teacher nevertheless needs these materials from the project, and they
can still rightly be called teaching materials. They should include guides for
the construction and use of apparatus for his courses; an example of this is the
guide to the construction of an internal combustion engine test bed, a piece of
equipment which costs considerably more to purchase complete than the
school-made item. The teacher also needs background reading on modern
developments; one example of the team's attempt to fulfil this need is the
handbook on *Computer and Control Logic*, another the journal *SATIS*, containing abstracts.

(b)   COMMUNICATION

The logical outcome of seeing the project's role as stimulating the teacher to
inject technology into his own courses in his own way was the realization that
communication between teachers is vital. The team devoted a considerable
proportion of their resources to collecting and diffusing the ideas of individual

teachers. With this philosophy, the project *Bulletin*, reaching 1000 schools, became an important teaching aid; it subsequently developed into a periodical, *School Technology*, which provided a national forum for the exchange of ideas. Films, slides and exhibitions were another aid for teachers; their provision again made heavy demands on the project.

(c) SUPPORT

At a local level the communication between teachers necessary to stimulate technological work in schools was achieved through 26 regional groups, covering the whole of England and Wales and involving 1000 schools. Their function was to support the individual teacher, through the interchange of ideas, in his often lonely and difficult task of developing technological awareness in his school. In some areas the idea has been carried further, and centres with staff and other resources have been established.

Another way in which the team endeavoured to support the teacher was through the provision of ex-government and industrial equipment. Available at several centres throughout the country, this provided a source of materials considerably cheaper than the traditional laboratory and workshop suppliers. A third means of teacher support was the promotion of examinations to test appropriate objectives over a suitable field of knowledge. One example is the CSE examination in control technology, another the Joint Matriculation Board's A level engineering science.

In summary, by no means all the energy and resources of the project were employed in producing teaching materials. The team saw the project's role less as the synthesizer of a course to be used by the teacher according to directions, than as a provider of intermediate products, of catalysts, of the right conditions and, in some cases, of the initial spark so that the teacher could make his own synthesis. Of course, no project team would accept the suggestion that they were providing a course which the teacher was forced to follow to a degree which stifled personal initiative, but nevertheless the Project Technology team demanded more of the teachers using its materials than most other projects so far. Furthermore, the process of trial was seen more as an opportunity to spread materials intended to stimulate technological work than as a test of the materials themselves. Whether or not these policies were justified was a question which fell to the evaluators to help answer.

Evaluation

A grant of £10 000 was awarded to the University of Keele to enable its Department of Education to carry out a two-year evaluation study of Project Technology; an existing member of the Department with experience in this field was to be honorary director. A full-time evaluator was appointed in

September 1969, when the project's secondary trials were due to begin, and a second part-time evaluator was appointed a year later.

The evaluation unit saw its function as the provision of information, as objective as possible, about the use of the project materials in schools. The information had to describe the conditions under which the materials were used, the ways in which they were used and the outcomes of such use. Furthermore, the information had to be of such a kind and produced at such a time that the central team could use it in preparing the final published versions of the teaching materials.

The evaluation unit has throughout worked in close consultation with the central team at Loughborough and with the Schools Council research staff, and the evaluators acknowledge the considerable help they have had from both. As a result of discussions in the autumn of 1969, the original proposals submitted by the Keele Education Department were developed and re-presented to the Schools Council Evaluation Committee (Science). Four areas of study were mentioned:

(a) the central team's feedback mechanism;

(b) pupils' and teachers' reactions to the materials;

(c) an investigation into the *Bulletin* and *SATIS*;

(d) the technological climate of the schools.

However, it soon became clear to the evaluators that, because of the nature of the project, they would have to develop an altogether more flexible and *ad hoc* approach than these proposals suggested.

In the first place, as a consequence of the project's policy of teacher autonomy, the team had not laid down behavioural objectives against which the outcomes could be evaluated. A working party of the project's consultative committee tried for some time to systematize the objectives which seemed to be the logical consequence of the project's overall aim, but as little useful seemed to be emerging, the attempt was dropped. Later on, with two years' hindsight, the evaluators came to consider that a guide along the lines of the Science 5–13 Project's *With Objectives in Mind* might have helped the teacher select first his own objectives and then the right teaching materials by which these objectives could be achieved. As it was, the evaluators, who were appointed two years after the start of the project, were advised by the Schools Council research staff not to spend their time in classifying the project objectives. Furthermore, teachers seem to have been divided in opinion as to the help which this approach, exemplified by the Science 5–13 Project, can give.

In addition, the regional group structure, although admirable for the diffusion of project ideas and for supporting teachers at the local level, was too cumbersome for the efficient organization of trials: it took too long to find out through regional conveners which schools wished to participate.

Moreover, in the first year of secondary trials and of the evaluation, 1969–70, the central team had insufficient manpower to support trial schools by visits or to organize the information feedback; this was a consequence of seeing the production of teaching materials as only part of their work. Thus, the evaluators had to be on the lookout for situations to occur which they could use for trials, and they had to be prepared to act quickly. They also bore the brunt of school visiting, so that, instead of being able to establish objective and systematic methods of observing the outcomes of the trials, they inevitably became occupied with collecting feedback information based on teacher opinion, and even supporting trial teachers with advice.

In order to stimulate activity and provide background information, to fertilize the project's grass roots in the regional groups, and indeed to meet the urgent request of these groups, the team deliberately supplied materials which they knew needed further editing; at the time, they did not have the staff to edit the materials rapidly, and the inevitable delay which further editing would have entailed was not considered justified. Thus, much of the information provided by the evaluators could have been provided at much the same level of validity by a small team of experienced teachers who had merely read the materials and expressed their opinions. Nevertheless, this policy of diffusing partially edited materials on a wide scale appears to have stimulated activity in a variety of institutions all over the country. What the evaluators have shown (see 'Photocell Applications', p. 169) is that such a policy is less successful with teachers inexperienced in this type of work, who found the partially edited materials difficult to handle.

Finally, the introduction of technology to the school curriculum is relatively new, so that the evaluators had difficulty in finding suitable test instruments. One of the aims of the project was to develop a favourable attitude towards technology on the part of pupils, but although a large number of scales were examined, one specifically designed for technology could not be found. Nevertheless, G. R. Meyer's *A Test of Interests*[1] had at least a face validity, which encouraged the evaluators to adapt it for their work on the CSE control technology syllabus. The advantages of using a scale which had been standardized outweighed the disadvantages of its being designed to test children's interest in science and only an indirect measure of interest in technology. The production of a test specifically for the purpose of this evaluation was ruled out as being too time-consuming.

The evaluators faced a more severe problem when they attempted to find a measure of skill in technological problem-solving. It was hoped that pupils who had followed the course in control technology, for example, would be able to transfer the problem-solving skills which they had developed in this field, and which were assessed for the CSE examination, to more general situations. The evaluators looked at several engineering aptitude tests which had been developed for vocational guidance. The method employed in the Purdue Creativity Test[2] seemed valid for the project's purpose, but unfortunately the items themselves were too difficult, being designed for professional engineers. Therefore the evaluators undertook to prepare a similar but easier test. They also decided to develop a test consisting of a series of little pencil-and-paper problems for much the same purpose. In this they were consider-ably helped by the work of M. T. Deere on the Design Line[3] and the tests which he and A. Carter have developed, which provided both a test structure and ideas for items.

Thus, because of the lack of suitable tests in this area, the evaluation unit was forced to produce instruments which its lack of resources would not allow it to standardize. Nevertheless, since only relative changes were being studied, the restriction of pre-trial tests to a small number of selected schools, followed by a simple item analysis, was not serious.

Despite these difficulties, the evaluators were able to carry out some work in three of the four areas mentioned on page 162. Readership surveys were carried out for both the *Bulletin* and *SATIS* (*c*); that for the *Bulletin* is re-ported on p. 165. Teachers' reactions to the material on *Photocell Applications* (*b*) were collected in twenty-four schools; these are discussed on p. 169. Separate reports of all these studies were completed and a report for the year, produced in July 1970, summarized the three separate reports and commented on the feedback mechanism (*a*).

The three separate reports were well received by the central team, although they were critical of the comments in the year's report on the way the trials had been conducted; they pointed out that these comments were made out of the context of the overall work of the project and ignored the change in the trial situation which would be brought about by the expansion of the team in the autumn of 1970. This kind of disagreement is inevitable when a separately funded unit is established to evaluate a project, and the evaluators have a particular responsibility to ensure that any tensions which arise are entirely constructive.

Another danger likely to occur from an independent evaluation was antici-pated early on: the unit might have become the sole channel of information from the trial schools to the central team, so that members of the team would have lost contact with the schools. Important though the evaluators considered their reports to be in the rewriting process, they nevertheless believed that the value of their work was enhanced by the opinions of the central team, formed as a result of school visits and of reading teachers' comments. Such direct impressions have a sharpness which is complementary to the more objective, but summarized and structured, information provided by the evaluators; both corroboration and disagreement between the two kinds of information can be fruitful. With the full agreement of the central team, therefore, the evaluators tried to separate information feedback from evaluation, seeing the former as primarily the responsibility of the team and believing that, while no sharp division is practicable, the project would benefit if both the team and the evaluation unit played complementary roles in obtaining information from trial schools.

By the autumn of 1970 the evaluation unit had been strengthened by the addition of a part-time helper. After consultation with the central team and the Schools Council research staff, the unit made proposals for additional studies:

(e) further investigations into the *Bulletin* and *SATIS*;

(f) an evaluation of the course in control technology leading to CSE Mode III;

(g) an investigation into the use of *Handbooks* for teachers and teachers' opinions on them:

    (i) *Gas Fired Muffle Furnaces,*

    (ii) *Bernoulli's Principle and the Carburetter,*

    (iii) *Engine Test Beds;*

(h) an investigation into the use of *Technology Briefs* (cards intended to stimulate project work);

(i) a pilot study into the regional group system.

By November work was in progress in areas (f) to (h).

Two of the evaluation studies are described in more detail below. They have been selected because they satisfy two criteria, namely, that they were complete at the time of writing and that they differed from other evaluation work currently in progress in the United Kingdom. (The author acknowledges his dependence for the next two sections on the reports of this work prepared by S. E. Gunn, evaluator.)

The readership survey of the 'Bulletin' (January 1970)

The *Bulletin* was distributed free six times a year to the project's associate schools and institutions, which numbered about 1000. Containing about 40 pages and a number of illustrations, it was produced by off-set litho from type-script. There was general agreement that it was most attractively produced and likely to make a considerable impact on its readers. Its purpose was to further the overall aim of the project by providing information on projects, examinations, accommodation, equipment and other information of direct use to teachers. Articles were also included on more fundamental matters relating to technology in the school curriculum and concerning the structure of the curriculum itself.

AIMS OF THE INVESTIGATION

These fell broadly into two categories:

(a) to discover which types of article were of most value to teachers and what use they were making of them;

(*b*) to discover whether there would be sufficient demand for the journal should it become necessary for readers to buy their copies in future.

METHOD

It was decided that two issues of the *Bulletin* would be investigated to reduce the risk of drawing conclusions about a particularly good or bad example; these would be the January 1970 and March 1970 editions. In the event, this plan was not adhered to; the November 1969 issue was used instead of the January issue, as the latter was felt to have atypical contents, and it was decided to postpone the second part of the survey because of other, more urgent demands upon the evaluators.

A postal questionnaire containing ten questions was used.

Questions 1, 2 and 3 obtained details about the respondent.

Question 4 attempted to find out whether the respondent had the *Bulletin* open before him as he filled in the questionnaire.

Question 5 required the respondent to rate each article in the *Bulletin*, using a three-point scale: worth while including, indifferent, not worth while including.

Questions 6 and 7 attempted to find out whether the respondent had used any article which had appeared in a previous edition of the *Bulletin* as a basis for work in schools or whether he was intending to use an article for this purpose.

Question 8 asked the respondent to name areas he would like to see dealt with in future editions of the *Bulletin*.

Questions 9 and 10 attempted to discover at what times of the year the *Bulletin* should be published, the price the reader was prepared to pay for it and the number of copies his school would require.

The questionnaire, together with an introductory letter and a prepaid envelope, was posted on 21 January 1970. If a reply had not been received by 16 February, another questionnaire, introductory letter and prepaid envelope with a follow-up letter were posted on 17 February. The closing date for replies to be included in the results was 16 March.

THE SAMPLE

There were approximately 5000 readers of the *Bulletin* at the time of the inquiry. The address list included headmasters, teachers of all subjects, LEA organizers and advisers, lecturers in colleges of education and universities, and some industrialists. It was thought that there were approximately equal numbers of teachers of science and teachers of technical subjects, and that the two groups together numbered about 3400. One member in ten was selected from these two groups for inclusion in the sample, as well as one headmaster in ten, by taking every tenth name from an alphabetical list. The teachers of subjects other than scientific and technical ones, colleges of education and university lecturers, and LEA organizers and advisers offered a market which could and should be expanded; therefore one member in two was chosen from these groups. Selection from all groups was on a random basis, with the provision that the number of schools whose staff received two or more questionnaires would be minimal. In the event, this only occurred in fourteen schools. The sample was constituted as follows:

Headmasters	78
Teachers	
Science	120
Technical subjects	106
Other subjects:	
geography	9
history	5
social studies, humanities, economics, etc.	21
art	11
domestic science	5
design and craft, etc.	5
English and other languages	8
Members of other organizations	
University lecturers	4
College of education lecturers:	
craft	4
science	4
Organizers and advisers	
craft	6
science	7
TOTAL	393

RETURNS

The response rate (52 per cent) was about the level expected and is reasonable for an inquiry about a widely distributed journal, some of whose readers were unlikely to feel committed to the project. Of the total number of replies (206), 107 were returned before the follow-up letters were sent. The lowest response rate was that of the headmasters (10 per cent) followed by teachers of 'other subjects' (23 per cent). The headmasters did, however, pass on the questionnaire to other members of staff, and if the teachers who returned the questionnaire on behalf of headmasters are included in the headmasters' group, the response rate rises to 55 per cent, which compares well with the 'members of other organizations' (56 per cent) and teachers of technical subjects (67 per cent) and is superior to the science teachers (46 per cent).

CONCLUSIONS

(a) The technical teachers had a higher rate of response than the science teachers. This might indicate that they received the *Bulletin* more enthusiastically. However, there was no significant difference in the answers the two groups gave to the questions, and therefore this hypothesis had to be treated with some caution.

(b) Almost all the readers who replied felt the articles in the *Bulletin* were worth while; only with two articles was any form of dissatisfaction shown.

(c) The value of articles appeared to have been judged by the quality of topic covered rather than by the type of article. No firm conclusion could be drawn because of the small number of articles involved.

(d) Of the respondents, 20 per cent had used *Bulletin* articles as a basis for work in schools or as a source of ideas. Nearly 10 per cent named articles which they intended to use in the future.

(e) Prominent among articles readers wished to see in the future editions were work for less able children, young children and secondary modern schools; more detailed descriptions of projects—method of teaching and pupils involved; and articles on specific topics, e.g. plastics in schools, electronics and materials testing.

(f) The most popular number of issues per year would be three and these would be of greatest benefit to the readers if they were published at the beginning of each term.

(g) Nearly half the respondents would purchase a copy of the journal for their personal use if it could not be supplied free of charge. However, the answers to the question did not show whether this would be the case if the school purchased copies also. Some 95 per cent of the respondents expected that their organization would buy a copy when it could no longer be supplied free of charge.

(h) Most readers would be prepared to pay £1 per year and schools would require on average just over two copies.

The *Bulletin* would thus appear to be popular with its readers, and almost all the articles were felt to be worthy of inclusion; many of the readers claimed to be using articles as a source of ideas. However, it must be remembered that only the more enthusiastic readers are likely to have replied.

COMMENTS ON THE EVALUATION

Within the limitations imposed by the method, the evaluators were reasonably satisfied with their survey. No question appeared to have been difficult to answer; the results, with the exception of that referred to in conclusion (g) were unambiguous; the response rate was reasonable. They regretted that the study was not repeated on another issue of the *Bulletin* but the information obtained by a second survey would have arrived too late for the immediate purpose of the team and other demands on the resources of the evaluation unit seemed more urgent. Nevertheless, it was hoped that a second study might be carried out at a later date.

A postal questionnaire has severe limitations, however, an important one being that only those teachers already interested in technology are likely to reply to it. While it was important that the project should support committed teachers, the survey gave little indication of how the *Bulletin* could be adapted to reach the unconverted. A postal questionnaire must also be quick and easy to complete. For this reason the evaluators asked the respondent to rate only the articles of an actual edition of the *Bulletin*; this might have been supported, had the above criterion not applied, by asking him to rate one or more hypothetical lists of contents, or even to give a list of contents of his own.

After the survey was conducted, the central team spent a considerable amount of time seeking financial support to enable them to continue issuing the *Bulletin* unders its new title *School Technology*. Despite the encouraging results of the survey, production of the journal did not become a commercial venture until 1971; up to that time the high esteem in which it was held by teachers, and which the survey so clearly revealed, undoubtedly helped the team to find funds to continue issuing it free.

'Photocell Applications'

INTRODUCTION

The evaluation of *Photocell Applications* was discussed with the central team at the end of the spring term 1970. Visits were made to schools during the summer term 1970, and in all twenty-four schools, in two regions, were visited; fifteen of these schools were using the material at the time of the visit; in the remainder the schools either intended to start work at a later date or had stopped using the material.

The draft had been distributed to the schools through the regional group structure. All the schools had been introduced to the material at regional group meetings, where they were addressed by the development leader responsible and shown an exhibition of demonstration experiments and pupils' work from pre-trial schools. The evaluators were given an opportunity to explain the purpose and nature of the evaluation. During the trials both regional groups held meetings to discuss the work; one group preferred not to meet as a whole but set up smaller groups of five or six schools.

Schools were not committed in any way to start work on the material, to work through it in its entirety (nor was it intended by the authors that they should do so), to complete the work in a given period or to use it with a particular age/ability group. The teachers were interviewed by the evaluator in their own schools for about $1\frac{1}{2}$ hours, and in some cases the evaluator saw the children working.

E.C.D.—7

METHOD OF EVALUATION

This material is concerned with one area in the field of electronics. Its aim is to provide background information and suggestions for producing certain electro-mechanical projects. It is designed for children of average ability in the middle of the secondary school age range but could also intrigue more capable or older pupils. The notes are primarily intended to be of help to both teacher and pupils. However, there are no clear divisions between those parts which are intended for teachers and those intended for pupils.

As these were the first trials held by the project, the evaluators felt that it would be advantageous to supply the central team with some feedback information on the reactions of teachers and pupils as soon as possible; this would enable the team to revise the draft quickly and would also show up any deficiencies in the trial situation before a large quantity of trial materials had been introduced into schools. This work would also provide the evaluators with a pilot study for the evaluation of later materials.

In view of the factors outlined above and in previous sections, it was decided to gain the majority of the information about *Photocell Applications* by interviewing the teachers concerned using a checklist. Any additional information which was not covered by the checklist was recorded as an extra comment. The evaluators were well aware of the limitations of this method of inquiry but they felt that it was the best possible method to adopt under the circumstances.

THE TRIAL CIRCUMSTANCES AND THE OUTCOMES

The first aim of the evaluation was to describe the situation in which the material was being tried and to provide a rough measure of its success; an example of the information obtained and the way it was presented is shown in Table 12.1. Much of it is self-explanatory, but three columns need further comment.

Successful/unsuccessful/intending

The success of the work was judged by the evaluators using the following criteria: teachers' comments; whether teachers intended to continue with the work or not; whether the work had already ceased through lack of materials, lack of success with projects, lack of success with pupils. The evaluators recognized the dangers of this type of analysis and the limitations which must be placed on any extrapolation made from it.

Three main categories were used:

Successful (some or all of the following): four or more projects completed successfully; teachers' comments like 'It's going well', 'I have managed to get a lot of the work covered'; intention to carry out work in future.

Unsuccessful: projects unfinished; only one or two projects completed and

Table 12.1 Specimen presentation of trial results from *Photocell Applications*.

| PUPILS | | | | | | | | TEACHER | | | |
Successful/ unsuccessful/ intending	n	Ability	Age	Pupils using material	Pupils' knowledge at start of course	Material part of another course	Time available per week	Subject	Experience with electronics	Training	Finance & materials
(Q) Partially successful (needed expert help)	18	CSE	11/12	No	No experience in electricity	Club activity	No precise times	Craft	Little previous knowledge*	C. of Ed.	Short of finance & materials; dislikes S-DeC†
(P) Successful	4	Very able	16/18	No	Basic course in electronics	Club activity	No precise times	Science	Very good	Univ.	Adequate; dislikes S-DeC
(S) Partially successful (work just beginning)	4	CSE	14/15	Yes	Some basic knowledge of electricity	Part class, part club activity	No precise times	Craft	Fair	C. of Ed., Tech.	Lacks gears, transistors, lenses; uses S-DeC
(T) Successful	11	Below CSE	14/15	Parts	Basic course in electronics	School leavers' course	6 periods	Craft	Good	C. of Ed.	Adequate; some S-DeC
(U) Successful	10	GCE & below	14/15	No	CSE Mode III electronics	CSE	2 periods	Craft, engin.	Very good	Univ.	Short of finance; materials adequate at present; prefers Radionic†

* Attended one-term course in electronics at an institute of education.
† S-DeC and Radionic are commercial electronic kits.

only after a considerable period of time; work stopped, or stopped and re-started after a long break, without adequate explanation; teachers' comments like 'Projects are not working well', 'I have not made much progress'; intention to discontinue the work.

Intending: schools planning to use the material in the near future.

Pupils using material
Were the pupils using the material themselves or was it used only as a teachers' guide?

Experience with electronics
This was really a measure of what teachers *claimed* to be their experience. The evaluators subsequently regretted that they had not established criteria here.

An inspection of the data, presented in the form shown in Table 12.1, revealed certain patterns which were strengthened when the information was summarized in Table 12.2.

It would appear from Tables 12.1. and 12.2 that where the material was being used successfully, the teachers had a good background in electronics and the pupils had some knowledge of electricity before starting the work. In four schools the material had been supplemented by the teachers, who had produced their own work cards. In four other schools the work was part of either a CSE Mode III course, in which electronics was included, or a basic electronics course.

The unsuccessful schools did not have teachers with a wide practical experience of electronics and, although some of the pupils had a knowledge of electricity before starting the work, in none of the schools was the material related to any form of course. In two schools sixth formers had shown little enthusiasm after seeing the material.

The schools which intended to use the material in the future all planned to start with children of CSE ability and above who would have some knowledge of electronics before they started the work. These schools were characterized by the care that they were taking in obtaining adequate materials and increasing their own knowledge of electronics before starting work with the children.

The age, ability or number of pupils involved in the work did not appear to have influenced the success of the material. In only two schools were the pupils working directly from the material (four CSE boys of fourteen and two sixth form boys, all in successful schools). The major factor influencing the success of the material seemed to be the teacher's experience in electronics; it did not seem to be very helpful to teachers with a limited knowledge. A term's basic course in electronics at an institute of education, although it had obviously increased the teachers' knowledge, had failed to give them sufficient experience and confidence to carry out work from the material successfully on their own. This was shown by the number of schools which were unsuccessful

Table 12.2 Summary of relevant factors from data illustrated in Table 12.1*

	Successful									Partially successful			Unsuccessful					
	H	L	M	N	O	P	T	U	X	Q	S	W	R	K	J	I	F	G
Ability of pupils																		
Very able					/											/	/	
GCE		/			/		/	/										
CSE	/				/					/	/	/	/					/
Below CSE			/	/		/								/	/			
Age of pupils																		
11/12										/			/					
12/13																		
13/14			/								/			/				
14/15	/	/		/	/	/	/	/		/			/					/
15/16																		
16/17						/												
17/18						/										/	/	
18+																		
Teacher's background																		
Good	/	/	/	/	/	/	/	/	/		/							
Theory only															/†	/†	/†	/
Poor										/†	/		/†	/				
Pupils' knowledge of electricity at start of course																		
Basic course in electronics	/	/	/	/	/	/	/	/	/									
Some knowledge of electricity											/	/				/	/	/
No knowledge of electricity										/			/	/	/			
No. of pupils	18	16	18	10	8	4	11	10	5	18	4	8	18	4	12	2	0	8

* Six schools, in the *intending* category, do not feature in this table.
† One-term basic electronics course at an institute of education.

although a member of the school's staff had attended such a course. Furthermore, these teachers had not extensively availed themselves of the expert help which was available from the institute of education.

Shortage of electronic equipment did not affect the successful use of the teaching material, although schools which were short had to carry out the work on a limited scale. The shortage of materials was caused by lack of finance, the delay between ordering and receiving components and the problems of buying through the local education authorities.

TEACHERS' VIEWS ON THE PRESENTATION OF THE MATERIAL

Part of a summary of the information in this area obtained from the checklist is given in Table 12.3. An inspection of this reveals that the teachers' views on the material, when considered in relation to their background, differed only in two areas. In general the teachers who claimed experience of electronics—not surprisingly—required less information about it and also less advice on how to teach it, compared to the others. Almost all teachers claimed to find the material easy to understand and all but one found the diagrams adequate. Seven out of the twenty-four would have liked more explanation of technical terms, but two-thirds of the sample wanted both more technical information and more advice, of a pedagogic nature, on how to carry out project work.

To give some examples of other information obtained and likely to be useful in the rewriting of the material, it was discovered that an overwhelming majority of teachers wanted the material more clearly classified into sections (e.g. ideas for pupils' projects, background information, pupils' experiments). However, there was not such a clear agreement on whom the material should be written for: eleven out of the twenty-five wanted it to have sections for both pupils and teachers, but seven wanted purely a teachers' guide and four material for use by pupils only.

As well as asking trial teachers for their replies to questions on his checklist, the evaluator invited them to express their views of the material in any way they chose. Most teachers expressed enthusiasm for the ideas embodied by the material but many made both criticisms, which supported the general conclusions given above, and suggestions for improvements.

TEACHERS' VIEWS ON OBJECTIVES

The part of the inquiry concerning the objectives teachers hoped to achieve by using the material was not successful. Teachers did not appear to have given consideration to this area: they were reluctant to express their views independently and only too willing to agree to a list of objectives suggested by the evaluators. While the evaluators felt that their attempt to elicit teachers' opinions in this area had been clumsy, it was clear that both the material and the meetings to introduce it must give much more guidance in this area.

In view of teachers' uncertainty over both objectives and appropriate teaching methods (see above), the evaluators felt that there was little purpose in proceeding with their original plan to analyse either the division of the time spent during work on *Photocell Applications* between the various learning experiences or the skills that pupils were developing during project work.

ORGANIZATION OF TRIALS

The evaluators' report to the central team also contained comments on how the trials were organized. Teachers, despite their criticisms of the presentation

Table 12.3 Teachers' views on presentation of material and teachers' backgrounds

Teachers' background		Ease of understanding			Information provided			Explanation of tech. terms			Diagrams			Advice on how to use material		
Subject (Science/craft)	Experience (Good/theory only/none)	Easy	All right	Difficult	Not enough	Enough	Too much	Inadequate	Adequate	Too much	Inadequate	Adequate	Too much detail	Too little	About right	Too much
(U) Craft	Good															
(L) Science	Good															
(H) Science	Good															
(M) Science	Good															
(N) Science	Good															
(O) Science	Good															
(S) Craft	Good															
(T) Craft	Good															
(W) Craft	Good															
(X) Craft	Good															
(P) Science	Good															
(A) Science	Good															
(V) Science	Good															
(I) Science	Theory															
(C) Science	Theory															
(D) Science	Theory															
(F) Science	Theory															
(G) Science	Theory															
(B) Science	None															
(E) Science	None															
(J) Science	None															
(K) Science	None															
(R) Craft	None															
(Q) Craft	None															
TOTALS		22	2	0	16	8	1	7	16	0	1	23	0	17	5	2

of the material, expressed considerable enthusiasm for the ideas it embodied. Nevertheless, the evaluators gained the impression that, in spite of the group meetings held, the majority of teachers felt they were far too isolated from the controlling body. All teachers indicated that they would have liked a visit from a team member: this would have raised their morale, and given them an opportunity to display their work, discuss further applications and receive expert advice where required. The evaluators felt that while teachers were reluctant to seek out expert assistance, they would have welcomed an opportunity to discuss problems with an expert should one have visited the school.

CONCLUSION

The evaluators considered that this study achieved a fair measure of success, despite the deficiencies already mentioned: the use of a checklist, with the rough-and-ready criteria they had established, enabled them to present a sufficiently objective picture of the trial situation; the information obtained was likely to be extremely useful in rewriting the material; finally, useful experience was gained both in organizing trials and in the conduct of an evaluation study.

Publishers for the project:
  Project Technology Handbooks and *Technology Briefs*—Heinemann Educational Books;
  course material—English Universities Press;
  review material—English Universities Press and the project;
  history units—Edward Arnold;
  Technology and Man (packs)—Blackie & Son/University of London Press.

Project periodicals:
  School Technology (quarterly);
  SATIS (six times yearly).

References

1   Meyer, G. R. *A Test of Interests* North Ryde, New South Wales: Macquarie University, 1969.
2   *Purdue Creativity Test* Industrial Relations Center, University of Chicago, 1967.
3   Deere, M. T. 'The anatomy of technology' *Studies in Education and Craft* 2 (1), autumn 1969.

13 Nuffield Secondary Science

Dorothy Alexander

Origin of the project

This project was set up at Mary Ward House, Tavistock Place, London in 1965, just as the Nuffield O level projects were on the point of publication; it emerged as a result of the preliminary work done by a group of HM inspectors under the chairmanship of L. G. Smith, and later published in Schools Council Working Paper 1, *Science for the Young School Leaver* (Schools Council, 1965). The work was built round eight major themes; from these a choice of materials could be made available for the teachers and the range of materials provided was expected to make it possible to find suitable material for a wide range of pupil ability. Initially, it was thought that these project materials would be suitable for the whole ability range with the exception of those expected to complete the full O level course, but in the event it may well be that it has wider-ranging possibilities even than this. Perhaps the simplest way of trying to crystallize quite a complicated situation is to quote directly from the Working Paper:

In brief, the basis of these suggestions is that there are certain major themes in science with which ... pupils might be expected to have some measure of acquaintance and, whilst it will be necessary to vary the manner and extent to which these are pursued in different circumstances and with different pupils, the themes themselves should largely be the same for all. Central to each theme will be those key ideas and areas of knowledge which lend it importance for the ... pupil and these mark out the broad directions in which emphasis needs to be laid to give significance to the theme as a whole. The cohesion which this should introduce into an individual theme, and the overall pattern of the themes collectively should give a significant underlying structure to the work. What is included will be chosen, not because it occurs traditionally in school science courses, but because of its relevance to the modern, adult world. It should therefore touch on matters of concern and interest to the pupils at many points.

During the course of 1966 certain pre-pilot testing of materials had taken place, and in the school year 1967–8 the first large-scale trials of themes were carried out with fifty-three schools, to be supplemented by an extended trial in over 150 more the following year. In 1967 also the project was transferred to Chelsea College of Science and Technology.

Officially evaluation began in January 1969, though in fact the work did not actually begin until February, by which stage there was to be but one short period of further trial during the year 1969–70. Feedback from schools in this last trial stage was likely to be useful only until January 1970, because of the need to get the books to the printers during that year for expected publication early in 1971. This may be thought to be a curious time for the insertion of an evaluation into the project's programme, since it could have little hope of being useful to the project team, or of taking a long enough look from a distance to judge the on-going effect of the project. In the event, however, the exercise had an unexpected value, as the group of schools involved had only a very short briefing conference in July 1969 and were not visited by members of the project team to give added support during the year. This meant that they could be regarded as 'first customers', obtaining their guidance almost entirely from the printed materials; reactions noticed during the period of this evaluation exercise might contribute useful pointers to any subsequent study, and indeed to the possible trends of in-service training. The time allowed for evaluation was expected to be two days a week for one year; in fact, this spread out to something more like one day a week for two years, owing to the nature of the evaluator's work and the pattern of evaluation which was eventually agreed—a pattern mostly enabling work to go on quite naturally without the evaluator. This was an important part of the strategy: the nature of the evaluator's work (and that of most additional helpers) meant that emergencies and crises were likely to arise unexpectedly; this arrangement meant that when problems did arise, they could be dealt with as a matter of urgency. Because of the easy relationship with the project team and the associated schools, it may be that the evaluator's activities at least reinforced for the project team some of the points already indicated by feedback of a different kind, and may also have illuminated certain sensitive areas from another standpoint. This was in addition to the 'first customer' effect outlined above and it was hoped that a simple pattern of observation and discussion would emerge, which might be of future use during a process of science curriculum change.

The evaluation pattern: evolution of the programme

The situation was somewhat daunting in February 1969 when the evaluator was faced with

(a) what could easily be a useless exercise because of its timing;

(b) a project which was producing a very large amount of material from which teachers could select, which meant that everybody was likely to be choosing something a little different;

(c) a project which aimed at providing useful material for some 75 per cent of the pupil population aged 13–16.

For the first three months the available one or two days a week were spent in trying to get the 'feel' of what was already being done; in meeting with the team members and worrying them about the meaning of the word 'significance' as this was something which appeared frequently in all the literature. For instance, to return once more to Working Paper I, this contains a whole section under the heading 'Significance', part of which runs:

Whilst it is platitudinous to say that the science done by these pupils should have significance for them, it seems that, because much of it at present has shortcomings in this respect, the most dramatic of the changes . . . envisaged could well arise from concentrating upon significance in all aspects of the work: by using it, indeed, as a touchstone at many points. This would involve taking a good deal less of the learning process for granted than is often the case at present. Relationships upon which significance will depend, which may arise spontaneously in the minds of their abler fellows, will need to be made abundantly manifest to Newsom pupils, particularly to those of lower ability.

The project team were very patient in what must have seemed to them a somewhat naïve approach to something they had been living with and had grown used to over nearly 3 years but by the end of March the evaluator was able to put forward the following notes for the benefit of the Schools Council Evaluation Committee (Science).

It would seem to me that the main points to concentrate on are: first, the question of significance, and secondly, the aspect of activity and element of investigation in the pupils' work, coupled with repetition and variety for consolidation. These are the items which seem to me most frequently referred to, both in the written materials, in the Schools Council publication and in the advice given by the team generally when discussing the project at their meetings and with the teachers. The word 'significance' has been difficult to pin down into any aspect which is capable of simple measurement, for it seems to have at least two parts to it: first, that there should be some immediate significance which perhaps may be described as meaningfulness as far as the pupils are concerned—that is to say, the materials shall relate to themselves at the appointed time when they are doing experiments—and further, that the materials should have some significance or purpose in relation to the life of the real world outside, into which these pupils will soon be moving. A further point in this long-term look at significance lies in the suggestion that the science the children do should add up to some sensible pattern, and this indicates that when the teachers choose from the eight themes, it is tó be hoped that they will choose such items that, over the period of three years, there will be some purposeful pattern in the schemes so evolved.

One evidence of the pupils' appreciation of their work, and thus perhaps an indication of the significance to the pupils of what they have been doing, may be found in their desire to have some more of it, and therefore it seems likely that one possible measure to help us may be in seeking to discover if there has been any change in the interest of the pupils. In other words, if they have been doing this kind of science for a year or two, do they want some more? This may perhaps be measured by the use of an interest test taken before the work is started and then at a later stage. This would mean using one of the interest tests which have already been prepared, probably by the National Foundation for Educational Research, and would need to be used in July of this year if we are to get any sensible value in terms of a pre-test and post-test situation. Further evidence of this kind may perhaps be gathered from the school in answer to such questions as:

What is the number of pupils choosing to do science when options are available, say at the end of the third or fourth year?   *or*

What is the number of pupils staying on and continuing with their science who could, in fact, leave by reason of age?   *or*

What about the absence rate—has it changed at all, perhaps as a result of this kind of activity?

Some collection of evidence might perhaps be possible along these lines through the medium of questionnaire.

On the question of the element of activity shown in the lesson, I think this might be approached by the use of classroom observation. If observation is to be used as an evaluation technique, it must of course be systematic; it must be recorded immediately; it must be structured and replicated, and this means an instrument must be devised which will be capable of use by one or two observers in the classroom or laboratory in which the work is being done, so that some continuous observations of the activities of the class may be made at frequent intervals. One of the major problems here would be to determine the sample of classrooms to be studied in this way, and to determine for how long it is necessary to keep up observation and how frequently. It would also be a good idea if it were possible to study a small group of pupils, together with the teacher, on a particular section of the work and to study them rather intensively. If this could be done, I think it might well be the most important of all things to do, as in this way one could see the relationship between the kind of work that was being done and the kind of learning that was going on very much more effectively: but this needs people really skilled in both knowledge of the science and knowledge of the psychology of learning.

Possible action

Using a sample group of the schools beginning to work with the material in 1969:

1 Give scientific interest test in July 1969.

2 See that questions are included in the project leader's questionnaire, which is planned to be sent out before the end of the summer term.

3 Carry out classroom observation during the autumn term or longer.

4 Study the teachers' purposes, partly from their returns to the project director when choosing their route and partly by discussion.

5 Repeat scientific interest test in July 1970.

Action undertaken

The first part of the work was concerned with drafting some questions to add to a questionnaire set out by the project leader later in the summer. This was sent to all schools so far involved in trials, namely, the fifty-three who had completed two years of trial work and about 150 more which were at that point completing their first year in this work. When analysed, the returns identified some of the reasons for choice of routes, showed the very strong influence of examination pressures in many of the schools, and also indicated that the trial work was making itself felt in classes and amongst teachers additional to those immediately involved. There seemed to be no falling off in the interest and industry of the trial classes thus far. In the summer of 1969 two people were invited to organize a special exercise to help schools wishing to prepare CSE Mode III schemes, and it was hoped that, when published, these would give advice on how to select a scheme in the spirit of the project instead of (as so often happens) choosing a scheme which fits in with examination requirements.

For the remainder of the evaluation work the population comprised those schools, some fifty in all, which joined trials in September 1969 for the first time. In the preceding June all pupils in these classes were asked to complete the NFER Pupil Opinion Poll: Science, no. 104, a questionnaire which had but recently completed its test runs. The evaluator was fortunate to find a ready-made instrument, even though there was little experience of its use for purposes such as this. The test booklet had to be rewritten to suit the circumstances of the experiment, but the questionnaire was used as it stood. The last twenty questions asked for pupils' opinions of their science teachers and in some areas this caused anxiety. One LEA returned all the forms as it was thought unwise to circulate them, and in some schools this section was deleted. Nevertheless, the majority of students seemed to have taken it all in their stride and when in June 1970 the same questionnaire was reissued to the same population, every school completed and returned the papers in good time. These papers were all marked and at the time of writing the process of computation to see if there had been any statistically significant change of attitude to science in the course of the year was well in hand.

The observation schedule

When the list of the 1969–70 schools were studied, it was found that the largest concentration of schools occurred in the Gloucestershire and London areas, and it was therefore decided to try and use schools from these two groups (five schools in Gloucestershire and five in Greater London for some more detailed observation. The problem was to try and devise the kind of schedule which could be used by people whose normal job included certain times when they went into the classes and observed them at work, but who were not necessarily trained for any sophisticated use of this kind of technique. Discussions with the project team members took place from time to time, in order to determine the kinds of activities which normally went on in lessons when classes were using their materials. What seemed to be a reasonable schedule was drawn up and then tried out by half a dozen people, only one of whom was involved with the team. They used it with a variety of classes just to see whether the schedule could be handled without undue fuss, and then, with one or two minor modifications, it was produced as the instrument to be used during 1969–70.

Each school had one observer attached to it. Those who took part as observers included Assistant Education Officers, science advisers, lecturers in colleges of education and wardens or leaders of teachers' centres, and in each case one person adopted a school and made arrangements to go in about three times a term, as and when his job permitted, to watch a lesson and complete the check list. This checklist was then sent to the evaluator, and various graphs were prepared, with the aim of making presentation of the information as visual as possible. It might have been easier in some ways if there had not been such emphasis on being simple; the end result was some hundreds of graphs drawn in different ways, leaving the problem of seeing which of them, if any, were likely to produce some useful insight. Once this problem had been solved, it was proposed to call together all the observers and teachers who took part in the exercise to show them the graphs and see what they made of them. Then, out of their joint observations and wisdom, it might be possible to see whether or not anything had been achieved by this method of describing a classroom situation. These meetings in fact took place in autumn 1971.

One administrative difficulty which sometimes caused problems was that until January 1970 the evaluator had no assistance. This meant that all typing and office work had to be done by the already over-burdened project secretaries, and evaluation had to take second place to their more immediate work. By planning some weeks ahead and letting them know what was needed, so that they could slip items in when time was available, it proved possible to keep things moving, but it was a great joy when, in January 1970, assistance was offered to get on with the processing of the Pupil Opinion Poll and other routine matters. Many of the staff at Chelsea College have been most helpful throughout, and a number of them became involved at different stages of the work. The work was, in fact, carried out by the voluntary efforts of something like twelve individuals (observers and Chelsea staff) and for this one year a full-time secretary-cum-research assistant.

Without all this good-natured voluntary help, nothing could have been achieved at all. The practical difficulties in organizing the observation were considerable, and until midsummer it was not certain whether there would be enough data flowing in through the observers to give any evidence at all. The major problems likely to have arisen were all completely outside the evaluator's control and therefore nothing could be done but hope, carrying on with the organization of other aspects of the investigation meanwhile. For instance, all the observers were key people in responsible jobs who were helping with the observation as an extra load in already crowded timetables. This meant that at any crisis point their main work had to take precedence and the evaluation exercise be relegated to second place. Teachers' strikes had to be coped with, as well as the usual winter ailments, and at a later stage there was a postal strike as well; in spite of everything most observers completed nine or ten observation schedules, which is a great tribute to their powers of organization and to their good temper.

It was initially planned to use the evaluator as a kind of moderator, since it was realized that in judgements of this kind there is a certain amount of variation from person to person. This, however, was impracticable for two main reasons: first, the evaluator would not have had time to do this as well as the remainder of her work, and secondly, it was quite out of the question to agree on days and times when all those involved could meet regularly. It was therefore decided to look for any signs of *change* in lesson pattern and see if such change could be examined in the light of the project objectives. The evaluator was able to meet each group of observers once a term to discuss progress, and one of the interesting aspects of these discussions was that no one really seemed to have problems in the handling of the schedule—only with their diaries!

Note: The present author's full report on the evaluation of the Nuffield Secondary Science Project is in preparation and will be published in the Schools Council Research Studies Series (Macmillan Education).

Publisher for the project: Longman.

14 Bilingual education in the anglicized areas of Wales: infant school project

C. J. Dodson

The teaching of Welsh as a second language in the schools of Wales has not prevented a decrease in the number of Welshman who can speak their language effectively after leaving school. The reasons for this are manifold. The pressures of the English advertising and communication mass media, as well as the requirements of industry, commerce and everyday living in Wales, tend to sap the will of many pupils to learn Welsh with enthusiasm, and weaken parents' determination to encourage their children to master the language. In the 1960s it became obvious to educationists that pupils starting to learn Welsh in secondary or even in junior primary schools would not be able to reach the level of proficiency in the Welsh language considered necessary for an acceptable degree of English-Welsh bilingualism in Wales.

In 1967 the Central Advisory Council for Education (Wales) recommended in the Gittins Report[1] that: 'As far as possible, Welsh should be introduced in the anglicized areas at the age of five, through activities, mime, song and rhyme in the context of a progressive infants school approach' (p. 244, para. 11.13.3). The report continues:

... the aim of full and adequate bilingualism can, perhaps, only be fulfilled by the development of the 'bilingual school' which would make systematic use of Welsh as part-medium of instruction at the junior stage. Such a school would be organized as follows, for English-speaking children:—

Nursery stage: (*a*) Learning Welsh through play activity.
                (*b*) Play activity through the medium of English.
5–7/8 years: (*a*) Learning Welsh through play activity and, where possible, play activity through the medium of Welsh.
                (*b*) Learning Welsh through peripheral subjects.
                (*c*) Other subjects through the medium of English.
8–11 years: (*a*) Working up to approximately half the time and subjects, including crucial subjects, through the medium of English and approximately half the subjects, including peripheral subjects through the medium of Welsh. [p. 245, para. 11.13.15]

As it would have been difficult for individual LEAs to implement such a scheme without a co-ordinating body responsible for methodology, in-service training, supervision of teachers and preparation of materials, the Schools Council decided to initiate a pilot Bilingual Education Project in schools in most of the Welsh counties. The Welsh LEAs responded well to requests from the Schools Council to initiate such a scheme in one or more of their schools, and twenty-five infant schools were asked to participate in the project. The Council appointed a director and an assistant in September 1968 to prepare the materials and to train and supervise the infant teachers who were to start the project in January 1969. The present author was approached in September 1969 with the request to act as evaluator of the scheme, the terms of reference being to make a judgement of the progress made so far and to assess whether the scheme was worthy of continuation and expansion at a later date.

Whilst the Gittins Report was being written, the University College of Wales Department of Education at Aberystwyth was conducting an experiment in the learning of Welsh as a second language at reception class level in order to develop a methodology which could blend in with modern developments in the infant school. As the evaluator was both director of the Aberystwyth experiment and a member of the Central Advisory Council for Education (Wales) working party on 'language', the findings of this experiment, together with observations made at infant schools where Welsh was being taught (the headmaster of one of these schools became the director of the Schools Council project) could flow directly into the Gittins Report, which in turn resulted in the setting up of the Schools Council Bilingual Education Project.

The Aberystwyth methodology is described in outline by C. J. Dodson[2] and in detail by Mrs E. Price[3] who, with Mrs E. Roberts, carried out the experiment in the classroom. It might be appropriate at this juncture to quote some of the major points of this methodology as described by Mrs Price, who became senior research officer of the Schools Council project from September 1971, because the Schools project was largely based on it and the evaluator used it as a yardstick for his assessment of the sample schools visited.

The Aberystwyth experiment had two specific aims:

The first aim was to evolve activities that can be used with children at reception class level, and the observations made in this field are applicable to both monolingual and bilingual schools. The second aim of the project was concerned with second-language learning in the Infants' School, and the combination of the two aims in the one project was deliberate. The present-day situation in Wales is such that, whereas many people would like to see all Welsh people becoming bilingual, if that could be done without any trouble, there does exist a good deal of opposition to devoting school time to the learning of Welsh as a second language, which is sometimes regarded as a waste of time and as a distraction from the more serious purpose of education. If, however, a second language could be acquired *at the same time* as the children are absorbed in activities aimed at widening their experience or developing their physical powers, then this objection would be removed.[4]

The teaching of the second language is divided into four phases. In phase 1 only non-verbalized activities, e.g. self-generating activities which are also independent of language, are used.

In this phase, the child need not verbalise at all, in order to perform the activity, though he may do so in the mother-tongue if he so wishes, and he need not understand the speech of the L2 [second language] teacher. The activity required of him should be self-evident, or be very easily demonstrable and imitated. This is a period of familiarisation with the second-language, during which understanding occurs, though lack of understanding on the part of the child should not cause insecurity or inhibition. Comprehension grows quickly, and many children are very soon ready to move into phase 2, when activities can be directed by a minimal use of the second-language spoken by the teacher, and reinforced by the teacher's gestures or actions. The children are still not required to verbalise, but most of them do so, either repeating words and phrases immediately after the teacher, or using them spontaneously later. Phase 2 is a long drawn-out period, during which the children acquire an understanding of a core of basic vocabulary and sentence patterns. Most children move, of their own accord, quite quickly into phase 2.

A considerable amount of immediate repetitive verbal response is made quite readily during phase 2, thus laying the foundation for the pupils' performance in later phases, during which verbal response will form part of an activity. Phase 3 is really a testing period, during which the teacher can try out the child's L2 comprehension. And at the same time, his comprehension can be both widened and consolidated by focussing attention on basic sentence patterns which can appear in many contexts such as games, books and songs. But it must be remembered that moving into phase 3 will occur in a piecemeal fashion. Each child will take the step in his or her own time. And even then, the individual may not be ready for phase 3-type activity in every sphere of interest. The building process will be gradual, and the pattern slightly different for each child. But as comprehension is widened and spontaneous verbal response increases, the children are ready for phase 4, when, for the first time, they can be required to make simple verbal responses, which will form an integral part of their activity.

It has been said above that the approach to phase 3 is made in a piecemeal fashion. This is true, to a varying extent, for each phase. It should also be made clear, that phases 1, 2, 3 etc. should not be thought of as following one another in strict chronological sequence. Even when all the children in the group have shown themselves able to take part in phase 2 activity, they will not all do so all the time. At every moment there will be some who revert to phase 1-type activity. Ideally, the child will strike a healthy balance and move from phase to phase, both backwards and forwards as his mood and interests dictate.[5]

The evaluator had therefore available a methodological framework which could be used as a model when comparing the progress made in schools. Although the Aberystwyth experiment had used a series of tests measuring general and linguistic progress, the results of which were obtained by daily observation and testing, no such tests could be applied in this initial evaluation of the Schools Council project for two main reasons. Firstly, the evaluator had not been appointed at the beginning of the project and had therefore missed the preparatory stage before the schools commenced with the scheme as well as the first two terms of the scheme's operation in the schools. Secondly, such tests would have required a large number of repeat visits to individual schools, which was not feasible in terms of time and expenditure.[6]

The evaluation therefore had to be based on careful observation and questioning, together with an examination of the materials supplied. The evaluating procedure was neither formative nor summative, as the visits made to different schools started in September 1969 and ended in March 1970. Each school had consequently reached different levels of development when any visit was made. During every visit the evaluator had to keep in mind the number of months the pupils had participated in the scheme, so as to reach valid conclusions concerning their proficiency levels. These levels were also influenced by the attitude, ability and expectation of the teachers, the availability of equipment, the background, attitudes and abilities of the children, as well as the attitude of parents. Obviously such an evaluation is not an easy one, and the evaluator has to know precisely where to look and what questions to ask as soon as he enters the school. He must therefore be a trained observer, who is thoroughly familiar with the aims of the project and the methodology used to reach these aims.

The Welsh session took up the whole of every afternoon. Whenever possible, the evaluator arrived before the afternoon session began, so as to make contact with the teacher outside the classroom. On one occasion the evaluator arrived unannounced approximately a quarter of an hour after the session had started. When the headteacher introduced the evaluator to the teacher in the classroom, the teacher began to show immediate signs of stress and loss of composure. This affected her classroom behaviour severely and it would have been foolish to let her continue under those conditions. Fortunately, the headmaster recognized the situation and offered to take her class, so as to give the teacher an opportunity to get to know the evaluator. Over a cup of tea the tension gradually disappeared. Nevertheless, it took three-quarters of an hour for the teacher to regain her equilibrium. On her return to the classroom with the evaluator, she had complete control of the teaching situation and the evaluator was able to make several observations which indicated that the teacher had both ability and an insight into the teaching and learning principles involved. This might seem to be a point of minor importance in an evaluation procedure, yet an initial insensitivity on the part of the evaluator could prejudice his judgement severely, especially if his arrival has been badly timed on several occasions.

The time spent by the teacher and the evaluator in getting to know each other, usually over lunch, was also valuable in detecting the teacher's attitude, grasp of the project's aims and methodology, and difficulties with pupils, parents and authorities, as well as her confidence and enthusiasm, or lack of them, and her general personality. During these conversations the evaluator had to be most careful to hide from the teacher what he himself expected to see and hear, as many teachers are able to adjust themselves quite readily to the evaluator's views concerning classroom procedure, thereby blurring to some extent the true potential and normal classroom behaviour of the teacher and pupils. When evasion became necessary, it had to occur in a way that would not make the teacher feel suspicious or resentful. In other words, the evaluator must show a great deal of human sympathy and understanding and, after these informal conversations, he himself undergoes a test considerably greater than that to which the teacher is subjected. Fortunately, the feedback procedures during these preliminary conversations are many, and he will soon recognize whether or not he is successfully putting the teacher at ease and take appropriate steps.

Preliminary conversations were also preferable to putting questions after the afternoon session, as the teacher's desire to leave school, perhaps to do her shopping and prepare her family's evening meal, acts as an inhibitor which could deny the evaluator valuable information.

During the conversations concerning this particular project, major points about in-service training and the role of local authorities came to light. Teachers admitted that they lacked confidence during the initial months, and felt that a far greater amount of in-service training should have been made available *before* they were expected to introduce the scheme into their classrooms. They had, in fact, attended a single conference lasting one session during which the scheme and materials were explained. The evaluator compared this with the three months made available to Nuffield Primary French teachers, and he was not a little apprehensive on the first few visits as to what he would find in the classroom. That he was pleasantly surprised will be explained later. Nevertheless, such a ridiculously short period of in-service training indicates that the project took a risk which could have caused the scheme to fail at the very start. That the project was a clear success was due to the zeal and hard work of the director and his assistant and to the resilience, flexibility and perseverance of the teachers. A more reasonable period of in-service training would also have made it clear to teachers that phase 2 is a long-drawn-out process. Many of them expected quicker returns for their efforts and had on several occasions been on the point of withdrawing from the scheme.

Although LEAs had welcomed the project in their schools, they had neglected to inform parents about the nature of the experiment. In certain parts of Wales this would have resulted in strong opposition by educated and articulate parents, who are conscious of their rights and the obligations of authority. There was considerable evidence that teachers did meet some parental opposition in all schools, but were able to alleviate the parents' fears about the scheme. Yet this could so easily have ruined the project in many areas, since teachers are not trained public relations officers. It was also difficult to ascertain what criteria had been used by local authorities in selecting the schools and teachers they considered suitable for the project.

Although the type of work done in a modern infant school could tempt an evaluator to begin questioning once more during the time when the teacher moves from one group to the next or from one child to another, close questioning of teachers had to stop as soon as the afternoon session began. It is felt that such interruptions are not only unwelcome to the teacher but tend to interfere with her planned sequence of methodological events, thus giving the evaluator a distorted view of normal teaching and learning behaviour. In the classroom the evaluator should rely on careful observation whilst making himself as inconspicuous as possible by blending in with classroom routine, e.g. during activity work by playing himself with the various groups whilst noting the verbal responses made by the children, or during more formal language work by sitting as low as possible to avoid the dominating effect a stranger can have on a class of children.

The evaluator should also train himself to retain in his mind most of the points he notices, as the sight of a stranger making copious notes in the classroom can unnerve even the most hardened teacher and consequently affect her teaching. Any reader who has undergone teaching practice during a teacher training course should not find it difficult to remember the agonizing moments when the tutor began to make written notes during a lesson, whilst the student wondered whether what was being written was in his favour or not. The evaluator should, of course, write up his notes as soon as he has left the school.

According to the methodology outlined previously, the children should have entered phase 3 and perhaps phase 4, by the time the evaluation began. Almost all the schools visited had in fact reached phase 3, and some schools had brought their children to a phase 4 bilingual level in given areas of activity. Yet in some schools it was not immediately apparent what level the children had reached, because in the teachers' eagerness to demonstrate the linguistic prowess of their pupils they demonstrated the work done so far by giving almost formal lessons, where spoken responses were elicited by means of verbal stimuli only. These demonstrations were reminiscent of the kind of language teaching given at junior and secondary levels and classified as 'oral work'. In only a few of the schools visited was a deliberate and unprompted attempt made to show how the children could apply in play activities the language material learnt during previous language-learning exercises.

This was significant, as it tended to indicate that some teachers had not grasped one of the major methodological principles of the project. It also showed that they had brought with them into the scheme a view of language teaching which was more relevant to junior and secondary schools; this again highlighted the need for more intensive in-service training at the beginning of the project so that teachers could accustom themselves more readily to a new methodology.

During such semi-formal lessons, an evaluator who was over-sympathetic to the scheme, or not too well versed in what is a new methodology hitherto not applied in schools at large, could easily have been deceived by the fluent and immediate responses made by children, and might have failed to recognize that many of these responses are well-drilled, parrot-like answers of extremely limited value for everyday purposes of living in a bilingual community. This is language at a very rudimentary level and does not enable the learner to cope with the ever-changing situations met in real life.

The evaluator had therefore to note carefully whether any of the sentence structures used during these pre-activity lessons were used during actual play activities, and whether the children were able to permutate the individual elements of speech patterns learnt, in order to cope with the activity. The more the children were able to demonstrate the skill of substituting vocabulary or elements in known speech patterns, whilst at the same time integrating the new language with the activities so vital for their general development, the higher the level of bilingualism reached.

It was possible to recognize three main groups. Firstly, there was the group of children with surprisingly good linguistic competence, exhibited mainly during activity work, especially when the children were left to themselves. These children had learnt to handle language in the flexible way described above and were able without prompting to communicate in Welsh in order to execute their activities. The second language was real and meaningful to them, not some superficial system of codes superimposed on to the vital business of playing and learning.

The second group, though they had worked diligently through the initial class exercises, were not always successful in adapting the basic language learnt when free activity work commenced. A further analysis showed that these children had in fact been taught and had thoroughly learnt a range of set sentences but they had not realized that the sentences belonged to pattern groups, the elements of which could be interchanged. Faced with a classroom procedure where the teacher gave a known type of spoken stimulus, the children would readily respond with the sentences learnt initially. They had learnt through constant repetition to respond to given situations. As soon as the spoken stimulus was changed to express an unfamiliar concept, the responses ceased. It was therefore difficult for these children to make a great deal of use of the sentences in subsequent activity work, which on most occasions was not predictable in detail. Nevertheless, this group had managed to learn a new set of sentences for their play activities, and in order to show that they were in fact using Welsh during these activities, they adjusted their activities to make the language material they had learnt relevant. This was in complete contrast to the first group of children, who adjusted their language to cope with the activities.

The third group consisted of children subjected to unimaginative initial teaching procedures. Lack of variety in presentation soon caused these young children to lose their concentration during classwork. It was noted that many of the children, when made to respond in chorus, would tend to learn Welsh sentences without being aware of their meanings. In subsequent question and answer work, wrong responses were frequent, though the actual sentences spoken by the children were linguistically correct. In other words, the children did not know the meaning of the sentences, the sounds of which they could speak perfectly. It is therefore understandable that there was little transfer of the language material into activity work.

This description of the three groups observed during the visits should not give the impression that there was a rigid division between these groups. All the children tended to operate at some time or other in one group or another, though predominantly in one of them.

In general, the children in any individual school tended to belong to one of the groups, indicating that their progress through the various stages of linguistic development was determined more by the quality of the teaching than by the IQ level of the children, though the higher a child's IQ, the more able that child is to handle language creatively in changing situations. The second group of children was found in the majority of schools visited. Only one school had children belonging to the third group. On the sample of schools seen it was possible that approximately a third of the schools in the project tended to produce children belonging to the first group. As the schools falling into the second group ranged from tolerably good to very good, though not outstanding, the scheme as a whole could be considered as a clear success.

If one considers that the majority of teachers were required to tackle the teaching of Welsh in a way strange to them, it is astonishing that such good progress was made in schools. Nevertheless, the levels reached in the majority of schools could clearly have been higher if there had been a greater amount of in-service training and supervision. The monthly visits made by two over-worked organizers, who were expected to prepare materials at the same time, were obviously not sufficient. It was also clear that teachers cannot be motivated to use new techniques merely by receiving printed information through the post. For instance, some of the older teachers had not grasped the difference between 'visual aids' and 'equipment' in infant school language learning.

For example, the equipment of a farm with its various animals, trees, etc., was used merely as a visual aid. The children would crowd around a table on which the different farm items were placed, and the teacher would ask questions in Welsh expecting Welsh answers in an almost parrot-like manner. The children, however, did not play with the farm after this drilling, so that a good opportunity for language consolidation and integration was lost. The second language would thus tend to be used by the children on a verbal basis only, completely divorced from the reality to which it belongs. There is a great deal of evidence which shows that language learnt and used merely at this verbal level will soon be lost.

On the other hand, some teachers showed a deep insight into the needs of children, and consequently developed activities, equipment and aids which would ensure that the second language could blend in with all the other work done at the school. Such teachers are able to work independently, foresee difficulties, linguistic or otherwise, and cope with any scheme without constantly being directed and fed with materials. Though such teachers may be blessed with above-average personality and intelligence, it would be folly to assume that a great deal of the knowledge shown by these teachers could not be shared by others if they were given an opportunity to acquire it.

It is interesting to note that the schools where the greatest amount of phase 4 work took place were those in which the widest range of suitable equipment was available, so that a great variety of activities could be introduced according to the needs of the children at any given time. Whilst the range of equipment available is no doubt a reflection of the teacher's insight into the principles of infant learning, it is also possible to deduce from this that children are best able to learn a second language in the setting of a modern child-centred infant school system rather than in a more traditional desk-bound environment. This is an encouraing correlation for both the linguist and the progressive infant teacher, and the general introduction of a second language in our infant schools might well be a necessary incentive to bring about more speedily the changes needed in the general education of the primary child.

During the evaluation of the materials supplied by the organizers it was found that a surprisingly large amount of materials had been written, invented and prepared. Listening books, tapes, songs and games all found great favour with the children and suited their general and linguistic needs admirably. It was found, however, that the books intended for the teachers were not used a great deal by them. This was confirmed by the project director. It was difficult to find good reasons for this, but an analysis of the books tended to suggest that there was too much in the teaching manuals so that teachers were not quite sure where to start.

Finally, it should be the evaluator's task to make alternative suggestions whenever he finds that certain items are lacking, that materials are either wrongly used or under-used, that methods are misunderstood and aims are wrongly interpreted. His recommendations should be brief and concise. Most of all he should know who will read his report and who will act upon it. Busy Directors of Education and Education Officers, for instance, for whom the evaluator's report may be one of many, cannot afford the time to read lengthy outpourings of eager evaluators wishing to 'put the world right'. Whilst the evaluator might have spent months or years in making his judgements, policy decisions are often made in a single meeting and a long report, no matter how interesting, may in the final analysis fail to persuade the decision-maker to take action. Perhaps the only reports excluded from this general principle are evaluators' reports on evaluation. This report is no exception.

Publisher for the project: not yet appointed.

Acknowledgements

The passages on p. 184 from the Gittins Report (see note 1 below) are reproduced by permission of the Controller of HM Stationery Office. Those on pp. 185–6, slightly adapted from Dodson et al. *Towards Bilingualism* (see note 3 below), are reproduced by permission of the University of Wales Press.

Notes and references

1   Central Advisory Council for Education (Wales) *Primary Education in Wales* [Gittins Report] HMSO, 1967.

2   Dodson, C. J. *Language Teaching and the Bilingual Method* Pitman, 1967, pp. 157–61.

3   Dodson, C. J., Price, E., & Williams, I. T. *Towards Bilingualism* Cardiff: University of Wales Press, 1968.

4   Ibid., p. 18, slightly adapted.

5   Ibid., pp. 24–5, slightly adapted.

6   With the appointment of a senior research officer at the start of the main project in September 1971, it has become possible to conduct tests measuring general and linguistic development in detail.

Further reading

The contributors were invited to suggest references to curriculum evaluation which they had found useful in the formulation of ideas. Their collected suggestions are given below.

Alexander, W. M. 'Assessing curriculum proposals' *Teachers College Record* **63,** January 1962, 286–93.

Alexander, W. M. *The Changing Secondary School Curriculum: Readings* New York: Holt, Rinehart, 1967.

American Educational Research Association monograph series on curriculum evaluation, Nos. 1–5. Chicago: Rand McNally, 1967–.

Atkin, J. M. 'Behavioral objectives in curriculum design: a cautionary note' *Science Teacher* **35,** 5, May 1968, 27–30.

Atkin, J. M. 'Some evaluation problems in a course content improvement project' *Journal of Research in Science Teaching* **1,** 2, 1963, 129–32.

Atkin, J. M. 'Research styles in science education' *Journal of Research in Science Teaching* **5,** 4, 1967–8, 338–45.

Becker, H. S. 'Problems of inference and proof in participant observation' *American Sociological Review* **23,** December 1958, 652–60.

Bell, C. 'A note on participant observation' *Sociology* **3,** September 1969, 417–18.

Benne, K. D., & Muntyan, B. *Human Relations in Curriculum Change* New York: Dryden, 1951.

Bennis, W. G., Benne, K. D., & Chin, R. *The Planning of Change: Readings in the Applied Behavioral Sciences* New York: Holt, Rinehart, 1961.

Bloom, B. S. (ed.). *Taxonomy of Educational Objectives: the Classification of Educational Goals* Handbook I *Cognitive Domain* Longmans, 1956. (For Handbook II, see Krathwohl et al.).

Bloom, B. S., Hastings, J. T., & Madans, G. F. *Handbook on Formative and Summative Evaluation of Student Learning* New York: McGraw-Hill, 1971.

Broudy, H. S. 'Mastery' chapter 5 (pp. 72–88) in *Language and Concepts in Education* ed. B. C. Smith & R. H. Ennis, Chicago: Rand McNally, 1961.

Broudy, H. S. 'Can research escape the dogma of behavioral objectives?' *School Review* **79,** 1, November 1970, 43–56.

Bruyn, S. *The Human Perspective in Sociology: the Methodology of Participant Observation* Englewood Cliffs, New Jersey: Prentice-Hall, 1966.

Campbell, D. T., Schwarz, R. D., Sechrest, L., & Webb, E. J. *Unobtrusive*

Measures: Nonreactive Research in the Social Sciences Chicago: Rand McNally, 1966.

Caswell, H. L. 'Difficulties in defining the structure of the curriculum', in *Curriculum Crossroads* ed. A. H. Passow, New York: Teachers College, Columbia University, 1965.

Chin, R. 'The utility of system models and developmental models for practitioners', pp. 201–14 in *The Planning of Change* (see Bennis et al.).

Cicourel, A. V. *Method and Measurement in Sociology* Collier-Macmillan, 1964.

Coleman, J. S., Katz, E., & Menzel, H. 'The diffusion of an innovation among physicians' *Sociometry* **20,** December 1957, 253–70.

Crombach, L. J. 'Course improvement through evaluation' *Teachers College Record* **64,** May 1963, 672–86.

Deutsch, M., Katz, I., & Jensen, A. R. *Social Class, Race, and Psychological Development* (especially part III), New York: Holt, Rinehart, 1968.

Dodson, C. J., Price, E., & Williams, I. T. *Towards Bilingualism* Cardiff: University of Wales Press, 1968.

Dressell, P. H. *Evaluation in General Education* Dubuque, Iowa: William C. Brown, 1954.

Dressell, P. H., & Mayhew, L. B. *General Education: Experiments in Evaluation* Washington, DC: American Council on Education, 1945.

Eggleston, J. F., & Kerr, J. F. *Studies in Assessment* English Universities Press, 1969.

Eisner, E. W. 'Educational objectives: help or hindrance' *School Review* **75,** autumn 1967, 250–82.

French, W. M., et al. *Behavioral Goals of General Education in High School* New York: Russell Sage Foundation, 1957.

Gagné, R. M. *The Conditions of Learning* New York: Holt, Rinehart, 1965.

Goodlad, J. I. 'The school scene in review: toward a conceptual system for curriculum problems' *School Review* **66,** 4, winter 1958, 391–401.

Gowin, D. B. 'Can educational theory guide practice?' *Educational Theory* **13,** 1963, 6–12.

Grobman, H. *Evaluation Activities of Curriculum Projects* (American Educational Research Association monograph on curriculum evaluation, No. 2), Chicago: Rand McNally, 1968.

Hastings, J. T. 'Curriculum evaluation: the whys of the outcomes' *Journal of Educational Measurement* **3,** 1966, 27–32.

Hedges, W. D. *Testing and Evaluation for the Sciences in Secondary Schools* Belmont, California: Wadsworth, 1966.

Hemphill, J. K. 'The relationships between research and evaluation studies' chapter 9 (pp. 189–220) in *Educational Evaluation: New Roles, New Means,* ed. R. W. Tyler, part II (68th Year Book of the National Society for the Study of Education), University of Chicago Press, 1969.

Herrick, V. E. 'The concept of curriculum design' in *Toward Improved Curriculum Theory* ed. V. E. Herrick & R. W. Tyler, University of Chicago Press, 1950.

Hudson, L. (ed.) *Ecology of Human Intelligence* Harmondsworth: Penguin, 1970.

Hughes, E. C. 'Social change and status protest: an essay on the marginal man' *Phylon* 1949, 58–65.

Hyman, H. H., & Singer, E. (eds) *Readings in Reference Group Theory and Research* Collier-Macmillan, 1968.

Inglis, F. *The Englishness of English Teaching* (Longmans curriculum reform series), Longmans, 1969.

Jackson, P. W. *Life in Classrooms* New York: Holt, Rinehart, 1968.

Janes, R. W. 'A note on phases of the community role of the participant-observer' *American Sociological Review* **26**, June 1961, 446–50.

Jones, R. *Fantasy and Feeling in Education* University of London Press, 1959.

Kerr, J. F. (ed.). *Changing the Curriculum* University of London Press, 1968.

Krathwohl, D. R. 'The taxonomy of educational objectives—its use in curriculum building' in *Defining Educational Objectives* (see Lindvall).

Krathwohl, D. R., Bloom, B. S., & Masia, B. B. *Taxonomy of Educational Objectives: the Classification of Educational Goals*, Handbook II, *Affective Domain* Longmans, 1964.

Lee, C. M. Bermers- *Models for Decision* English Universities Press, 1965.

Lindblom, C. 'The science of muddling through' *Public Administrative Review* **19**, 1959. Reprinted in *The Making of Decisions*, ed. W. J. Gore & J. W. Dyson. New York: Free Press of Glencoe, 1964.

Lindvall, C. M. (ed.) *Defining Educational Objectives* University of Pittsburgh Press, 1964.

Merton, R. K., & Kendall, P. L. 'The focused interview' *American Journal of Sociology* **51**, May 1946, 541–57.

Metropolitan Toronto Board Study of Educational Facilities. *Educational Specifications and User Requirements for Intermediate Schools* (SEF report E2). Toronto: Ryerson Press, 1968.

Moore, W. E., & Tumin, M. M. 'Some social functions of ignorance' *American Sociological Review* **14**, 1949. 787–95.

Musgrove, F. 'Curriculum objectives' *J. Curriculum Studies* **1**, 1, 1968, 5–18.

Oldfield, R. C., & Marshall, J. C. (eds). *Language* (items 14 & 23) New imp. Harmondsworth: Penguin, 1970.

Pace, C. R. 'Educational objectives', chapter 4 in *The Integration of Educational Experience*, ed. P. L. Dressel, part III (57th Year Book of the National Society for the Study of Education), University of Chicago Press, 1958.

Peters, R. S. 'Must an educator have an aim?' in his *Authority, Responsibility and Education* Allen & Unwin, 1959.

Popham, W. J., Eisner, E. W., Sullivan, H. J., & Tyler, L. L. *Instructional Objectives* (American Educational Research Association monograph on curriculum evaluation, No. 3) Chicago: Rand McNally, 1969.

Review of Educational Research **40**, 2, April 1970: *Educational Evaluation.*

Rogers, E. M. *The Diffusion of Innovations* New York: Free Press of Glencoe, 1962.

Schwab, J. 'The concept of the structure of a discipline' *Educational Record* **43**, July 1962, 197–205.

Skilbeck, M. 'Curriculum development: the nature of the task' (unpublished paper), University of Bristol, 1968.

Smith, B. O., Stanley, W. O., & Shores, H. J. *Fundamentals of Curriculum Development* New York & Burlingame: Harcourt, Brace, 1957.

Smith, E. R., & Tyler, R. W. *Appraising and Recording Student Progress* New York: Harper, 1942.

Stake, R. E. 'The countenance of educational evaluation' *Teachers College Record* **68,** April 1967, 523–40.

Taba, H. *Curriculum Development* New York: Harcourt, Brace, 1962.

Thorndike, R. L., & Hagen, E. *Measurement and Evaluation in Psychology and Education* 3rd ed. New York: Wiley, 1969.

Tyler, R. W. *Basic Principles of Curriculum and Instruction* University of Chicago Press, 1950.

Tyler, R. W., Gagné, R. M., & Scriven, M. *Perspectives of Curriculum Development* American Educational Research Association monograph on curriculum evaluation, No. 1), Chicago: Rand McNally, 1967.

Weiss, R. S. 'Issues in holistic research' in *Institutions and the Person* ed. H. S. Becker, B. Gear, D. Riesman & R. Weiss, Chicago: Aldine, 1968.

Weiss, R. S., & Rein, M. 'The evaluation of broad-aim programs: a cautionary case and a moral' *Annals of the American Academy of Political and Social Science* **385,** 1969, 133–42.

Wheeler, D. K. *Curriculum Process* University of London Press, 1967.

Williams, J. 'The curriculum: some patterns of development and design for evaluation', pp. 185–208 in *Educational Research in Britain,* ed. H. J. Butcher, University of London Press, 1968.

Wiseman, S., & Pidgeon, D. *Curriculum Evaluation* Slough: National Foundation for Educational Research, 1970.

Wittrock, M. C., & Wiley, D. E. (eds) *The Evaluation of Instruction* New York: Holt, Rinehart, 1970.